THE
FUTURE
AS IF
IT REALLY
MATTERED

JAMES
GARBARINO

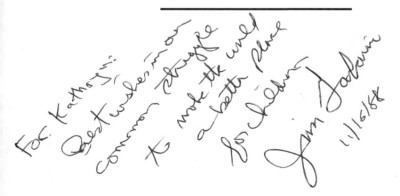

THE
FUTURE

AS IF
IT REALLY
MATTERED

*JAMES
GARBARINO*

Bookmakers Guild, Inc.

Published in 1988 in the United States of America by
Bookmakers Guild, Inc.
1430 Florida Avenue, Suite 202
Longmont, Colorado 80501

Printed and bound in the United States of America

Library of Congress Cataloging-in-Publication Data

Garbarino, James.
    The future as if it really mattered / James Garbarino.

    Bibliography: p.
    Includes index.
    ISBN 0-917665-17-1 : $22.00   ISBN 0-917665-20-1 (pbk.) : $13.95
    1. Social policy.   2. Economic policy.   3. Family policy.
I. Title.
HN18.G266   1988   88-5059
361.6'1—dc19   CIP

For
Josh and Joanna
Ben and Noah
and Ashley

Contents

Preface

This book began in 1979, in a taxicab. Having landed in Houston to attend the Woodlands Conference on Sustainable Societies, I found myself sharing a cab with Don Lesh (then Executive Director of the U.S. Association of the Club of Rome; now Executive Director of the Global 2000 Coalition). I was in Texas to receive a Mitchell Prize for my essay "The Issue is Human Quality: In Praise of Children." Hearing of Don's affiliation I expressed interest in learning more about sustainable societies, societies that are economically, environmentally, demographically, and ethically sane. Don directed me to Aurelio Peccei's book *The Human Quality.* I read the book and went on to other publications of the Club of Rome, including the ground breaking *Limits to Growth.* Before long I was a member of the U.S. Association for the Club of Rome being exposed to a wealth of ideas and information about the prospects for a sustainable society. As I listened and read I found myself wondering what all this implied for families. I recalled an article my wife Nan and I had written together some years earlier entitled "Where Are the Children in the Sustainable Society?" Utopia? This book is the result of asking that question, and thus owes its origins to my serendipitous conversation with Don Lesh. I needed to write this book to put together what I read with what I was seeing in my travels across the United States (39 states) and Canada (6 provinces) and around the world (four continents). Looking at the future in the faces of children I met, I felt something growing in my mind and my heart. This book is that something, something personal and professional both.

I think this effort to bring together personal and professional concerns is natural for me in part because of who I am and where I come from—the merging of an Italian and Anglo-Saxon ethnic heritage. I have always been aware of my strong family orientation, but have never understood it so well as when I saw it reflected in Stephen Hall's 1983 *New York Times Sunday Magazine* article "Italian-Americans Coming into Their Own." He asks:

"Is there is single thread that runs through these people?" and answers: "If anything, it is the unusual propensity to merge, rather than separate the professional and the personal." (p. 31) Family is at the heart of my personal and professional identity, and this book is testimony to that. I look at my children and I see my grandchildren to be. But, I also see the grandchildren to be of the children I met in cities, towns, and villages in South America, in Asia, in Europe and in Africa. And I see a thread connecting together all the people who have helped me in this task.

Pediatrician Robert Aldrich played a big role. He took me under his wing and arranged for me to travel to Japan in 1981 to participate in an international Symposium on "The Child in the City." Visiting Japan was a decisive experience. Aurelio Peccei helped me in our one brief face-to-face conversation in Washington, D.C. in 1982. Nicholas Geogescu-Roegen helped me in one short letter of encouragement.

The Kellogg Foundation played a facilitating role by supporting me as a Kellogg National Fellow from 1981–1984. I used my Fellowship resources to read and travel as I have sought out ideas and experiences to help me answer my questions about the place of children and families in the sustainable society. The Kellogg Fellowship took me to Brazil, China, and Hawaii. All three trips helped me see things more clearly, and have found a place in the book. The Kellogg Fellowship allowed me to seek the help and advice of many individuals much more knowledgeable than I about the economics, demographics, physics, biology, and politics of the sustainable society and the interrelated issues we call the "world problematique." This process has reinforced and strengthened my belief in the collective nature of the struggle to understand and nurture the world and its living beings. I am grateful for all the help I have received from the Foundation.

Foster Parents Plan International helped by hosting my trip to Sudan in 1985. In the midst of political turmoil (President Nemerye having just been overthrown) and devastating drought and economic dislocation I saw a demonstration of hope and concrete statement of what "meeting basic human needs" really means. I was helped in the field by PLAN's staff of genuine do-gooders, really doing good.

A special group commented upon the first version of this book, and I want to acknowledge their help: Rob Abramowitz, Umberto Colombo, Bob Cory, Duane Elgin, Liz Dodson Gray, Jay Forrester, Bob Garretson, Nicholas

Georgescu-Roegen, Ann Heider, William Henry, John Hershberger, Gary Hirshberg, Michael Hoffman, George Mitchell, John Ogbu, Dana Raphael, John Scanzoni, Townsend Scudder, Bob Stecker, Jess Stein, Joan Vondra, Page Wilson, and my favorite in-house critic Nan Garbarino. Others have helped through chats on buses driving the backroads of Brazil, around the dinner table in China, in land rovers in Sudan, in the classroom, and anywhere else I could learn something I needed to know.

Jim Garbarino
Chicago, Illinois

CHAPTER

1.

November 1979:

Houston, Texas

An Introduction
to Limits:
Have We Sold Out
Our Children's Future?

H OUSTON CLAIMS TO BE THE
oil capital of the world—a dubious honor, it seems to me. I am at "The
Woodlands"—a pleasant residential and commercial enclave of affluence
developed near Houston by my host, George Mitchell, whose commercial
activities involve oil exploration and real estate development. Both are
primary forces shaping life in the modern era, and therein lies both the
promise and the problem. I am there as winner of one of eight Mitchell
Prizes awarded for essays on the theme "Building a Sustainable Society."
Paul Ehrlich, author of The Population Bomb, has won first prize for a
piece on diversity and its value to a sustainable society. My essay is entitled "The Issue Is Human Quality: In Praise of Children." All the winning
essays emphasize conservation and doing more and better with less. The
conference's keynote address, delivered by U.S. Senator Lloyd Bentsen,
does little to alter my stereotyped view of Texas as a metaphor for America: "More growth! More oil! More production! More land development!
More! More! More!" Afterward, there is talk in the bar of the prize winners
signing a petition to disavow and contradict the Senator's remarks. I recall
a joke heard long ago, in a very different context:

PATIENT: Doctor, I have a problem. I feel anxious, worried, overbur-
           dened, and generally miserable.
DOCTOR: Why is that?
PATIENT: I don't know exactly.
DOCTOR: Well, tell me about your life.

> *I live in a nice neighborhood in a big house full of expensive*
> *furniture. We have two cars—a station wagon and a sports*
> *car. The kids have all the toys they could ever want. We eat*
> *out at nice restaurants several times a week. My wife*
> *dresses in the newest fashions and so do I. We belong to the*
> *country club and have a condominium at a ski resort.*
> DOCTOR: *That all sounds wonderful. So what's your problem?*
> PATIENT: *Well, Doctor, I only make $100 a week.*

Sitting here listening, I think America is the patient and the Senator is the
doctor. And he doesn't get the joke. (Nine years later, with the oil boom
gone bust—for the moment at least—and Texas experiencing a severe re-
cession, I wonder if he gets it now.)

The Meaning of Social Welfare

The term "social welfare" refers to a society's ability and willingness to protect and care for its members, particularly its more dependent members—children, the frail elderly, the physically and mentally disabled, and anyone else who needs special assistance in meeting basic needs. Even healthy adults may need social welfare systems when faced with special crises, for example when mothers are left alone to care for young children. These systems come into play in modern society when workers are unemployed and thus deprived of their regular income, or when sick parents are unable to meet their child care responsibilities. Social welfare systems may be formal (government food stamp programs) or informal (neighbors or church members stepping in to help a family hit by disaster). We know that the public institutions of state, church, and philanthropy are critical pillars for social welfare in modern societies. We also recognize as such pillars the multitude of social support networks formed by kinship, friendship, and membership in self-help groups, clubs, neighborhood associations, and churches.

The adequacy of social welfare systems depends upon several things. One is the nature and quality of the economy. Does it meet subsistence needs for food, shelter, and clothing? How much wealth does it generate? How is wealth distributed? What is the society's class structure? Of course, once we move beyond basic subsistence (and even before we do), wealth is quite a relative term. This comes sharply into focus when we recognize that a family of modest means in the United States enjoys a luxurious standard of living by Third World standards, as anyone will attest who has traveled to the refugee camps of Ethiopia and the Sudan or the slums of Brazil or Ecuador. In a modern society we should always be skeptical—even suspicious—when we are told that we "can't afford" to support social welfare systems.

Thus, a second factor in shaping social welfare systems is politics. Does the political system serve the interests of a small ruling class at the expense of the larger population? Is social justice a high political priority? Is there a commitment to meeting basic human needs for dependent individuals and their families? A third factor is knowledge. Do the institutional leaders possess and bring to bear a valid understanding of how society works and changes, of what children and adults need to advance developmentally? Do they understand the relationships between economic and political forces in maintaining social welfare systems? Do they understand the long-term implications of short-term decisions?

The history of social welfare systems reflects the interplay of economics, politics, and knowledge. For the most part, *formal* social welfare systems are a modern creation. They depend upon an economy capable of producing sufficient wealth to permit redistribution to those in need, and to support those whose job it is to redistribute it. Further, they require a political system capable of establishing and maintaining social welfare systems. Finally, they require a knowledge base for policy and program development. All three preconditions are primarily modern creations (Rostow, 1972). Like the complex, high-powered societies they represent, social welfare systems are in their infancy when contrasted with the span of human history behind and ahead of us as a species.

Against the backdrop of human tenure on Earth, the modern period is but an eyeblink. Only in the last few moments of human history have the powerful economies, the complex governments, and the sophisticated data bases we take for granted appeared. Economic, political, and intellectual growth has accelerated astronomically in the centuries since Columbus crossed the Atlantic, the decades since the Wright Brothers flew at Kitty Hawk, and the years since Neil Armstrong stepped out onto the moon. What does this acceleration mean for families? What does the future hold for social welfare systems if current trends continue? What limiting factors in the Earth as a set of environmental systems will shape this process of change? How will families fare in the future? These are the questions before us. We begin with a look at the hypothesis that our current foundations for social welfare are fraught with danger.

Giants Walk the Earth

"Limits to Growth," "Small Is Beautiful," "Doing More with Less," "Voluntary Simplicity," "Beyond the Age of Waste," "A Sustainable Society." All these slogans respond to the challenge of adapting modern civilization to its startling success in transforming the planetary relationship between the naturally occurring and the humanly built environment. They presuppose that we have failed to develop a physically and morally sustainable relationship with the Earth—a failure that undermines the economic and environmental foundations for social welfare, and ultimately for family well-being. Commentator after commentator remarks on the astounding success of human ingenuity, industriousness, and brute force in wresting a dominant place for humanity on Earth. Until recently, most Western or Western-oriented observers have watched this process with awe and pride as it literally conquered the world. This attitude approaches reverence in *The Ascent of Man* (1974), in which Jacob Bronowski glorifies the scientific and technocratic genius of the human species. He rightly saw that humans stand in unique relationship to the Earth because of their intellectual resources.

> Man[1] is a singular creature. He has a set of gifts which make him unique among the animals, so that, unlike them, he is not a figure in the landscape—he is a shaper of the landscape. (p. 19)

Bronowski sees human cultural evolution as a series of technological breakthroughs that have brought humanity into a position of dominance over all creatures great and small. In his eloquent essay, he examines the evolution of the human mind through its long childhood, in its interplay with the physical and social environment. His voice is one of praise for human accomplishment, of exhortation to go beyond the present and challenge the future. It is the modern voice speaking for mankind as the cultural giant, as Lord of the Earth and the skies and all that is. Though more eloquently than most, Bronowski speaks in a voice familiar to us. But it is not the only voice.

Another voice is wary of giants. Psychologist Carol Gilligan (*In a Different Voice*, 1982) hears it in Anton Chekov's *The Cherry Orchard*, in which:

> Lopalin, a young merchant, describes his life of hard work and success. . . . he reveals the image of man that underlies and supports his activity: "At times when I can't go to sleep, I think: Lord, thou gavest us immense forests, unbounded fields and the widest horizons, and living in the midst of them we should indeed be giants"—at which point Madame Ranevskaya interrupts him saying, "You feel the need for giants—they

are good only in fairy tales, anywhere else they only frighten us."
(Gilligan, 1982, p. 5).

There has long been a second voice, crying out *for* the wilderness, questioning humanity's process of global domination—indeed, seeing the assertion of human power as a threat to the social fabric into which children and adults are woven through the day-to-day business of family life. This voice has come from those in more harmonious relationship with the land (e.g., Native American Indians); from those who more naturally emphasize social harmony over competitiveness (what Gilligan calls "the feminine perspective"); and from those sensitive to the spiritual costs of human power (e.g., the Sino-Confucian "conservative" philosophers).

In the past decade, the first voice has continued its cheerleading for "more! more! more!" But as the degradation and destruction of the physical environment becomes more evident through increasingly sophisticated documentation and analysis, the second voice has spoken with renewed persuasiveness for "living lightly upon the Earth." It argues that the energy-intensive, environmentally degrading, and socially imperious "modern industrial order" will lead to cataclysmic global consequences which will erode environmental and economic foundations for social well-being. The futurist Aurelio Peccei (1976) calls this growing crisis in the relationship between human civilization and the Earth's resources "the world problematique."

The World Problematique

The harmonious use of human power would create a sustainable society, one that establishes justice and holds the material world steady and constant so that creative, spiritual, intellectual, and interpersonal worlds may flourish. Movement toward a sustainable society would strengthen the foundations of social welfare so that families could proceed with the important business of transforming human organisms into human beings. Technologically and economically advanced societies must shed their role as environmental brute and become instead the world's nurturers, while the less industrialized must avoid becoming brutish in the first place. Perhaps the image of the garden is apt.

Having cut back the underbrush, plowed the fields, and established our human plantings, we must tend and care for these plantings in a way that harmonizes our immediate needs with the future well-being of the garden itself. This task requires a special blend of far-seeing idealism and concrete planning and analysis. It requires a hard-nosed but warm-hearted look at our place in the world—a kind of visionary pragmatism. It requires not that we blindly turn away from modern technology but rather that we harmonize its ends and means. An important aspect of this challenge lies in the recognition that families are the headquarters for human development, the lifeboats[2] for the human species in the modern era.

Every social, economic, and political perspective, if its adherents are to bring their plans to fruition, must make its peace with the family or make war upon it in as far reaching struggle. For some, the durability of the family as a social and biological unit is a source of hope and confidence: The family will survive and see us through. Others, who would restructúre society to liberate individual children and adults—and perhaps realign them into new social entities—find the family a frustrating roadblock to progress. The family, an enduring set of relationships among biologically or legally connected adults caring for dependent generations younger or older, can fulfill a holding function while other socioeconomic relationships are reformed to meet the needs of a sustainable society. Families echo the past, inspire the present, and portend the future. They are our most direct connection with historical time, and the focal point for motivating the changes needed to bring about a sustainable society.

The Need for a New Economic Perspective

Recent history provides a flawed model of economic civilization, one that cannot continue humanely. Future generations will require an expansion and transformation of the kind of economic thinking that provided the foundation for the Industrial Revolution in the seventeenth, eighteenth, and nineteenth centuries. "Old" economic thinking may have been adequate to create the banking and accounting systems that transformed agrarian barter economies into industrialized cash economies. The old model focuses exclusively on "monetarized" aspects of the environment. Anything with a cash price attached becomes a factor in calculating cost; anything without a cash price is "free." Thus, dumping waste from a factory into a river is "free," while hiring someone to cart it away is a cost. Activities that do not generate cash income are economically invisible. But if someone can find a way to attach a cash price to them and cause people to pay it, they enter the monetarized economy.

The monetarized model provided a gross approximation of the actual costs of production for its times—particularly the period 1750-1950. Those times were characterized by "free" raw materials, including petro-energy, and "free" waste disposal, as well as an enormous reservoir of "free" *social* resources to absorb the psychological and interpersonal side effects of industrialization. When these "free" factors were added to clear increases in day-to-day material well-being brought about by industrialization, the net result was improved social welfare, judged by most criteria of human quality. It resulted in lower monetarized production costs per unit produced, in more monetarized wealth for societies that succeeded in industrializing, and in population growth. This last point is an important one. After thousands of years with only a tenuous hold on the planet, the human species established itself in a supreme position. But that very success and the means used to establish it now threaten to overwhelm and destroy civilization, rather than sustain it.

As the magnitude of Western industrialization and cash economy has increased since 1950, several of its critical assumptions have begun to crumble in the technocratically developed nations, and have shown signs of being untenable in the preindustrial Third World. In many cases we have reached and even exceeded the point of diminishing returns. Costs of increased monetarized wealth are being offset in both the already monetarized and the as yet unmonetarized domains of human existence. This has imposed a socioeconomic injunction on modern industrial development and has brought about a growing threat to the foundations of social welfare systems. Raw materials are no longer "free." Waste disposal is an ever-increasing cost, and—in the case of nuclear wastes—a problem with no good solution at any cost. The concepts of cost and value that served us well for nearly two centuries have become increasingly inaccurate, even obsolete, because changing conditions have exposed their long-term invalidity. The conventional short-term economic view is now neither life-giving nor a valid picture of reality, but instead a demonic force. If we cannot change our thinking, we will face a future ever more brutal as the "haves" seek even more ruthlessly to maintain the status quo, and the "have-nots" try more desperately to grab more for themselves. The social consequences for families include alienation, disorganization, dissatisfaction, and disruption, as the foundations for social welfare systems crumble and erode.

Shifting our economic thinking requires shifts in our basic concepts about the nature and function of human institutions in relation to human enterprise. It requires that we make decisions and policies based on their total contribution to our store of physical and social resources, rather than on what they appear to cost in dollars. We must examine both aspects of the economy, those with a cash price tag and those yet outside the realm of monetarized accounting (such as housework and child care provided by a family member). Economist Orio Giarini (1981) calls this total worth our "dowry and patrimony," and it is one foundation for social welfare (the others being political will and knowledge of how social systems work). It underlies the wealth of families. To develop a sustainable society, domestically and internationally, we must evaluate human activities by the criterion of their net contribution to total wealth and ultimately to social welfare, rather than by the increasingly unrealistic criterion of monetarized value. We seem to be in a pivotal period in human history.

The Role of Great Men and Women and Great Books in History

Much has been written about the role of "great men" in historical transformations, but great ideas often play as important a role. Consider John Evelyn's *Sylva: A Discourse of Forest Trees and the Propagation of Timber,* published in London in 1664.[3] As Evelyn wrote, deforestation was proceeding at an alarming rate in seventeenth-century England, and he sought to demonstrate the need to reverse this trend. His book stimulated widespread planting of trees; even King Charles II took notice and ordered that the royal forests be replenished. Evelyn's book was so successful in its aim that one historian (Robert Southey) has observed that it stands as "one of the few books in the world which completely affected what it was designed to do."

As we face the current immensely complicated crisis of the world problematique, another book occupies a critical historical position. In *The Limits to Growth,* published in 1972, Dennis and Donella Meadows and a team of investigators presented a gross empirical analysis of the recent past and projected future course of human civilizations, taking into account population and resources. It throws down the gauntlet to the modern industrial order: reform or destroy, redirect or self-destruct.

> Man possesses, for a small moment in his history, the most powerful combination of knowledge, tools, and resources the world has ever known. He has all that is physically necessary to create a totally new form of human society—one that would be built to last for generations.[4]

The Limits to Growth reached millions of people, but it remains a secret to most people in most places. And it appeared in a historical moment of the greatest importance. As we look at the world more than a decade after its publication, we still see a mixed picture. The causes for hope and despair are, as ever, abundant and in dynamic tension. A colleague of mine was fond of telling his students that to deal with the twentieth century one needs to be an ambulatory schizophrenic. That is to say, one needs to acknowledge the craziness, but continue trying to lead a sensible life.

Finding a Sensible Path in a Crazy World

The threat of nuclear annihilation itself is sufficient cause for despair. The world's nuclear arsenals threaten to do unholy violence to human life, and indeed to the very life of the planet. The current stock of some *fifteen thousand* deliverable megatons is enough to deliver a one-megaton bomb to each community of 1,500 or more inhabitants in both the United States and the Soviet Union.[5] Scientists now believe that nuclear war could generate a global environmental disaster. Clouds of dust would blanket the planet, leading to a cold and dark "Nuclear Winter" resulting in massive famine and an end to human civilization as we know it. Recent hypothetical analyses suggest that even a "limited" nuclear war would disrupt society to such a degree as to neutralize or incapacitate it. If we add to the prospect of nuclear horror the less dramatic but nonetheless terrible toll modern civilization takes on water, soil, and air, it becomes clear that the psychological basis for pessimism and despair is in place, and in more than adequate supply.

What stands against these negative forces within and around us? Hope, imagination, and human will to survive. The very human genius that has brought on the crisis can provide the resources to solve the problems before us. We must neither despair nor believe that somehow we can muddle through doing business as usual. Neither "doom and gloom" nor "boom and bloom" will do the trick. The solutions we need must arise from the application of intelligence, imagination, love, work, and the will to survive.

Families provide an anchoring point for our efforts. They are the natural context in which to pursue issues of human quality and the best place to see what is really happening. They are organized around basic and enduring human dynamics. Meeting the needs of families will take us far toward creating a sound foundation for a sustainable society. If we fail them, our other efforts at social engineering will crumble or be torn down. Families, as lifeboats for the human species, are at the center of our analysis of the economic and environmental foundations of social welfare systems. This focus on their needs and wealth provides a perspective with which to understand both the present and the various alternative futures that present themselves. It is a fulcrum with which we may move the problem of a sustainable future.

Social Welfare as the Foundation
for a Sustainable Future

We need a new synthesis that builds upon two foundations. The first is an ethic of accountability. Individuals, corporations, and governments must assume full social and ecological responsibility for their actions. Is this possible without an elaborate and intrusive governmental bureaucracy? In his comparative look at societal blueprints for the future, Bohdan Hawrylshyn (1979) concludes that it is—if we work toward values and institutions that encourage cooperation and pluralism. And, I would add, the family is central to these values and institutions. It is a culturally invigorating challenge, a new frontier that can bring into play all the resources of human hearts and minds.

In addition to accountability, we need a community-oriented perspective on social welfare systems. This requires that major institutions within communities act in concert to develop plans consistent with local resources—material and human. In *Cities and the Wealth of Nations* (1984), Jane Jacobs presents the view that primary economic transactions occur between cities and between the regions that coalesce around them. Cities and their regions—not societies—are the actual and appropriate units for economic analysis. This community focus makes some sense from the perspective of understanding and sustaining social welfare systems. Whether it be child protective services, education, or food support, what matters is the ability and willingness of *local* systems to implement social welfare policy.

A sane planetary strategy for human survival and quality of life implies national and international planning, of course. But just as one recognizes the virtue of individual initiative in regulating day-to-day enterprise, one also sees that community-based effort is necessary for a safe and sane world order. Trade is essential; but it must be trade among cooperating and independently sustainable communities. This is not a chimera. Sustainable communities are feasible. In the realms of energy, housing, health, and food production, even cold-weather climates permit self-reliance when cooperation and innovative thinking are the norm. Bruce Stokes discusses "local solutions for global problems" in *Helping Ourselves* (1981), for example computer links between urban industrial plants to recycle waste. Third World countries may have a more natural basis for trade among themselves than with industrialized nations of the first and second worlds. Small-scale family and neighborhood projects involving recycling, food production, and child care can be productive and sustainable. Herein lies the wealth of families.

As the mother and father are parents to the child, so the community is parent to the family. A family-oriented society built upon collective accountability is the necessary successor to Adam Smith's invisible guiding hand in transforming the social savage into the noble caretaker who will tend our planetary garden. If we realize this concept in an ecologically sound fashion, the sustainable society will come to pass. If not, modern civilization will degenerate into a new, more pernicious form of barbarism.

The Concepts of Limits to Growth: Coping with the Finite in Human Affairs

The limits-to-growth thesis seems elegantly simple and undeniable[6] in principle: the material Earth is finite. One wonders how anyone could disagree. But how relevant are the limits to growth on a day-to-day, year-to-year, and decade-to-decade basis? Generally we accept the counterproposition of "the inexhaustible supply of solar energy." The difference between the limited material Earth and the limitless sun lies, of course, in order of magnitude. Both are limited—every thing is limited from nearly any theological or teleological perspective. (Perhaps only regarding the concept of God do we really speak of the infinite, now that astronomers tell us that even the universe is finite.) For almost any practical purpose we can disregard the sun's limits (it will last five billion years at current levels of solar activity), but we must take into account the Earth's limits—perhaps in year-to-year, probably in decade-to-decade, and certainly in century-to-century calculations and operations. The issue, then, is the nature of the limits to the material Earth.

It is ironic, however, that it is the Earth's limits and not the sun's with which we must be concerned. Viewing them as "systems," it is the sun, not the Earth, that seems less promising (in principle). The sun is a system so enormous in relation to astronomical bodies near it that it has virtually nothing to gain from them. It is essentially a "closed system." On the other hand, with respect to what it provides its neighbors, the sun is a benevolently open system. It radiates the energy upon which all the other systems depend (the third planet—Earth—is the most graceful recipient, according to our astronomers). And its enormous mass establishes a gravitational locus for the dependent entities that cluster around it to form the solar system.

As one of those entities, the Earth is a system very open to input. Economist Nicholas Georgescu-Roegen (1976) tells us solar energy is enormous in its direct impact—the Earth reflects back half but "accepts" roughly 2,650 Q of energy (a Q is about 10^{18} BTU; current earthly energy use per year is about .2 Q). This solar energy reverberates through the Earth's systems in many ways—wind, waves, and wood, to name the three most prominent. What is more, the Earth could theoretically be open to input from other entities in its near environment—for example, minerals from the moon or other planets and additional direct solar radiation captured by orbiting space stations.

In principle it seems we should be concerned with the sun when we discuss limits. The sun seems so very finite, with its massive consumption of matter to produce outgoing energy, while the Earth is open to alternative solutions to its energy and materials problem. In practice, of course, the tables are turned. Limits to growth is so much an earthly concern that the most apt metaphor for the planet is "Spaceship Earth."[7] The planet is a self-contained habitat. We, as crew, must husband our provisions and expect little help from the void outside, except whatever solar energy we can capture using the ship's ingenious equipment and whatever we can rig up with the materials at hand.

The limits-to-growth thesis rests ultimately on the principle of "entropy," one of the keys to thermodynamics. Georgescu-Roegen (1976) has pointed out its critical importance in relation to sustainable societies. Entropy refers to the fact that energy exists in two states. One is "available" or "free" energy which we can use to accomplish work. The second is "unavailable" or "bound" energy which we cannot use. For example, the chemical energy in a piece of wood is available to us: we can burn the wood to produce heat, which we can then use. The energy needed to light the fire is small compared with the energy it releases. But the heat from the fire disperses, and once dispersed it is no longer free. That is, greater energy is required to recapture it than we will have available once we do so. Free energy is organized and concentrated; bound energy is chaotic and dissipated. Put most simply, the law of entropy tells us that the movement of energy within systems is from free to bound energy, from available to unavailable, from order to disorder. This phenomenon may become more and more relevant to daily life as wood to burn becomes less readily available, and large amounts of energy are required to find, obtain, transport, and ultimately burn it for heat. In some parts of the world women may spend most of their time (and energy) gathering firewood.

The Implications of Entropy for Social Welfare

In principle, entropy is always critical for understanding the past, analyzing the present, and predicting the future of systems. Relative to other systems, human beings are energy eaters. We live off available energy and leave waste (bound energy) in its place. This is human life in its least flattering, most prosaic sense. Procreation is miraculous, but it sets in motion what is essentially a parasitic process that the institutions we call social welfare systems are designed to facilitate. The fetus lives off available energy from the mother, who serves as host. The mother lives off the energy of other biological systems, such as plant and animal food, and nonbiologic sources such as minerals in her diet. Social welfare systems are designed to help her serve this function. Indeed, many of the most persuasive arguments in favor of social welfare systems demonstrate the positive cost-benefit ratio of the community's investment in support for pregnant and lactating women. Prenatal investment is a demonstrably elegant and cost-effective strategy for enhancing human development. In conventional economic terms, every dollar invested in supportive early care saves four dollars in later rehabilitative and compensatory care.

Once weaned, the child becomes a direct user of free energy, and again requires social welfare systems to protect its energy supplies. And so the life cycle continues. In death, the body may return its residuals to the Earth (cultural practices permitting), but most likely it will consume one last portion of free energy to avoid even this payback, by cremation (transforming the body into bound energy) or casket burial (making the dead body a closed system by using a barrier against the Earth's biologic systems). No matter how you look at it, it costs the Earth plenty to support the human race[8]—not even considering for the moment the vast differences in such cost between the haves and the have-nots of the world.

Of course, the dynamics of entropy are exceedingly complex and open to disagreement even among experts. The mechanics of calculating free and bound energy within systems, the flows across systems, and the process of energy degradation on any large scale are staggering. When population was small and human tools rudimentary (that is to say up until about 300 years ago), we were a negligible influence on the planet. Crises of energy, material, and population were few and localized: a village might overgraze or overplant surrounding fields; a clan might deforest a small area; a town might pollute a small body of water. But the effects were confined to a small space and were short-lived, because the massive supply of free energy permitted the Earth's systems to respond effectively. Limits were present, but they consisted mainly of the constraints imposed by the minimal size and power of the human race individually and collectively. Discussions of social welfare systems could proceed without taking entropy into account, because the world was so big and human communities so relatively small.

Now, though, entropy is a real factor, and limits are a matter of acute concern in social policy. As Georgescu-Roegen makes clear, even if we are able to achieve a "steady-state" socioeconomic order, we must still acknowledge entropy as a historical threat. That is, while the sun's projected five-billion-year future makes it "permanent" by any human scale, the enormous energy flow from free to bound forms generated by modern urban-industrial societies brings the end of civilization, even existence itself, within historical view. Unless we accept entropy's relevance, we face the prospect of a world bereft of the means for releasing and using free energy from sources such as coal and even "renewable" sources such as the sun.

The human race has no ultimate control over its eventual fate. Entropy is the eventual "victor," even over the sun. But by most ethical standards, an undeniable moral superiority is inherent in a society that sustains human enterprise for hundreds of thousands of years rather than devouring the world in hundreds.

How Long Is the Future?

In his science fiction novel *Galaxies Like Grains of Sand*, Brian Aldiss (1973) puts the law of entropy in unusual historical perspective. His story chronicles the decline of our galaxy after thousands of centuries. A humanlike being who appears on the scene proclaims that the very matter of our galaxy has worn down and run out, an illustration of entropy at its grandest. In a clever twist, the book ends with a postscript from a succeeding species paying its respects to the new defunct, formerly "new" superbeings who had succumbed to relentless entropy. Human history may be less than an eyeblink in the span of the galaxies, only a moment in geologic time, but our time is ours. How we live on Earth will go a long way toward determining how long we do so.

While some people are willing to think about the fate of Earth and of human societies in general, most are not prepared to do so. Their concerns are limited by the boundaries of kinship, friendship, and self-interest. For most people, the family is the best opening subject for a dialogue on the future. While many of us may be willing to turn away from the extinction or impoverishment of others, particularly those removed in time or space, few of us are indifferent to the destruction of *our* posterity—our children, their children, and their children's children. Family can be the motivator and social welfare systems the vehicle for understanding and improving the way we are living. If we understand how we live upon the Earth, we will be in a position to project how well our families will live in the future.

How *are* we living upon the material Earth? This question sustains the debate about "limits to growth." The debate begins once we move beyond the necessary recognition that entropy imposes inevitable limits. The imminence of these limits is debatable, but the accumulating evidence documents that we are living off capital at an ever-increasing rate because of the increasing population's increased demand for important materials. And we cannot be confident that some magical technological fix awaits just over the horizon to deliver us from our earthly limits. Apologists for the modern order such as Herbert Kahn (1982) and Julius Simon (1983) would have us believe that entropy and limits to growth are irrelevant, that the current order has a long and indefinite future. Critics of the modern order reject these claims. Our task is to understand the basis for acknowledging limits to growth and the need for transition to a sustainable society.

Origins of the Limits-to-Growth Thesis

Since the nineteenth century, scientists, artists, and others have seen that modern industrial civilization was becoming untenable, that population growth, pollution, and material consumption were propelling us toward catastrophe. Some of these precursors of the limits-to-growth hypothesis based their judgments on an intuitive distaste for the modern industrial order. Some observed the transformation of a particular community; others took a broader perspective and analyzed changes in an entire society. From these limited observations they extrapolated to larger units, even to the entire world. Some were elitists concerned about threats to their class's dominant position. Some were social democrats concerned about mass social welfare systems.

English essayists John Stuart Mill and John Ruskin explored the mistaken concepts of wealth that permeated their society and institutions in the nineteenth century, when England dominated the agenda and mechanisms of the modern world. Gerald Smith (1980) has concluded that these nineteenth-century thinkers were on the mark in their efforts to project a wise course for economic development. Ruskin, for example, urged his countrymen to work toward "true wealth," and saw in it a basis for human betterment and justice. Moderation, generosity, and satisfaction are the hallmarks of true wealth, as he saw it.

In the United States, patrician historian Henry Adams (1914) found cause for alarm when he considered the industrialization and urbanization of America as the century turned from the nineteenth to the twentieth. He wrote of this age:

> Power seemed to have outgrown its servitude and to have asserted its freedom. The cylinder has exploded, and thrown great masses of stone and steam against the sky. The city had the air and movement of hysteria, and the citizens were crying, in every accent of anger and alarm, that the new forces must at any cost be brought under control. Prosperity never before imagined, power never yet wielded by man, speed never reached by anything but a meteor, had made the world irritable, nervous, querulous, unreasonable and afraid. (p. 499)

In *The Theory of the Leisure Class* (1912), economist Thorsten Veblen introduced the concept of "conspicuous consumption." Veblen and others saw the cultural dangers and the essential falsity of aggressive Western materialism, which reached full bloom with the mass consumption of the twentieth century. The Versailles court of King Louis XIII was lavish and exploitive, but it was trivial compared with today's mass-oriented shopping centers marketing plastic, metals, fibers, and electric- and petrol-powered experiences to hundreds of millions. Moving one small stream and a few hills to create the palace at Versailles was child's play compared with diverting major rivers and moving whole mountains to sustain today's urban centers, suburban developments, and agribusiness enterprises.

Artists like D. H. Lawrence, who were aware of the threats to culture posed by the modern industrial order, could evoke an image of change, but few could foresee the physical threats as well. And no one had the tools to document their criticisms. Ruskin was, after all, something of a romantic crackpot. Lawrence could write the following passage (1928), but he was not equipped or inclined to document his analysis scientifically.

> This is history. One England blots out another. The mines had made the halls wealthy. Now they were blotting them out, as they had already blotted out the cottages. The industrial England blots out the agricultural England. One meaning blots out another. The new England blots out the old England. And the continuity is not organic, but mechanical. (*Lady Chatterley's Lover*, 1928, p. 146)

One of the biggest problems facing such analyses is that throughout history, dire predictions of catastrophe have proved incorrect because a technological breakthrough altered the course of social and economic development, thus invalidating a projection of the future based on previous trends. This is the principal rationale used to dispute the relevance of the limits-to-growth thesis.

Those in privileged positions have always tended to see social change as social catastrophe. That observation may be justly applied to those named earlier, the patrician Henry Adams being a prime example. Rejoinders to such critics have sometimes rightly been able to portray them as the boy who cried wolf or as Chicken Little mistakenly thinking that the sky is falling. Contemporary debates are often cast in this light. But what if the wolf really *is* coming? Or, as a bit of bathroom grafitti put it, what if Chicken Little was right?

In 1962, Rachel Carson published *Silent Spring,* a landmark analysis of the concrete effects of powerful modern technology on the biological environment. The pesticide DDT served as an excellent symbol of the modern era. It exemplified the clearly benevolent intent of modern advances in their early stage (it kills insects that harm crops), their ambiguity in the middle stage, when it becomes apparent that they involve costs as well as benefits, and, finally, their demonic character (when they destroy that which they are supposed to serve, protect, and enhance).

It was not until the late 1960s that systematic efforts began to develop an empirical, comprehensive methodology for projecting the future of the modern industrial order. Aurelio Peccei and his colleagues formed the Club of Rome to generate, coordinate, and disseminate their understanding of the global prognosis. They started with four powerful, intertwined forces of the modern order—population growth, resource use, energy consumption, and pollution. These, they said, were part of a broad syndrome, global in its origins and consequences, which they called "the world problematique." The result of an interdisciplinary effort called the "Project on the Predicament of Mankind" was the historically significant report to the Club of Rome entitled *The Limits to Growth,* cited earlier.

Inspired by pioneering systems analyst Jay Forrester (1980) and under the direction of Dennis Meadows, the researchers developed a complex set of equations to relate five global trends: accelerating industrialization, rapid population growth, widespread malnutrition, depletion of nonrenewable resources, and a deteriorating environment. A computer analyzed the available data and projected what would happen in the event of various contingencies. They hoped in this way to predict the future of economic and environmental foundations for social welfare.

THE FUTURE AS IF IT REALLY MATTERED

A key feature of the model was its recognition that some variables change at a percentage rate rather than by the addition of the same fixed sum, for example when bank interest is compounded and one receives interest on the interest. This exponential growth can boggle the mind. Consider this classic example: if a man is paid a penny on the first day of the month and his wages are doubled every day, he will receive $5,368,708.80 on the twenty-ninth day of the month and $10,737,417.00 on the thirtieth! Half the total growth occurs near the very end of the process. Percentage growth rates produce massive increases in the *amount* of change. This is a key element in the concept of limits to growth and one reason people find it so difficult to grasp.

Lester Brown (1980) offers several helpful metaphors. One invokes the image of lily pads in a pond, starting with one and doubling each day; the pond is half covered on the twenty-ninth day and completely covered on the thirtieth. The point is that *crisis can arise precipitously out of seemingly low-grade chronic problems.* On the basis of such a model, *The Limits to Growth* concluded:

- Exponential growth in population and material production is a dominant force in socio economic change in most contemporary societies.
- Current rates of population growth and material output cannot be sustained indefinitely. Probably, growth will overreach important physical limits if continued in accordance with present patterns for another 50 to 100 years.
- Growth may end either through orderly accommodation to global physical limits (a transition to equilibrium) or by overshooting those limits and collapsing, producing a major world catastrophe.
- Because of the many delays in complex systems governing material output and population, the most probable result of current global trends is overshooting of limits and collapse.
- Technological solutions designed to reduce pressures caused by growth (starvation, pollution, rising costs of food production and research, etc.) may only postpone the collapse unless accompanied by changes in social, economic, and political factors stimulating growth.
- It seems possible to identify alternative stages of global equilibrium in which population and material output remain essentially constant and are in balance with our finite resources. They would satisfy man's most

fundamental needs, permit cultural progress, and sustain societies indefinitely.

- There is no unique, optimal long-term population level. Rather, there are many trade-offs involving personal freedom, material and social standard of living, and population level. Given our finite and diminishing resources, we must recognize that inevitably, a larger population implies a lower material standard of living.
- Delays of 50 to 100 years are involved in negotiating an orderly transition to a state of equilibrium, however defined. Thus, nations must begin now to recognize that progress cannot eternally be equated with growth, and must stop the implicit and explicit encouragement of population increase and material expansion. Each year of delay decreases man's long-term options and lessens the likelihood of orderly transition to equilibrium. (Lesh, 1978)

The Fate of the Limits-to-Growth Thesis

The years since publication of *The Limits to Growth* have been characterized by intense debate in some quarters and oblivious silence in others. Subsequent reports to the Club of Rome have sought to clarify issues and rectify technical and conceptual weaknesses in the original. For example, *Mankind at the Turning Point* (1974) examined implications of global trends in various regions of the world. The authors (Mihajlo Mesarovic and Edward Pestel) concluded that industrial history, resources, and demographic character produce different projected paths, in different regions—but paths that will eventually converge in disaster, collapse of social welfare systems, and a retreat into barbarism. In the meantime, the prognosis is for an increasingly unjust world order as the haves struggle mightily to preserve their privileged position in relation to the have-nots. Both reports must be understood as projections of what will happen *if fundamental policies and trends continue.* Of course, both are calls for action to change these policies and trends; here, science and propaganda are comrades in arms. Subsequent reports to the Club of Rome are testimony to this (e.g., *Reshaping the International Order,* 1976; *Goals for Mankind,* 1977; *No Limits to Learning,* 1979).

In March 1982, the Smithsonian Institution in Washington, D.C., recognized and celebrated the tenth anniversary of the publication of *The Limits to Growth.* At the meeting many leaders of the movement to seek a sustainable society heard Dennis and Donella Meadows and their colleagues say that events of that decade had reinforced their belief in the validity of their thesis and in the need for global action to avert catastrophe. They reported the results of a 1982 conference on efforts around the world to develop global and regional models. Despite differences in focus and technique, these groups all affirmed that current trends (particularly the population-industrialization-urbanization complex of forces) portend collapse of the global socioeconomic order and social welfare systems in the twenty-first century. What is more, they reaffirmed the conclusion that *social* changes, not technological fixes, are the primary vehicle for averting disaster and placing humanity on a sustainable ecological and socioeconomic footing (Meadows, Richardson, and Bruckman, 1982).

Social welfare ultimately depends upon how well underlying economic, political, and intellectual models correspond with the realities of the environment. The law of entropy tells us that the physical environment imposes limits on these models. Figure 1.1 describes two scenarios. The first assumes that limit-setting takes place far from the boundaries of environmental tolerance, both now and in the next hundred years. The second assumes that we are close to environmental boundaries, may actually be bumping into some of them already, and will certainly collide with them massively in the decades of the twenty-first century. The first model divorces social welfare systems from environmental systems (at least in principle and in general). The second tells us these two areas will become ever more inextricably linked, as physical and political resources are absorbed in a struggle to maintain a social life increasingly brutish, nasty, and short.

Opponents of the Limits-to-Growth Thesis

Two counterviews dispute the validity of the limits-to-growth thesis, one that argues for business as usual and one that proposes a popular revolution to free us of limits. Both groups argue for more rather than less population and industrial development, for more consumers and more consumption. Both say that current models of economic life promise to enhance, not undermine, foundations for social welfare systems.

Those boosting "business as usual" maintain that things are getting better for everyone under the current world order. They cite worldwide increases in per-capita income, improved health, and progress in telecommunications, transportation, electronics, robotics, agricultural techniques, and petroplastics as harbingers of an even grander future for Earth and its people. They are confident that human ingenuity will produce technological

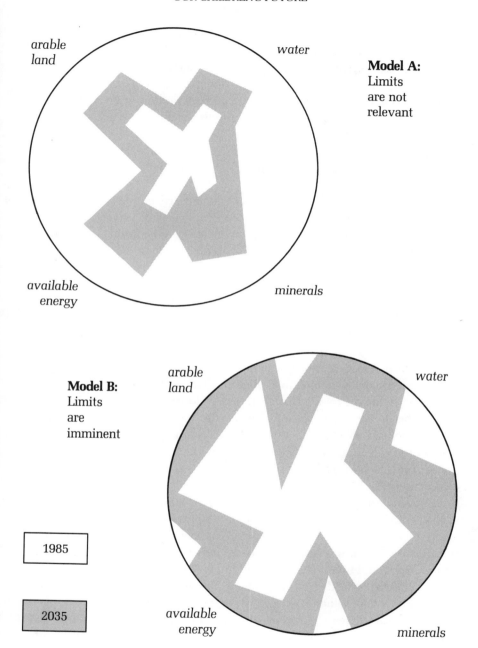

Figure 1–1: Two Alternative Models of "Limits to Growth"

fixes as needed: new substitutes for exhausted mineral supplies, new energy sources such as nuclear fusion to replace petrofuels, new food sources to augment or replace conventional agriculture, space colonies to relieve earthly overcrowding. Herbert Kahn entitled his "booster" book *The Coming Boom* (1982), while Julius Simon calls his *The Ultimate Resource* (1982). Both seek to reassure us that the present path of growth is sustainable and wise. Both have been criticized and repudiated by those who recognize the limits to growth; one review of Kahn's thesis calls it "Prayerful economics," because it seems to be based upon a "miraculous" deliverance from the natural process of the world.

These boosters from the Right have counterparts on the Left who argue that the limits-to-growth thesis is a conservative ploy to keep down the masses, that it simply rationalizes an unjust status quo. In its most extreme form, this argument says limits to growth translates as genocide and oppression. It proposes a political revolution to replace the current world order with a radical socialist society in which environmental and economic issues—like the state in the classic Marxist conception—will wither away. Donella Meadows summarizes (but does not endorse) this socialist perspective with the statement, "since each new mouth comes equipped with two hands, overpopulation is unthinkable" (p. 21). One might characterize Simon's view, "since each mouth comes equipped with a brain, technological inadequacy becomes unthinkable." Rejections of limits to growth from either political extreme are fatally flawed, however, for both sides fail to recognize that neither labor (the Left's solution) nor technology (the Right's solution) is an unlimited substitute for the physical systems of the Earth. We cannot stop entropy. It always costs something to conduct an economic activity. There really is no such thing as a free lunch. We cannot indefinitely use cheap "available" energy. Running power plants, factories, or households requires ever more costly efforts to use available energy. The more sophisticated our technologies, the higher the energy cost to cope with the waste products that result. The cost of radioactive and chemically toxic waste will be with us and future generations long after we have used the energy. To dispute the validity of the limits-to-growth thesis is to gamble with the future. Some do so disingenuously because they stand to profit from business as usual. Others refuse to recognize the practical implications of entropy. In future years our great-grandchildren may look back on us and say, "How could they have been so blind!? How could they not see that limits to growth were inherent in their society and its economic and technological principles?"

How indeed. Listen to the following story:

A skillful trader is intent upon selling his horse. The beast appears to be a prime physical specimen, tall and strong, who can run like the wind. His only defect is that he is blind as a stone. But the trader, a man of P. T. Barnum–like commercial convictions, does not despair. He invites a prospective buyer to examine and observe the horse in the paddock. All goes well until the horse begins to gallop around the field. Crash! He runs into a tree. Dazed, he gets up, shakes his head, and gallops off. Blam! He runs headlong into the fence. He gets up and gallops off, headed straight for an enormous boulder in the middle of the field. "Why, that horse is blind as a bat!" yells the prospective customer. "No sir," replies the trader. "He's not blind. He just don't give a damn."

Are we blind or don't we give a damn? It's often hard to tell. Some of the problems we face in accepting the concept of limits to growth are understandable. Traveling across the North and South American continents, and even in Western Europe, one sees vast stretches of forest and farmland. When we in the affluent modern world want something material, it's always available. Even the "gas crisis" of the early 1970s was a relatively minor inconvenience in the grand scheme of things. We naturally assume that our children will have all that we have, if not more.

Is Conventional Economic Thinking Terminally Ill?

Heidegger explored the proposition that one never becomes truly aware of life until one profoundly accepts the inevitability of nonbeing, the idea that one will cease to exist. Often, people who have had a brush with death experience a renewed appreciation for living. Yet most of us adopt the "personal fable" (Elkind, 1980) that we are immortal, and we live each day as if our lives—like our resources—were unlimited. The enormous psychological challenge of recognizing our personal limits somehow complicates our ability to recognize societal limits. It is hard to accept the idea of our personal death, and even harder to accept the idea that our children's society will die. Just as our failure to accept the "limits-to-life" thesis distorts how we account for each day, so our failure to accept the limits-to-growth thesis distorts how we account for each economic transaction. If we psychologically accept the *fact* that our time on this planet is limited, we are less likely to squander it. If we politically accept the *fact* that our access to the physical Earth is finite, so too are we less likely to squander our resources. A mature person gives up the personal fable of immortality on Earth; a mature society gives up the economic fable of infinite resources.

Later we will examine the assumptions behind conventional concepts of economic development. Here, let it suffice to say that most conventional economic analysis operates in an ecological vacuum, not recognizing the long-term historical issues posed by the laws of entropy and the limits-to-growth thesis (Georgescu—Roegen, 1980). Only the last 300 years have been examined in any real detail by conventional economic analysis. But this "long run" is an inadequate basis for understanding the future. The next 30 years will produce more industrial economic activity than has transpired in all human history to date. This is not surprising; more people will share the Earth in the latter twentieth century than in all previous centuries combined. And human economies are enormously more powerful than ever before. As we saw in Figure 1:1, the relation between economics and ecology has created a whole new ball game. Conventional economic thinking has not adjusted to this new state of affairs.

The conventional economic model is not equipped to describe and analyze what we face in the long term now that the old context of free resources, unlimited waste disposal, and low-impact economies is gone. It simply doesn't consider the real, elemental world of material stocks, energy flows, biological systems, and human capital. If we accept the limits-to-growth thesis, we must conclude that conventional economic thinking is wrong, no matter how accurate its short-term predictions may have been or may continue to be regarding isolated issues such as domestic banking or corporate marketing. This recalls an aphorism attributed to the French philosopher Albert Camus: "Just because we are precise does not mean we smack of the truth." We will return to the problem of economics again (and again), but first I want to explore two prior issues: the concrete nature of a sustainable society and the central position of families in discussions of human quality and quantity. Both are essential steps on the path that leads us to understand the environmental and economic foundations of social welfare systems.

Footnotes

[1] I shall have much to say later about the masculine gender of this "Man" who is at the center of Bronowski's vision of the human enterprise as "he" is in conventional economic thinking as well.

[2]I shall consider at a later point how this use of the lifeboat metaphor resembles and differs from Garret Hardin's (1976) concept of "the lifeboat ethic."

[3]By John Martyn and James Allestry, published under the sponsorship of the Royal Society of London for Improving Natural Knowledge.

[4]Meadows, Meadows, Randers and Behrens, *The Limits to Growth*, 1972.

[5]Jonathan Schell, *The Fate of the Earth*, 1983.

[6]Which is not to say that it is not denied. I shall discuss later Julius Simon's and Herbert Kahn's challenges to the limits-to-growth thesis.

[7]Bartlett's attributes the metaphor to R. Buckminster Fuller in his 1964 book *Prospect for Humanity*: "For at least two million years men have been reproducing and multiplying on a little automated Spaceship Earth." Some (e.g., Hardin) oppose the metaphor because it implies that someone is captaining the ship. But as Robert Heinlein has suggested in some of his novels, a spaceship planet might function for long periods on automatic pilot before the crew realizes its guidance responsibilities.

[8]The anthropomorphic overtones involved in any discussion of this sort are nearly unavoidable, put potentially dangerous. Does the Earth "care" whether human beings (or any beings, for that matter) continue to exist? More on this later.

CHAPTER

2.

December 1974:
Chichen Itza,
the Yucatan, Mexico

What Is
a Sustainable Society?
Do We Live in One?

I CAME TO THE YUCATAN TO SEE
the restored traces of Mayan culture left after centuries of neglected history.
In the Mayans I see a foreboding predecessor of our own society—indeed,
of the modern way of life. They originated in what is now Guatemala, and
for many centuries they thrived and dominated this world. Why did such a
powerful culture collapse? Our best guess is that soil erosion precipitated
an agricultural crisis that incapacitated the whole society. For all our attention to the rise and fall of the Roman empire, it's not the only story worth
knowing. In some ways it's probably not the most accurate analogy to our
situation. Rather than reading Gibbons on the Roman empire, perhaps we
should read E. S. Deevey's treatise on the cataclysmic consequences of the
ruined Mayan agricultural base.

I came to see Chichen Itza, this ancient Mayan city, with dozens of affluent tourists from societies currently dominating the modern world. How
much we Americans, Germans, and Japanese all have in common with each
other. But with the Mayans?

Chichen Itza is architecturally superb with its pyramids, markets,
sports arena, houses, and observatory. It's humbling, or at least ought to be.
Can any of us see ourselves and our societies here? Do the Germans see
Berlin—where they, like the Mayans, performed human sacrifices? Do the
Japanese see Toyko—where they, like the Mayans, ran death camps for
prisoners of war? Do I see Washington—where the extinction of peoples
(like the American Indians) and cities (like Hiroshima) was ordered? Do
any of us see our own societies reduced to ghost towns because of an unsustainable relationship between the human community and nature's
ecosystems?

I do see an exciting moment. Three men are restoring an original column of what must have been an archway. It is in four pieces of stone, and they hoist and push to recreate this small piece of the city toppled hundreds of years ago by who knows what forces, human or otherwise. I notice that the foreman speaks Spanish to one man and an Indian dialect to the other; the two workers communicate only through him. It adds to my excitement. Contemporary society in the Yucatan has exactly this task of bridging the gap between Indian and Spanish, of mobilizing these two traditions on behalf of today and tomorrow. And here is ancient history literally being put back together before my eyes as the column rises again. It's a treasured moment I capture on film, and it seems as real and exciting viewed now as it did when I was there.

But no one else is watching with me. Some Germans pause briefly, and one says, "Nothing's happening here." Then they move on. Ironically, of course, he's right. It's already happened here. Where it is happening is in Berlin, and in Toyko, and in Washington.

What Is a "Sustainable Society"?

What makes a society sustainable? *Webster's* tells us that to sustain a thing means

- to give support
- to provide for the support or maintenance of
- to cause to continue
- to support the weight; hold up
- to prevent from sinking or giving way
- to endure
- to support as true, legal or just

To sustain then means to help a thing continue over time; to support something else, to legitimize. Each meaning is relevant to the concept of sustainable societies. They have a long life in the span of human history; they support a particular and desirable way of life and social order, offering more than mere survival; and they have moral legitimacy, higher values. Each of these is important.

How Long is Long?

For millions of years, human societies were barely sustainable, in the sense of enduring. For most of our species' history, the issue was whether we could establish an ecological niche large enough and stable enough to permit collective functioning beyond the level of family or clan. Disease, predators, climate, and limited food supply always threatened to overwhelm us, and the long-range survival of human communities was in doubt. Only in the last few thousand years has our tenure on the planet seemed assured.

Considering social welfare systems and families against this backdrop cautions against simplistic nostalgia for "the good old days." Only about half the children born in medieval Europe survived infancy and lived until their fifth birthday. In the United States before 1900, so many women died before marriage, perished during childbirth, were widowed very soon after marriage, or remained single that only about 40 percent of America's women experienced a sustained period of married family life as adults. The modern era is the first age in which human communities have laid the demographic and economic foundations for social welfare systems that support families.

Before we glorify the good old days, we might recall family planning pioneer Margaret Sanger's account of life in the impoverished tenements of New York City at the turn of the twentieth century. Sanger wrote:

> Each time I returned to this district, which was becoming a recurrent nightmare, I used to hear that Mrs. Cohen "had been carried to a hospital, but had never come back," or that Mrs. Kelly "had sent the children to a neighbor and had put her head into the gas oven." Day after day such tales were poured into my ears—a baby being born dead, great relief—the death of an older child, sorrow but again relief of a sort—the story told a thousand times of death from abortion, children going into institutions. I shuddered with horror as I listened to the details and studied the reasons back of them—destitution linked with excessive childbearing. The waste of life seemed senseless. One by one, worried, sad, pensive, and aging faces marshaled themselves before me in my dreams, sometimes appealingly, sometimes accusingly. (Sanger, 1938, p. 89)

These conditions continue with a vengeance for today's American "underclass" and for much of the impoverished Third World. Poverty is hardly uplifting, rarely noble.

Today's Challenges

Having established our presence on Earth despite dangers from predators and the environment, we found that we faced the threat of self-destruction. The Mayan debacle was such a case. After enduring for a historically significant period, Mayan society collapsed, even though Mayan peoples continued. Because Mayan agriculture could not support its population, a kind of social Dark Ages ensued.

As we seek to understand historic sustainability, we certainly need to wrestle with the question, "how long is long?" Is a society sustainable that can only project its social welfare systems for 50 years? If we start by looking at our own families, we must answer "no." Who is willing to say that one's children will be the last generation to live within a civilization's social welfare systems? Would 500 years do? That sounds more like it, so long as we are not speaking of the end of humanity as well as of the society in question. Our sense of historical time has withered, of course. Hitler boasted that his Third Reich would last 1,000 years, but it was toppled in less than 15. Post–World War II boosters of the United States proclaimed "The American Century," and American hegemony lasted a decade. Our sense of forever has become trivialized in direct proportion to the pace of social change.

The family is the most potent means of linking today with yesterday and tomorrow. It is the natural focus for analyzing and planning for our social welfare. If we think of the family as not just parents and children, but also ancestors and descendants, it offers a psychologically powerful answer to Groucho Marx's question, "What did posterity ever do for me?" We need to celebrate the family forward and backward in time to counteract the trivializing of history inherent in modern life, with its emphasis on transience, change, and the interchangeability of people, places, and things. A strong focus on family helps us see beyond the end of our noses.

The dynamics of oil prices in the mid-1980s illustrate this need for a longer perspective. As the Club of Rome has made abundantly clear, current oil consumption patterns are one very important aspect of the world problematique. If petroleum is to continue to be available as the cornerstone of modern affluence, we need to conserve it. Because of a short-term decrease in consumption of crude oil (linked more to worldwide recession than to successful conservation efforts), OPEC and other oil "producers" lowered their prices. A collapse of the pricing structure followed, and "cheap oil" returned as "producers" competed for sales. The public cheered, despite the need for *higher* prices to encourage a more realistic approach to petroleum and other nonrenewable resources. The drop in price can only be temporary. The availability of gasoline at less than a dollar per gallon is a trivial gain when it means our grandchildren will have limited access to petroleum products at all.

When economist John Meynard Keynes was asked how his pump-priming approach to government spending would work in the long run, he replied, "In the long run, we shall all be dead." This dismissal of the long-run problem looks more and more like a prophecy. With a trivial sense of the future we certainly *shall* all be dead—or at least plunged into that social and cultural death foreseen by *The Limits to Growth*. Family provides a potent counterweight to this fatal gap in our ability to imagine the future, because few of us will accept the end of our children's children's children. Based on data on life expectancy, many of the young children who witnessed Halley's Comet in 1985-1986 have a good chance of seeing it again. Any concept of the sustainable society *must* include the prospect that our civilization will be around to witness several visits by the venerable comet.

There is no obvious answer to the question of "how long." Given our history and traditions, it's fair to say that a society suited to a 50-year lifespan is not sustainable, but one with a 500-yearlife span is. The benchmark for human societies is, by most western accounts, the Roman society that arose and continued over roughly half a millenium. Chinese society has a still longer track record, so 500 years should serve as a minimum standard.

What Is Society Good For?

A sustainable society offers more than mere biological continuity of the human species. The prospect of nuclear war emphasizes this point. All but the most apocalyptic visions of nuclear holocaust conclude that the human species would survive—albeit in small numbers, in shockingly impoverished circumstances, and plagued by deformities and cancer. This hardly constitutes a sustainable society. Nuclear war would plunge us into a "worthless state of existence" (to use the phrase employed by *The Limits of Growth*) more quickly than any other environmental catastrophe. Recent analyses of the prospect of "nuclear winter" tell this story all too well.

Jonathan Schell's book *The Fate of the Earth* (1982) pictures a human race beaten in the wake of even a limited nuclear war. He portrays the human race struggling to maintain itself on an environmentally shattered planet—a situation far different from that faced by humanity in the relatively benign world of hundreds of thousands of years ago. Schell foresees an end to civilization in all areas receiving even a fraction of the megatonnage of nuclear weapons currently targeted at them. Formal social welfare systems would no longer exist in those areas.

Injuries would probably be compounded by epidemics. Dr. H. Jack Geiger described the likely conditions after a limited attack: "The landscape would be strewn with millions of corpses of human beings and animals. This alone is a situation without precedent in history." Water and food would be polluted. As is always the case in disasters affecting the water supply, the risk of cholera and typhoid would be enormous. Disease-bearing insects would have a field day, feeding on the tens of millions of corpses. Public health facilities would have been destroyed as part and parcel of the general destruction of institutional life. Radiation sickness, wounds, and depression would sap the strength and resistance of survivors. Whatever society remained would be a sick society. Geiger paints a bleak picture.

A society thus ravaged would be unable to maintain social welfare systems, the economy that fed and clothed us having been shattered. As Schell put it:

> If the economy in question is a modern technological one, the consequences will be particularly severe, for then the obstacles to restoring it will be greatest. Because a modern economy, like an ecosystem, is a single, interdependent whole, in which each part requires many other parts to keep functioning, its wholesale breakdown will leave people unable to perform the simplest, most essential tasks. Even agriculture—the immediate means of subsistence—is caught up in the operations of the interdependent machine, and breaks down when it breaks down. (pp. 68–69)

We might foresee an eventual resurgence of civilization as survivors cut their losses and threw themselves into the task of constructing new institutions, new social relationships, a new economy, and a new network of social welfare systems. But the grim reality of undertaking such a task amidst such devastation is too much for most of us to comprehend, let alone endorse in the name of political ideology or national interest.

Nuclear conflagration aside, there is still the prospect of environmental catastrophe. The horrible events in Bhopal, India, in 1984 bear witness to this possibility. Accounts of a city devastated by the leak of methyl isocyanate gas from a Union Carbide plant give us an inkling of what we would face if environmental degradation accelerates, as many fear it will. The Indian government acknowledged 1,431 deaths (although some groups claim the figure is more than 2,000). Health officials document five to ten times that number of permanently disabled persons who cannot seek employment.

The Bhopal disaster is a microcosm in some respects. But it fails as a model because it was an isolated event. The social welfare systems of surrounding communities and the larger society were available in the crisis. Even in an impoverished nation like India, they are substantial. Imagine the challenge of responding simultaneously or sequentially to hundreds or thousands of Bhopals. That is what we would face in the event of even the most limited nuclear war or dramatic environmental degradation. And such degradation may well be the outcome of the "economic war" in which more and more of us are combatants or victims.

An economic war, like a shooting war, can produce social and ecological death. The nuclear scenario is so awful that few will endorse it. However, in the pursuit of affluence, many more may accept the risk of environmental breakdown and the cost to quality of life (particularly what they perceive to be other people's life). A visit to a strip mine, toxic waste dump, or urban slum shows us that. They exist, and are usually placed in close proximity to those with the least political clout. Most people survive these travesties most of the time, but such environments are hardly sustainable, because they undermine the existence and operaton of essential social welfare systems.

"Sustainable" implies more than mere survival of the species. A sustainable society supports a way of life organized around ethical and operational principles. It implies the existence of a culture and a social network within an economic system. Our concern is, after all, with sustainable *societies*, and they are nothing if not socioeconomic organization.

The endurance of a socioeconomic order depends upon its relation to the physical and social environment. If the United States were the only society consuming petroleum and other nonrenewable materials, our society's prospects for a long life would be much greater than they are, with more and more other societies also claiming access to material affluence. We can see this clearly with the success of Japan and the Pacific Basin countries in the 1970s and 1980s. A particular society's sustainability depends to an ever increasing degree upon global context. For example, a report by the Washington-based Environment Fund estimates that in 1980 the energy consumed per capita by the United States population was five times what it was for the rest of the world—333 million versus 66 million BTUs. By 2030, however, the massive increase in the world's population will increase demand elsewhere for energy (even without a rise in the standard of living) by a factor of more than five. Any one society's sustainability depends partly on the extent of its competition with other societies for resources and partly on the extent to which it can be self-reliant. Brazil, for example, is seeking to opt out of the competition for petroleum by converting to domestically produced alcohol. But this is no magical quick fix. Converting from petroleum to alcohol has its own massive social, economic, and environmetal costs. For one thing, it diverts land away from food production.

Some societies have operated on a technologically primitive, labor-intensive basis for periods of historical time that begin to qualify them as sustainable. The Aleutian Inuit (the name preferred by natives for people commonly called Eskimos) and the pygmies of New Guinea are two examples. However, these societies were small by most standards and geographically isolated in a way that *was* rarely feasible then and *is* now virtually impossible. At least under the current world order, being a closed system is rarely permitted. Except for feudal Japan under the Tokugawa Shogunate from 1603–1867, few large societies have managed this. What is more, small-scale premodern societies rarely, if ever, remain sustainable once they come into contact with more modern societies.

The case of the Aleutian Inuit exemplifies the problem. One sees this when contrasting Inuit life as presented in the 1920s documentary *Nanuck* with that portrayed in the 1976 film *From the First People.* In the 1920s Nanuck and his family were self sufficient, although the tide of modern life was rising around them. They lived in dynamic harmony with the natural environment. The Shungnak family of the 1970s is tied to the modern world with its technological benefits and costs—radios, processed food, snowmobiles, and electricity. If anything, the Shungnak community is so removed from its self-sufficient and sustainable past that it is now hyper-vulnerable. It depends upon imports to meet virtually all its basic needs. What is more, the old skills needed for sustainable self-sufficiency are dying with the elders. Life is "easier"—after all, Nanuck died in the winter following the filming of his story. But, the Shungnak community remains a metaphor for us all: we have increased our power and productivity by substituing petroleum- and electrically-powered machines for human and animal power, but in doing so we have increased our vulnerability to any kind of socioeconomic disruption. We have constructed elaborate formal social welfare systems to cope with life's inherent vicissitudes and the complexities introduced by modern societies. Now we must find a way to pay for them, because we can no longer live without them.

What Does It Mean To Be Modern?

For all practical purposes, the issue of socioeconomic order boils downs to this: can a given society support its socioeconomic order over the long run in the global context of that particular length of time? Historical comparisons are important, but the big challenge comes in looking toward the future. The long run with which we are concerned is the period from the mid–twentieth century onward to the twenty-fifth. To earn the label "sustainable," a society must meet the stiff 500-year test. As currently constituted, few if any societies do.

This, of course, was the message of *The Limits to Growth* in 1972, *Mankind at the Turning Point* in 1974, and *Groping in the Dark* in 1982. "Modernized" societies fail the 500-year test because their socioeconomic orders are unsustainable—even if current relations between technologically modern and unmodern societies remain unchanged. Modern societies can continue to do well for the next half century if they're lucky and if they can keep the poor societies down. But they face an erosion of wealth in the latter half of the twenty-first century, when the children of today's youngsters will be babysitting for their grandchildren.

How do today's very rich and poor societies contribute to each other's social welfare? Modernized societies provide money and models for economic development. They also provide models for social welfare systems. They provide technical assistance and medical care. In some cases they provide food directly. But they also exploit poor societies as markets and as sources of raw materials, including labor. Indeed, modernized economies depend upon international trade and the development of markets in other societies for their economic life blood, and ultimately for resources for their social welfare systems. This is precisely one of our concerns in this book.

Just as we have come to see that our military and economic future is globally interconnected, so we must see that supply and demand for social welfare systems are related to the global order. This new challenge arises not only from our economic and environmental interdependence, but from moral issues raised by modernization. The modern "way of the world" is taking an ever larger place in the day-to-day life of societies all over the world. It is evident in lively international trade of high-technology articles for mass consumption—e.g., ratios, televisions, and automobiles.

This is the most visible sense in which modernized societies have penetrated the unmodernized world. Poor societies are ripe for this penetration; they may even desire it. But once in the industrialized export business they are hooked into a game in which someone must lose (import) if someone else is to win (export). Balance-of-trade surpluses and deficits are not the whole story, however. Behind them are more basic human realities that influence the meaning of sustainability.

In his introduction to Duane Elgin's *Voluntary Simplicity*, Ram Dass, a Western-style intellectual turned Eastern-style mystic, recounts the following story, presented in a narrative form compatible with its content.

> I look out over a gentle valley in the Kumoan Hills at the base of the Himalayas. A river flows through the valley forming now and again man-made tributaries that irrigate the fertile fields. These fields surround the fifty or so thatched or tin-roofed houses and extend in increasingly narrow terraces up the surrounding hillsides.
>
> In several of these fields I watch village men standing on their wooden plows goading on their slow-moving water buffalo who pull the plows, provide the men's families with milk, and help to carry their burdens. And amid the green of the hills, in brightly colored saris and nose rings, women cut the high grasses to feed the buffalo and gather the firewood which, along with the dried dung from the buffalo, will provide the fire to cook the grains harvested from the fields and to warm the houses against the winter colds and dry them during the monsoons. A huge haystack passes along the path, seemingly self-propelled, in that the woman on whose head it rests is lost entirely from view.
>
> At a point along the stream there is laughter and talk and the continuous slapping of wet cloth against rock as the family laundry gets done. And everywhere there are children and dogs, each contributing his or her sound to the voice of the village.
>
> Everywhere there is color: red chili peppers drying on the roofs and saris drying by the river, small green and yellow blue birds darting among the fruit trees, butterflies and bees teasing their way from one brightly colored flower to another.
>
> I have walked for some five miles from the nearest town to reach this valley. The foot path I have taken is the only means of exit from this village. Along the way, I meet farmers carrying squash, burros bearing firewood or supplies, women with brass pots on their heads, school children, young men dressed in "city clothes." In all of these people I find a quiet shy dignity, a sense of belonging, a depth of connectedness to these ancient hills.
>
> It all moves as if in slow motion. Time is measured by the sun, the seasons, and the generations. A conch shell sounds from a tiny temple, which houses a deity worshiped in these hills. The stories of this and other deities are recited and sung, and they are honored by flowers and festivals and fasts. The provide a context—vast in its scale of aeons of time, rich with teachings of reincarnation and the morality inherent in the inevitable workings of karma. And it is this context that gives vertical meaning to these villagers' lives with their endless repetition of cycles of birth and death.
>
> This pastoral vision of simplicity has much appeal to those of us in the West for whom life can be full of confusion, distraction, and complexity. In the rush of modern industrial society, and in the attempt to maintain our image as successful persons, we feel that we have lost touch with a deeper, more profound part of our beings. Yet, we feel that we have little time, energy, our cultural support to pursue those areas of life that we know are important. We long for a simpler way of life that allows us to restore some balance to our lives.

Is the vision of simple living provided by this village of the East the answer? Is this an example of a primitive simplicity of the past or of an enlightened simplicity of the future? Gradually, I have come to sense that this is not the kind of simplicity that the future holds. Despite its ancient character, the simplicity of the village is still in its "infancy."

Occasionally, people show me their new babies and ask me if that peaceful innocence is not just like that of the Buddha. Probably not, I tell them, for within that baby rest all the latent seeds of worldly desire just waiting to sprout as the opportunity arises. On the other hand, the expression on the face of the Buddha, who had seen though the impermanence and suffering associated with such desires, reflects the invulnerability of true freedom.

So it is with this village. Its ecological and peaceful way of living is unconsciously won and it is vulnerable to the winds of change that fan the latent desires of its people. Even now there is a familiar though jarring note in this sylvan village scene. The sounds of static and that impersonal professional voice of another civilization—the radio announcer—cut through the harmony of sounds as a young man of the village, holding a portable radio to his ear, comes around a bend. On his arm there is a silver wristwatch that sparkles in the sun. He looks at me proudly as he passes. And a wave of understanding passes through me. Just behind that radio and wrist watch comes an army of desires that for centuries have gone untested and untasted. As material growth and technological change activate these yearnings, they will transform the hearts, minds, work, and daily life of this village within a generation or two. (1979, pp. i–iii)

Ram Dass sees the vulnerability of this unconsciously "simple" society to the calculating complexity of modernization. Elgin says the answer lies not in unconscious simplicity, but in integrating the benefits of technology with the demands of the future and the wisdom of the past. He calls this "voluntary simplicity"—a kind of "informed consent" to live in a sustainable society. It takes a special brand of cultural intelligence to master the forces of modernization.

The Revolution of Rising Expectations and the Tidal Wave of Wants and Demands

Japan is being put to this test. Robert Christopher (1983) provides a timely scorecard on its efforts to harmonize forces of modernization with the cultural wisdom of a stable past. He chronicles the firestorm of affluent modernization that erupted in Japan in the post–World War II era. By 1981, the per capita number of color televisions in Japan was 1.4! Women are entering the paid labor force in dramatic numbers, and the number of day care centers has followed suit. Young people emphasize individuality and personal privacy more than ever before. Christopher reports on a 1980 poll in which 71 percent of youth aged 15–19 said they have "an individual life style" and fewer than 10 percent indicated a desire to lead "a life useful to society." These results reversed the findings of a similar survey in 1960. Juvenile crime and drug abuse have risen dramatically in recent years. These changes reflect a general shift in orientation that seems a nearly universal response to affluence: "As commitment to work begins to diminish, the emphasis on personal desires increases" (p. 87). The average number of hours Japanese spent on the job dropped from 186 per month in 1970 to 175 per month in 1980 (still at the high end of the scale for modernized societies). Borrowing rather than saving for consumer purchases is becoming the dominant pattern.

Nevertheless, Christopher does not foresee an easy and total victory of modernization over traditional Japanese culture.

> Despite the self-absorption of so many young Japanese these days, the great majority of the population finds it almost impossible to conceive that anyone can achieve real stature or success except as part of a group. . . . One of Japan's greatest strengths in its extraordinary evolution from the feudal society that it was at the time of Commodore Perry's arrival to the advanced technological one it is today has been that instead of totally accepting destabilizing and often unsuitable Western ideas and institutions, the Japanese have been remarkably successful in adapting these influences to their own needs and imperatives. (pp. 90, ff)

Once released upon the world, modernization is a force so far reaching and powerful that it stands almost beyond human control. Harlan Cleveland's classic image (1949) was of a "revolution of rising expectations." With that phrase he meant to convey that the people had a new vision of material possibilities and potential for enhanced social welfare. Today the phrase seems too tame to convey the intensity of this force. Perhaps "a tidal wave of wants and demands" is nearer the mark. In any case, changed expectations after World War II have made it more difficult to conceal or rationalize the distinction between modernized "haves" and unmodernized "have-nots." How can you keep them down on the farm after they've seen TV? This change places new constraints on the third component of sustainability, namely that society be just.

The Just Society: Spaceship Earth or Slaveship Earth?

Modern industrialized societies are living off their capital—nonrenewable sources of energy, arable land, and drinkable water. Even worse, our high-powered societies are living off the *global* capital and encouraging others to do the same, an intolerable situation given the vested interest of current *and future* generations in nonmodernized societies. One strategy for sustaining socioeconomic order is to live off the resources of others. But this does not meet the third condition for sustainability: moral legitimacy.

Mere physical survival of the species and maintenance of order are insufficient to make a society sustainable. It must also meet the criterion of justice. A society may endure, but without an ethical core, it is not sustainable. This ethical imperative must permeate our analysis of economic, environmental, and social welfare issues. Some foreseee that the most powerful modernized states will endure through exploitation and suppression. In such a worst-case moral scenario, the elites within those societies would maintain an affluent life style by forcing other societies to provide the necessary resources yet forego participation (with the exception, perhaps, of co-opted managerial elites). Within the powerful societies, the elites would extend affluence as widely as would be consistent with maintaining their own privileged positions, relying upon coercion to make up the difference.

One could accurately call such a world "Slaveship Earth," (Paarlberg, 1975) but certainly not a world of sustainable societies. Are the foundations laid for Slaveship Earth? The vast majority of citizens in industrialized societies seem ready to accept rationalizations for their privileged position, and the performance of many local elites in primitive societies argues that Slaveship Earth is a most persuasive scenario for the future. But it is not the sustainable society, no matter how long it endures. One can foresee it but not accept it, for it has no moral duration, whatever its historical scope. It is without sufficient commitment to the moral imperative to build and maintain social welfare systems to sustain families.

Slaveship Earth exists already in the day-to-day lives of millions of Earthlings. And it exists in the visions of negative utopian literature ("dystopias," as they are sometimes called). Huxley's *Brave New World* (1948) and Orwell's *1984* (1948) are most well known. Harry Harrison's *Make Room, Make Room* (1962), which became the film *Soylent Green*, is perhaps most to the point. It portrays precisely the political, economic, ecological, and ethical bankruptcy of a society that endures by cannibalizing the world and its people. The elite live in opulent enclaves protected by police. The masses are destitute, often homeless. The countryside is intensively farmed by chemical high-tech methods to provide marginal food for the urban masses and luxuries for the elite. With the oceans dead, the managerial elite turn to high-tech cannibalism; human bodies are recycled to become a protein-rich food source called "soylent green." The state encourages suicide to relieve crowding and maintain the food supply. Hardly the sustainable society we want, but not a gross exaggeration of conditions in some societies at present.

Reports from Mexico City tell of pervasive crowding and destitution. Brazil's three largest cities—Sao Paulo, Rio de Janeiro, and Belo Horizonte— have *millions* of abandoned children. Brazil, with a population of 130 million (sixth largest in the world), an affluent minority, and a severely impoverished majority, offers many working models of the society envisioned by Harrison. That viewers could be horrified by the fiction of *Soylent Green* yet oblivious to the facts of life for hundreds of millions worldwide agues that Slaveship Earth is a plausible, realistic model for the future. We can't take sustainability for granted; it is not an inevitable result of social evolution.

Various forms of the sustainable society are possible so long as they meet three basic conditions: historical scope, social coherence, and moral legitimacy. Some may last longer than others. Some may have traditional class structures; others may be more egalitarian. Some may be primarily rural, while others will be urban. Some may be richer than others. But all will live long and prosper, to nurture the best humanity has to offer, and to respect the human spirit. All will maintain social welfare systems upon a sensible economic and environmental basis. All will sustain the wealth of families.

Do We Live in a Sustainable Society?

Having said all this, the first issues we confront are these: do we North Americans currently live in a sustainable society? Could most societies around the world readily become sustainable? Let's assume that everyone is commited to a long history for the human race, to a coherent social order, and to justice. Many doubt the validity of this benign assumption of universal good intentions, and with good reason. But for the sake of argument, suppose it is true, and that current debates over nuclear power, conservation of natural resources, population, and economic development are debates of means rather than ends. What then?

Then we must look at our society and world to see whether our situation is, indeed, sustainable. Those who think it is propose four arguments. First, the population "problem" is self correcting. Second, technological innovation eliminates constraints on natural resources by substituting abundant resources for scarce ones. Third, the cluster of life styles in an urban industrial society is suitable to human development over the long haul. And fourth, the current situation offers the best long-term prospects for justice.

Population: It is commonly argued that rising affluence and a declining birth rate go hand in hand. As societies mature economically, so the analysis goes, family size shrinks. Proponents of this view cite as evidence case studies from around the world—but clustered, of course, in modern industrialized/urbanized societies. This view offers demographic hope rather than despair. It evokes the image of a population computer rather than a population bomb, as people adjust (calculatingly) to the joint phenomena of lower mortality rates and capital-intensive life styles that make children more costly.

In 1982 the United States Census Bureau projected zero population growth for the United States by the 2050s, with a peak population of 309 million as deaths exceed total births and net immigration (*New York Times,* November 4, 1982). The population in 2050 would be older (22 percent aged 65 or over versus 11 percent in 1981), and the ratio of elderly to working-age members would shift from 5.4 to 1 (in 1982) to 2.6 to 1. Such a society could be feasible within limits set by available resources, provided assumptions hold about industrial productivity and accessibility of resources—that is, that the world order regarding who gets to use what remains roughly intact, that potential sources of energy pan out, and that immigration does not grow significantly. In fact, the low national birth rate has led more than one observer to argue that we have overcorrected demographically, that we need to *increase* the birth rate among affluent modernized populations.

Looking beyond the United States, analysts who say sustainability is here project that population increases will level off *within acceptable limits* through a variety of automatic processes. In the already and the soon to be affluent nations, Western attitudes toward economics and family size will do the trick. Parents will choose to have fewer children and will act upon that decision effectively because of the availability of reliable contraception. In less affluent countries (whose numbers vary depending on the estimate), the population boom of the post–World War II era will prove to be a relatively short-lived phenomenon. How? They see an end to the "demographic euphoria" that greeted declining death rates. These death rates had declined due to improved basic health care and an upsurge in the availability of food (because of improved agricultural practice and aid programs). A policy of demographic restraint will take hold and stabilize population within limits set by the planet's ecology, according to this view, and we will avoid overshooting the mark. Thus, our current situation is already sustainable, given the inevitable trends built into the social system. This view has been well publicized in the writings of economist Julian Simon (*The Ultimate Resource*, 1979), the late think-tanker Herman Kahn (*Global 2000 Revisited*, 1983, and *The Coming Boom*, 1982), and Ben Wattenberg (*A Dearth of Children*, 1987).

Technological innovation: An economic analog to the self-correcting model of demography is the self-sustaining trend of techological innovation. In this view, each economic breakthrough of the past has arisen from a new organizing technology that permitted and even stimulated beneficial economic transformation. Some (e.g., Kondratieff) have gone so far as to plot "long waves" of economic development of roughly 50 years' duration directly linked to the interplay of technological innovation and investment of capital. Hydro-powered machinery, steam engines, the railroads, petroleum-based industry—each technological breakthrough created economic reorganization that increased society's wealth. Economic historian Walter Rostow integrates these developments into a coherent picture in *Stages of Economic Development* (1964).

In this view, high tech microelectronics will stimulate the next advance as we move into the future. Just as the burning of coal solved the energy problem in a deforested England in the seventeenth century, so new technologies will overcome the problem of declining oil reserves in the twenty-first. This theory relies on historical extrapolation and profound confidence in our scientific and engineering ability. The attitude is, "if we did it before we can do it again"; "if we *need* to create a solution, we *will.*" It's the familiar adage: "necessity is the mother of invention."

Most of these analyses focus on the industrial sector, and therefore emphasize the root problem of finding enough energy to fuel the transformation of raw materials into goods. The new energy technologies are typically high-tech, industrialized power generation ranging from nuclear fission to nuclear fusion to the large-scale capture of solar energy. For nuclear fission, the answer is breeder reactors to generate power and atomic fuel, although few experts now see this as an option beyond 2025.

For nuclear fusion the key is to find a way to transform globally abundant hydrogen into usable energy. For solar energy, it is the construction of vast installations on Earth (or in orbit around Earth) to collect sunshine and transform it into usable energy. Perhaps nuclear fusion has the greatest appeal, as is evidenced by the following "public service" advertisement from Gulf under the headline "Gulf People: Energy for Tomorrow." In the ad, Tihiro Ohkawa, vice president for fusion power research at Gulf's General Atomic Company, says:

> Our research programs, sponsored by the Department of Energy and others, could lead to construction of an experimental fusion reactor within a decade. . . . Both fusion and conventional fission reactors produce heat, which can, for instance, generate electricity. But fusion produces less radioactive waste than fission. It can't get out of control. And it uses cheaper fuel—hydrogen instead of uranium. In fact, fusion reactors can make fuel for fission reactors, and possibly will even burn the fission reactor's wastes. . . . It's a tremendous technological challenge, but the reward is tremendous, too: inexhaustible energy.

The modern life style: Modern industrialized/urbanized societies offer successful individuals an unprecedented range of options about how and where to live. Indeed, one justification for these societies is that they free people from the constraints of the past, and offer mobility in all its senses. Yet, despite their apparent diversity, it is fair to say that these societies, when contrasted with past societies and with nonmodernized, nonindustrialized societies, offer only one life style.

This life style is founded upon a wide range of consumer goods for homemaking (food-related and cleaning appliances), recreation and entertainment (television and water skiing), and travel (automobiles and airplanes). It substitutes capital- and energy-intensive activities for labor-intensive activities—a vacuum cleaner for a broom, a video game for a walk in the woods, a snowmobile for a pair of snowshoes. Those who think our society is now sustainable argue that this life style can be a permanent feature of human life. Some, like Alvin Toffler, may see humans themselves changing, becoming more adapted to this life style, but in any case they see it as the wave of the future. They see it penetrating more and more societies and becoming the basis for a world culture. What is more, they see this life style dominated by consumer goods as consistent with basic human needs and thus psychologically sustainable. Its demographic and ecologic sustainability rests upon solutions to the population and energy problems already considered. The "American way" that Alan Potter (1954) described more than three decades ago as the natural destiny of a "people of plenty" will become common worldwide. This is evident already. One can drink

Coca-Cola in China, eat a Big Mac in Brazil, play PacMan in Nigeria, and direct-dial home from Khartoum.

Justice: Those who say current modern society is sustainable say it meets the criterion of justice. Because they assume population and resource problems are being solved "automatically" by the existing socioeconomic order, they see no threat to future generations. "Use more now, have more later" is a crude rendering of this view of intergenerational justice. As for the justice of the system with respect to the current individuals on Earth, they answer that it is more just than it was in the past, and more just than the realistically available contemporary alternatives. What is more, it offers the greatest hope for the future, for the rest of the world as well as the United States. Current approaches do as much as is humanly possible for as many as is humanly possible—their imperfections are just that, and not fundamental flaws.

In sum then, on one side stand those who argue that we live already in a sustainable society, in a world destined to become composed of ever more similarly sustainable societies—if only everyone will keep their faith in the processes of modernization. Tinker if you must, they say. If necessary, fine tune for greater efficiency. But don't meddle with the basic mechanisms, because they are working. We have a sustainable society in the making if we only stay the course.

But Do We Live in a Sustainable Society?

But do society and the current world order predict sustainability? The answer to this question appears to come from how we interpret our most recent past. Were the 1970s an aberration, or a portent of things to come? Those who foresee sustainability see the 1970s as a temporary deviation from the course, one that is being corrected in the 1980s. They see the 1970s as a temporary recession rather than a symptom of profound crisis, and the 1980s as a permanent return to good times. In the year 2000, they believe, we will look back to see upward progress from World War II toward an affluent, just, and permanent world order, progress interrupted by only brief setbacks in the 1970s. They point to the fact that policy makers responded to danger signs as they became evident during that decade. For example, DDT and PCBs (two dangerous toxic pollutants) were the target for legislative and executive action in many modernized societies. The attention led a 1982 UN environmental program to announce that progress had been made in dealing with these pollutants globally, and to conclude that the world's oceans were successfully withstanding contamination by waste dumping and agricultural runoff.

In contrast, those who disagree that sustainability is upon us argue that we will see the 1970s as signaling a decisive downturn that invalidated old models of investment and development. They conclude that environmental awareness, improvements, and control are importantly positive, but are only the beginning of fundamental shifts in policy and practice. In the long run, they argue, many of the improvements noted in the 1980s are not of sufficient magnitude to stabilize human communities. Proudly proclaiming that you have slowed a runaway truck from 60 to 40 miles per hour is almost meaningless if there is a dead end 100 yards ahead. There are grounds for disputing the notion that sustainability is upon us.

Population: Official estimates by the UN and the World Bank in the late 1970s do project that the world's population will stabilize below 10 billion early in the twenty-first century. According to the Environment Fund, the low estimate (based upon reaching replacement level fertility by 2000-2005) projected an addition by 2075 of 3.9 billion people to the 1983 figure of 4.6 billion. The high estimate (replacement by 2040-2045) was for 8.9 billion by 2150. By 1988, however, global population had already reached 5.1 billion! What is more, some demographers maintain that the connection between affluence and decreased birth rates does not automatically and necessarily hold. In Brazil, for example, the booming economy and dramatically increased per-capita income of the 1960s were accompanied by an equally large population increase and (through the 1970s) actual *declines* in basic social welfare for 80 percent of the population.

Are the estimated upper limits for population sufficient reassurance that the population problem is solved? Perhaps not. The estimates project massive population increases in some of the societies least equipped to deal with them in a humane and dignified way. Already the Indian subcontinent can only marginally meet basic needs for a population of roughly 850 million. What will it be like with the middle range estimate's 2.3 billion? The same is true of Central America and Africa. Even China, which has already exceeded the 1 billion mark, is concerned, although it has an aggressive population control program. With 22 percent of the world's people on only 7 percent of the available land, even China—with its high level of governmental commitment and powerful infrastructure for exerting social control—is struggling to stabilize population at a sustainable level.

All this leads Lester Brown (1980) of the Worldwatch Institute to conclude that the population problem is not "solved" simply because under existing trends and policies population will stabilize at about 10 billion. Ten billion may be "survivable," although that is debatable considering the demands such a population, even if most of it lived in poverty, would make on the Earth. But it is hardly sustainable if it means giving up a humane life style and justice. He and others argue that a population of 10 billion will exact those costs and will not endure for long, because it will require cannibalizing the planet for maintenance, even if technological innovation leads to new economic wealth. Brown argues instead for a goal of 6 billion, and it's a modest proposal at that.

> Supporting even six billion people at acceptable consumption levels will not be possible without widespread rationing, more careful management of biological systems, stringent energy-conservation measures, materials recycling programs, and a more equitable distribution of vital resources both within and among societies. On the other hand, stabilizing world population at six billion will not require any country to do what several countries have not already done. (Brown, 1980, p. 146)

To achieve such a goal with a life expectancy of 70 years would require birth and death rates in balance at about 13 per thousand. Current death rates range from about 6 to about 15; birth rates from about 10 to nearly 50 per thousand.

Is the population problem solved? World population has already exceeded 5 billion. There is no permanent solution in one sense, of course. Birth and death rates can always vary. There are upper limits on birth rates, set by the physiology of fertility, of course, but they are much too high to be of any practical value. We are talking about birth rates that must eventually work out to about 2 per woman, although biological limits do not usually begin to operate until we reach a figure higher by a factor of 5. Active, comprehensive contraception is fundamental to any plan for stabilizing population. Access to contraception is a key feature of social welfare for the individual family and for the community.

A growth rate of zero is possible, but extremely improbable. Rarely in history have birth rates declined below replacement levels and stayed there. The 1980 rate of 1.8 in the United States is historically noteworthy and, of course, doesn't include the effect of immigration. The price of population stability will be eternal vigilance. One aspect of a sustainable society is relative stability in birth and death rates and prompt public response when they get out of line.

The nurturance we provide to families is critical to population control. UNICEF executive director James Grant (1984) reports that health and nutrition services aimed at increasing the odds of survival in the first years of life are a consistently effective stimulus to limit population. *The State of the World's Children 1982-1983* concluded that if we cut the infant and child mortality rate in half, we would reassure parents sufficiently to motivate a decrease of between 12 and 20 million births each year. This estimate is based on the fact that family size decreases when parents see decreased risk to each child, they are less inclined to produce large numbers of offspring. This is particularly true in societies with few formal social welfare systems.

The impact of migration in calculations concerning sustainability is not yet fully appreciated. The decrease in United States birth rates in the 1970s is widely recognized, yet not the impact of immigration, most notably from Mexico and Central America. Such immigration is hard to monitor and control, and its long-range impact is unknown. With Mexico's population alone predicted to rise from 70 to 205 million by 2000, such immigration may increase dramatically. The projected economic climate in Mexico lends credence to such a prediction. No one seems to know how emigration from Mexico will affect population growth in Mexico, let alone in the United States. In any case, it seems extremely risky wishful thinking to believe the population problem is solved, even for the United States, even under the best of technological and economic conditions. And optimistic forecasts concerning those conditions are themselves suspect.

Technological innovation: While those who believe sustainability is upon us look to technological innovation as a permanent savior, others are doubtful. Few who have explored "the technology issue" foresee a return to the low-tech, low-power technologies that dominated the period before the Industrial Revolution. The genuine progress offered by many technological breakthroughs is hard to deny. Umberto Colombo (1983, personal communication), for example, cites three areas in which technological innovation can help lead the way to a truly sustainable society: biotechnologies that use microorganisms and genetic engineering to reduce energy consumption and pollution; information-processing technology that facilitates decentralization and greater equity between urban and rural areas; and new materials that increase the life and utility of goods requiring fewer nonrenewable materials to produce. But the law of entropy warns against techniques that promise something for nothing. We must look at the *net* energy produced by high-tech power plants, which require massive investments of resources before they break even and exact great maintenance and waste disposal costs after they become operational (and sometimes even after they are defunct).

Some observers have examined efforts to create an atomic "breeder reactor" that could generate its own plutonium to fuel fission that produces commercially usable energy. Billions of dollars have been invested over three decades into what some call "the dream machine," and the net result is a dead end. Even the more sensible photovoltaic cell, which transforms sunlight into electricity, must face up to the limits imposed by entropy upon its production and use in reality. There is no perpetual motion machine, no formula for creating gold from lead. There is no free lunch. No technology will free us from the reality of limits.

Beyond the problem of entropy stands the proposition that we face a law of diminishing returns. The massive needs of a population numbering in the billions ensure that the costs of *any* new technology for mass use will be so large that they are probably prohibitive (Orio Giarini, p. 146).

Giarini argues that the economy becomes unstable when scarcity arises because technological innovation cannot generate accelerated surplus production. In short, there arises a crisis of diminishing returns from technology. Here the historical crunch comes, for Giarini sees the mid-1970s as the time when the diminishing returns of technology began in earnest. Why? It is partly because new technologies are based in sophisticated science, which means it takes longer to move from idea to implementation. Fusion seems to be the worst case thus far. Just as we were told for years that policy makers could see "the light at the end of the tunnel" in the Vietnam War in the 1960s, so now we are told that fusion will deliver "inexhaustible energy for tomorrow" (Ohkawa, 1981). But that "tomorrow" seems always to be receding into the future, and meanwhile each today brings another cost in the form of toxic waste, pollution alarm, and recognition of environmental limits.

The long lead times required for technological research do not fit well with the supply-demand equilibrium of the economic process. Technological change has its own cycles, and tends to produce more waste and require more capital allocation. And sophisticated technology tends to make systems more vulnerable to human limits. This is evident in military equipment. High-tech weapons are often beyond the capacity of soldiers to operate and maintain effectively. Giarini argues that the only technological innovation not yet experiencing diminishing returns is the computer microprocessor (although others might add the bioengineering noted by Colombo). This may be one of our few aces in the hole in redirecting society towards sustainability—a bargaining chip in negotiating a way to avert disaster.

The law of diminishing returns seems to have reared its ugly head in the 1970s. The catalog is extensive: per-capita food production peaked; most industrial applications of post–World War II technology were in place, and yet they have not delivered quick, dramatic payoffs for the masses. In the case of energy, utilities *cannot* make an adequate profit by investing in new generating plants, only by investing in conservation and efficiency. As noted before, one reviewer called Herbert Kahn's prediction of economic boom and a technological Eden "prayerful economics," in the sense that it hopes for a miracle that will transcend the normal workings of the world. All in all, the most hard-nosed practical analyses available suggest assumptions by the "sustainability-is-upon-us" school regarding technology are untenable.

The modern life style: Is the modern life style sustainable? Those who think it is rest their case upon two assumptions: first, that the material basis exists for consumer-oriented affluence to become the standard way of life for everyone; and, second, that consumer-oriented affluence rests upon a sound psychological foundation.

Can the modern life style be sustained as the dominant motif for the entire world? The issue raises a dilemma of sorts, for it appears that efforts to spread the North American way of life throughout the world eventually undermine its viability in North America. Our success in Westernizing Japan, Brazil, and other societies seems to be one factor depressing American industry in the 1980s. The consumer-oriented modern life style is truly "living off the fat of the land." Not everyone can live so. It requires a favorable balance of trade between the affluent and the nonaffluent, the haves and the have-nots. One country's solution is another country's problem. The same is true *within* societies as well.

The United States is the most successful modernized nation in many respects, and yet about 25 percent of its children lived below the poverty line in 1986. In the 1980s poverty is growing, especially among children and their mothers in single-parent households. The various "economic miracles" of Latin America, such as Chile and Brazil, tell similar though more dramatic stories; not 25 percent but 75 percent are likely to experience real poverty amidst an outburst of apparent affluence. The Asian miracles (Singapore, Taiwan, South Korea) are beginning to show the same weaknesses. As the good times of the 1960s came to an end, the 1970s saw an outbreak of economic deprivation. Worldwide unemployment reached 30 percent, and in the United States rose above 10 percent. The "normal" unemployment rate for the United States was held to be 4.5 percent only a decade ago, yet in 1985 7 percent was accepted politically as normal. There is every indication that this figure will continue to climb, as it has done already in most Third World and many modernized countries. The 1980s have seen ever higher "normal" levels of unemployment in European countries as well: 13 percent in Belgium, 11 percent in Britain, 9 percent in France, 10 percent in Italy, and 15 percent in Turkey, for example.

More and more workers will, at age 35, experience the prospect of being unemployed for the rest of their lives or at age 18 of never holding a real job at all. What is more, monetarization means that more and more families experience "modern poverty," defined by the inadequacy of *cash* income to meet *cash* expenses. Had they been less tied to the cash economy, these families need not have experienced "classical poverty," defined by the inadequacy of total resources to meet basic needs (Giarini, 1981). When what once was "free" now has a cash price, the danger is that those who once could afford the cost in terms of labor now cannot generate enough cash to pay the price. This critical dynamic profoundly affects the wealth of families. It is evident in the United States as more and more families cannot "afford" child care—because what once was outside the monetarized economy is now rapidly becoming part of it.

Families suffer casualties in the economic wars that are part of monetarizing and modernizing a society. Chronic economic deprivation elevates the rate of family violence and neglect; episodes of acute deprivation precipitate still further increases in assault. Even periods of dramatic economic change typically viewed as positive (e.g., the energy boom towns of the American West) produce increases in child maltreatment. Families require a *stable and supportive* economic climate. Economies that jeopardize this climate jeopardize their own sustainability.

As Giarini states (1981), total welfare equals the value of the nonmonetarized economy plus the value of the monetarized economy. When monetary value increases without producing an equal or larger decrease in nonmonetary value, total welfare improves. When increases in monetary value produce offsetting decreases in nonmonetary value, total welfare remains unchanged. When costs to nonmonetary value exceed gains in monetary value, total welfare declines. This equation sets the parameters for the macroeconomy of the society and the microeconomy of the family. It finds its expression in the actual wealth of families. It defines the terms for debate about the relations of economic and social welfare systems. The modern life style seems best suited to single people and childless couples, who can run the rat race unimpeded by meeting the day-to-day needs of children. First and foremost, children cost time and personal investment. It is the time spent listening to, talking with, caring for, playing with, and responding to children that produces good child development and family well being. All this means little or nothing in immediate monetary payoffs. It's all too easy to borrow against this necessary but non-monetary investment if doing so will allow a parent to earn more cash income.

It seems that the continued existence of the modern affluent life style presupposes a predatory relationship with the rest of the world and with future generations. This is true within families and in the society as a whole. The process of consuming and degrading resources to provide the material underpinnings of that life style often produces offsetting or even larger costs to those features of life that are outside the cash economy, most notably the intimacies of family and community. Were this life style confined to a small elite, the damage might be manageable. But widespread affluence suggests a cannibalizing of the Earth's resources to feed the consumer's habit, with a corresponding degradation of social life. We have already witnessed this in North America. There is reason to believe that the "total welfare" of Giarini's equation may be on the way down.

In modern societies, the marginal participants often use the least ecologically viable products. They rely heavily on petro-plastics—cheap, nonreparable items with a very short useful life and inefficient energy consumption. The high-class modern materialist is more likely to use products of wood, glass, and gold that are more durable and efficient. Perhaps the most damning indictment of the modern life style is that only the richest can meet their desires for quantity in ways that are sound qualitatively.

Beyond the issue of the modern life style's material sustainability is its psychological sustainability. Modern affluence seems profoundly unfulfilling to many people. Particularly among the marginal participants, life seems frustrating and unsatisfying. One suspects that you can fool some of the people all of the time and all of the people some of the time. But one worries (or is it hopes?) that many realize they have been fooled when cheap affluence breaks down. Having been fooled, they are resentful. The expectations created by merchandising are very high: people take for granted what were once thought to be luxuries. If not grounded in economic reality, high expectations are socially and psychically dangerous. Observers report growing numbers of homicides because of disputes arising from minor conflicts. Senseless violence is high both in boom towns where unrealistic expectations are high and in bust towns where previously high expectations have set people up for severe disappointment. Much of this turmoil derives from frustrated expectations and the resulting stress. Materialism literally drives people crazy, and both the social and physical environments pay the price.

Justice: Certainly most premodern or unmodernized societies were and are unjust; justice is not the sole province of traditional societies. But does modernization bring justice? Is the current world order just? Modernization offers the *prospect* of justice, the prospect of replacing exploitive relationships of the past with more humane ones. The wealth of the modern economy makes possible extensive formal social welfare systems. Professional human services—in the form of teachers, day care providers, nurses, psychologists, and social workers—become possible. Yet modern society can become an engine of social injustice if it develops a standard life style that is untenably materialistic. In such a case, the indigent are likely to become worse off as the gap widens between them and rest of society. In such a climate a growing perception arises that "society" (meaning affluent taxpayers) cannot afford to support social welfare systems. This is painfully ironic, of course: the incredible wealth of North America belies the claim that basic social welfare systems are beyond its means.

As daily life comes more and more within the constraints of a cash economy, marginal elements fall into an ever more degraded position. One sure sign of this is when elite groups retreat to enclaves of affluence and rely upon security forces to protect them. We see this in both West and East. Indeed, one of the great historical ironies is to see the elites of the United States and the Soviet Union in ever more similar positions: living in enclaves of affluence while the masses exist in shoddiness. In both societies, these enclaves are institutions within institutions, all set within an egalitarian ideology. In the Soviet Union certain stores, neighborhoods, and services are open only to the certified elites. In the United States exclusive schools, neighborhoods, tax policies, shops, and clubs pretend to be open to all, yet they are closed to those without money. Both the United States and the Soviet Union have stood Marie Antoinette on her head. We no longer say that "both the rich and the poor are prohibited from sleeping under the bridges of Paris." We now say that "all are free to cross the bridge, so long as they can pay the toll."

Internationally, the justice of the modern order is even more suspect.

Each affluent member of the modern world consumes many times the resources of a counterpart in the "other" world. This is not simply because some nations are better endowed with natural resources; it reflects an exploitive policy in which Third World elites are bought off by affluent societies. The problem is magnified in countries, such as Brazil, with a historical tradition of economic and political oligarchy. The trend in Brazil and elsewhere has created two societies—one rich, one poor—within one nation. In the case of Brazil we might think of Belgium within India— although using current population figures, we might do better to speak of a prosperous Canada (25 million people) existing within a desperately impoverished Bangladesh (105 million).

Justice is at a premium in the current world order. Ruth Sivard's *World Military and Social Expenditures* (1982) documents this. Military forces in Third World countries have doubled in the past 20 years, and in 1980 totaled about 15 million—almost two-thirds of the world's armed forces. Expenditures for arms in these countries was about $20 billion. Fifty-two of these 113 nations are under military rule, and most routinely engage in extreme repression, including torture. More than 10 million people have died in wars since 1960. Yearly world public expenditures average $19,300 per soldier and $380 per school-age child. Infant mortality in some war zones (such as Afghanistan) is 50 times what it is in modern societies, and much higher than in neighboring poor societies "at peace." The United States and the Soviet Union combined spend an estimated $250 billion annually on their military establishments. The five major possessors of nuclear devices jointly hold about 40,000 tactical and 20,000 strategic weapons. Injustice is not new to the modern era, of course. But the struggle between self-interested competing forces and between forces of justice and injustice has never before been so destructive to human life.

Are We Living in a Sustainable Society?
We Are Not.

The population problem remains unsolved, because its likely "natural" leveling-off point would be too stressful for global resources. The prospect of unlimited technological innovation and economic growth is unreliable in the long run (if not the short run). The modern way of life is a material aberration; it cannot be generalized to the family of humanity across the world and through the decades. It works against the psychic needs of parents and children. And it is spiritually and psychologically risky. What is more, the current order is unjust, both within and across societies. It undermines essential social welfare systems.

We do not live in a sustainable society. How do we make the transition to one? First, we must suspend our willing belief that it is at hand. Terrible as it is to look global disaster in the face, we must not shy away. To avert our eyes now would be to deny the best of the human tradition and surrender to what has now come clearly into focus as the worst. It would lead to ever more serious erosion of the economic and environmental foundations for social welfare systems and the wealth of families. Deathship Earth? Slaveship Earth? Spaceship Earth? Which will it be for the family of humanity, for our children, and for their brothers and sisters around the world today and yet unborn? To understand this we must understand how human families themselves operate in the scheme of things.

CHAPTER

3.

July 1983:
Rio de Janiero,
Brazil

The
Family
Lifeboat

ABOUT 20 MILLION ABANDONED
children and youth live in Brazil (which has a total population of some 130
million), according to some estimates. I had my first encounter with some of
these kids within hours of my arrival in Rio de Janeiro. After settling in at
the hotel, my companions and I set out to test the surf.

At Ipanema Beach, a group of boys who appeared to range in age between 11 and 15 swooped down on our towels and clothes, surprising our
two volunteer guards and running off with our money and valuables. We
were lucky and learned our lesson cheaply; little was there to be taken. We
doubled our guard and successfully defended our property for the rest of
our time there.

As we were leaving the beach, we saw again what many Brazilians
call the "informal income redistribution system." A youth ran by, fleeing
from a man who shouted, ladrão! ("thief!") as he pursued. In an apparent
ritual of negotiation, the young thief first dropped the man's ID, then his
credit cards. The victim slowed, then stopped to retrieve these critical parts
of his stolen property. The bargaining completed, the thief ran off unmol-
ested, as if to say, "I have the money and the wallet; you have the rest. Fair
enough?" It almost seemed so—an informally negotiated truce between one
of Brazil's haves and one of its have-nots.

Millions of children and youth are abandoned to the streets in Brazil
because of family breakdown. Why else do parents give up their children or
children their families? The magnitude of the problem reflects the level of
social and economic stress. It recalls descriptions of the civil war that
wracked the Soviet Union in the 1920s, when some nine million children
and youth were left without families. Economic war destroys families now

as the shooting war did then. When families come unglued, it signals pro-
found crisis, a breakdown in fundamental social welfare systems. Does
what I see in Brazil portend the future? With three million new Brazilians
each year, the answer is critical to the family of man and to the wealth of
families.

What Is a Family?

What is a family? Families are the thread that holds the human race together (Garbarino and Associates, 1982). Through our families we are connected to the past—the distant times and places of our ancestors—and to the future, the hope of our children's children. Although family life exacts psychological costs, families are the bedrock of human social life, a potent force for social stability and meaning. They are neither the reactionary and oppressive trap that some radicals see nor the bastions of sweetness and light that some ultraconservatives see. But they *are* our best hope for humanity's efforts to achieve a sustainable society and guarantee social welfare systems. The challenge is to equitably balance power in families that now oppress women and children, and to enhance the power of family relationships to teach empathy, sympathy, and ecology. Thus we may create ethical and psychological foundations for social welfare systems in a sustainable society.

Who is not moved by the excitement of discovering one's ancestors? Who is not enriched by uncovering connections of kinship? My wife searched through old and faded archives in a small Scottish parish church and tracked down the rector, who suggested she search among the gravestones for a relative who had been dead some two hundred years. The search was rewarded. The moment was magnificent. Equally so was her paternal grandmother's expression when she saw pictures of the gravestone and the parish records. This feeling of wholeness and connection with the past through our families is central to the human experience, and it can inspire us to build the institutions and nurture the values we need for a sustainable society. It should guide our social welfare systems as well.

When we see a young child struggling to master a skill we now possess, we realize what enormous growth takes place in the everyday lives of our fellow human beings. Parents share the infant's unbounded glee at accomplishment. Ah, to be able to turn over! To sit unaided! To stand unassisted! And, miracle of miracles, to walk! To talk! We all can appreciate these wonders, but the special bond between parent and child goes further.

To be a parent is to have a special, "irrational" feeling of responsibility for a special being. Tolstoy captured the parental perspective in his epic *War and Peace:*

> The universal experience of the ages, showing that children grow from the cradle to manhood, did not exist for the Countess. The growth of her son had been for her at every stage as extraordinary as though millions and millions of men had not already developed in the same way. Just as twenty years before it had seemed unbelievable that the little creature lying under her heart would ever cry, nurse at the breast, or talk, so now she could not believe that this same little creature could be that strange brave officer, that paragon of sons and men, which, judging by his letter he now was. (pp. 291–292)

Definitions of Family

Sociologists and anthropologists have long searched for an all-purpose, universal definition of "family"—one that would apply to all cultures and communities across time and space. In North America, recent social changes legitimizing new family forms are pushing traditional definitions to their limits and beyond. New actors have joined the effort to define the family, as city planners, politicians, judges, legislators, the clergy, and others are asked to legitimize some relationships and not others. Three common themes are clear in most definitions. Family implies a household founded in marriage, child rearing, and kinship. Within the family, adults contract with each other to assume economic and social responsibility for each other and for children, and to become part of a larger network of kinship. Sociologist Ira Reiss defines the family as "a small kinship-structured group with the key function of nurturant socialization" (1980, p. 29). Much as we should be responsive to changes in family forms, we need to retain a profound respect for the accomplishment of creating and sustaining a family. Political scientist Jean Bethke Elshtain captured this feeling when she wrote:

> To throw the honorable mantle "family" over every ad hoc collection of persons who happen to be under one roof at the same time is to diminish the genuine achievements of family men and women who have retained their commitments to and for another. (1983, p. 25)

Like "sustainable society," "family" is something with such moral force and profound significance that when we apply the term to human arrangements we must do so with an appreciation for its far-reaching implications.

The poet Robert Frost spoke of the emotional significance of family as home for the heart in *The Death of the Hired Hand:*

Home is the place where
When you have to go there
They have to take you in.

Anthropologist Margaret Mead spoke eloquently about family as our personal connection with history:

As in our bodies we share our humanity, so also through the family we have a common heritage. . . . the task of each family is also the task of humanity. This is to cherish the living, remember those who have gone before, and prepare for those who are not yet born. (1965, p. 11)

Can we call social relationships that don't stretch across generations "families"? This is a troublesome point. Speaking of her work with the religiously oriented "Commission on Today's Families," Elizabeth Dodson-Gray (personal communication) notes that the group agreed on a definition of family as "a household joined by ties of blood or commitment." This resonates with the standard dictionary definition of family deriving from the Latin *familia* for a household's members, and encompassing fellowship as well as kinship. Can homosexual couples form families? Surely, if they assume responsibility across generations by raising (if not necessarily bearing) children. Is a couple whose children have grown up and left the nest still a family? Yes, but it is through their connection to their children.

Who may say that someone else's relationships do not constitute a family? The answer must lie in the historical meaning of the word. Formats do change for accomplishing the basic business of forming households to create and nurture human life. But it is inappropriate to apply the label "family" to any socially desirable relationship just because the label has positive connotations and conveys legitimacy. If everything is family, then nothing is family. This is particularly true because family alone usually does not constitute an adequate social environment. Other powerful relationships, such as friendship, are important as well. This becomes apparent as we consider the costs as well as the benefits of family.

The family is not all sweetness and light. The very intensity of family life means that malfunctioning in a family is likely to have devastating impact on the development and psychological well-being of its members. This dark side of family life includes physical, emotional, and sexual child and wife abuse. Wife abuse particularly testifies to the cost of male domination (patriarchy) for families. Likewise, sexual abuse of children reveals the danger of masculine imperiousness and aggressiveness. Of course men, too, may be oppressed by the family. But when families oppress women and children, it is more likely a result of the culture that places them under male domination. And even a nice master can be oppressive. For all its potential and actual oppression of individual members, family remains a central facet of human experience and one of its greatest sources of meaning and value.

Families are life, and no program of social engineering will alter that. Even in the sustainable society there will be sibling rivalry, blocked relations between parent and child, conflicts between grandparents and parents over child rearing, and marital conflict. Loved ones will grow old and become sick. However, in a sustainable society, in an ecologically sane social order, we will be able to concentrate more on harmonizing family relations, on equalizing masculine and feminine power, and on directly facing basic issues of human quality, because we will not be sidetracked by a host of fundamentally irrelevant material dilemmas as we are today. What is more, our other important relationships will improve to complement and augment families as social support systems.

Whatever definition of family we use, we need to recognize that kinship is the foundation of the family. Individuals are born into the "family of origin" and eventually may start a family of their own (the "family of procreation"). Wherever individuals may go with their lives, their actions reverberate through kinship directly. Thus, for example, whether one's parents will ever become grandparents, and one's brothers and sister's uncles and aunts, depends upon one's own childbearing—particularly in modern small families. In China, under the One Child Policy, the roles of cousin, aunt, and uncle may be eclipsed in the next generation if the policy is fully implemented.

Embracing their families of origin and procreation, most people spend most of their lives in family units, and virtually all of their lives as part of an active kinship system of some sort. We rely upon families for identity, relatedness, intimacy, and growth, our most profoundly human qualities. They are the root of social welfare, and through family life we share most directly in the miracles and tragedies of human experience. Even adults who are not themselves parents can play an important role in the families of which they are affiliate members, as aunts, uncles, godparents, and the like. What is more, they can support public policies and institutions that aid parents, and single adults can do so with the recognition that a pro-family stance is a good investment in the quality of their society.

Frost's conception of home and Mead's of family are particularly relevant to modern North America, where traditional models of the family have come to be less and less in accord with the realities of day-to-day life. In the United States, for example, most people traditionally define the ideal "normal" family as a man and woman in their first marriage plus dependent children in a household in which the man works outside the home for income while the woman manages the household and provides child care. Yet more than one-fifth of American children at any one time live in single-parent households. Ninety percent of the time, that one parent is the mother. About half of all American children will spend some of their first eighteen years of life in such a household or in families created by second marriage. Thus, many children and youth have one or more stepparents. Also, one-fifth of couples forming households elect not to have children at all. And finally, more than 60 percent of all mothers of dependent children are employed outside the home, many full time. Thus, families conforming to the "normal" model are a very small minority, perhaps 15 percent. Processes of modernization have displaced the traditional "normal" family—which was never so predominant as nostalgic myth would have it anyway.

A Continuum of Families

The modern family is usually small—perhaps only a mother and her child. Such a small family is obviously at one end of the continuum, but we need to recognize it as a family. Toward the other end of the continuum stands the extended family, a composite of intergenerational relationships including children, parents, grandparents, and other relatives. Beyond that stands the clan, a confederation of related families. Modernization has meant a movement away from the clan toward the small "nuclear" family—or perhaps we should call it the "atomic" or "elemental" family, because it is the smallest unit of family possible. Modernization has also meant the growing importance of family surrogates, adults not part of a bona fide family who desire the close support a family can offer. Many such people form attachments to these friends with a warmth and a sense of commitment that is familylike. We humans need those connections, in families and in familylike relationships, to encourage, support, and guide us. Such relationships are primary support systems. When they are impaired, we call upon social welfare systems to compensate.

With families in such a central position, it is little wonder that the health and welfare of the family is always a topic of discussion, a matter for concern, and an issue for debate, particularly in times when family forms and functions are changing. Social historian Colin Greer (1976) points out five common views on the condition of "The American Family":

- "The family is decaying." In this view, the traditional family is falling apart, and the security of the national community is in jeopardy as a result.
- "The family is evolving." Adherents of this view say the family, like any institution, must keep up with the times to do its job.
- "The family is not changing much at all." In this view, all the anxiety is misplaced—what is called the crisis of the family is simply a version of usual intergenerational conflict.
- "There are changes in the family, but there is no need to worry about them." In this point of view, the institutional structure of society is always changing, and family changes simply reflect that.
- "The family is in retreat, defending itself against the power of the human potential movement." From this perspective, the family is the oppressive agent of an oppressive social system that is being beaten back by the positive, progressive forces freed in a postindustrial society undergoing liberation.

Obviously, family forms have changed and still are changing. Yet the essentials of a healthy, strong family remain stable and relevant to the needs of a sustainable society—commitment, caring for the generations, making a protected place for children, and nurturing all concerned. Research by Nick Stinnett and his colleagues (1979) offers a good picture of the characteristics of families well equipped to meet the challenges of the modern world. Stinnett found six common elements in families identified by community agents as strong:

- *Appreciation:* The members regard each other warmly and positively, and give support to each other as individuals.
- *Spending time together:* Strong families spend time together and enjoy it.
- *Good communication patterns:* Family members are honest, open, and receptive toward each other.
- *Commitment:* The family unit is important to its members, as are the interpersonal subsystems within the family. The family is the principal focus of its members' activities.
- *High degree of religious orientation:* Strong families seem anchored in a sense of purpose that is often religiously based. A spiritual approach

toward life gives family members a common belief and promotes family values.

- *Ability to deal with crises in a positive manner:* Strong families are able to deal with conflicts and band together in mutual support when bad times arise.

Other efforts along these lines have added to the above openness to the outside world, a positive attitude toward affiliation, and fairness in allocating tasks, esteem, and authority to females and males in the family. A well functioning family should open doors to the world, not be a closed room that stifles its members' development. Most strong families excel in providing nurturance and constructive feedback to female and male, adult and child members. This emphasis on nurturance and feedback directs our attention to families as informal social welfare systems.

The Nature of Social Support

Many terms exist to describe the people in one's life who provide the meat and potatoes of social existence—whose presence, concern, and feedback are a valued part of day-to-day life across the years. Some researchers speak of a range of interpersonal exchanges that provide an individual with information, emotional reassurance, physical and material assistance, and a sense of the self as an object of concern. Others just speak of "caring." The social institutions and networks of relationships that provide these critical psychological elements form the social fabric of the family and ultimately, the community. Maintaining their vitality is one of the major challenges in times of social change.

The social fabric of families is determined in large part by social support systems, the sets of interconnected relationships among a group that provide its members with enduring patterns of nurturance and feedback for efforts to cope with day-to-day life. Gerald Caplan (1974), a pioneer in outlining the importance of social support systems to mental health, defines these systems as enduring relationships that provide a sense of belonging, caring, concern, feedback, identity, and self-worth. These support systems may compensate for the impersonal character of other more formal relationships. As Caplan puts it:

> People have a variety of specific needs that demand satisfaction through enduring interpersonal relationships, such as for love and affection, for

intimacy that provides the freedom to express feelings easily and unself-consciously, for validation of personal identity and worth, for satisfaction of nurturance and dependency, for help with tasks, and for support in handling emotion and controlling impulses. (1974, pp. 5-60)

Of course, the family is our first support system, usually foremost among all others. But few if any families are enough in and of themselves. We need relationships outside the family. We need friends, neighbors, and colleagues. The quality of social support actively available among individuals and their families is a good indication of the human quality of the social environment. A high-quality environment enhances mastery and social competence, which we need to encourage if we are to meet the challenges of creating a sustainable society.

Mastery is the joint product of personal and social resources. The help available to individuals consists both of the competence they bring to a situation and the resources in the social environment. Families are central to both. An effective family teaches personal competence and offers access to social resources. It provides an entryway to the world.

Social support is the major currency of value in the environment; families are the chief bankers in this psychological economy. And if social support is the currency, then children are the principal "commodity," that which is of intrinsic value. Yet we know that male domination of society and its institutions leads to a devaluing of children, because "children are women's work." The patriarchal society values what men do more than what women do, and the crucial function of nuturing children suffers as a result.

Bringing men into the business of nurturing children is one way to create a more family-oriented ethic which can then support the thinking, feeling, and action needed for transition to a sustainable society. As Elizabeth Dodson-Gray (1982) persuasively argues in her book *Patriarchy as a Conceptual Trap*, until women and their work have the same status as men and theirs, social quality will take a back seat to aggressive material expansion. By putting families first, we may place *quality* of human relationships in its proper position of ascendancy. Both require that we end masculine domination in the family and in society. That revolution will produce a cultural climate in which the sustainable society can exist.

The Fate of the Family and the Fate of the Earth

Concern for the fate of families in the process of modernization is well grounded. The principal investments of self in others are made in the family and in familylike relationships. What we have experienced from our caregivers determines what we offer to those for whom we care. How we nurture the world reflects how we ourselves were nurtured. Families provide motivation for the extremely demanding role of caregiver, be it for the child or the feeble elderly. Commenting upon the realities of trying to substitute paid care for family care, a Soviet psychologist observed: "You can't pay a woman for what a mother will do for free." Of course it's not "for free," and it's not just mothers. Families are bound up in an intense psychological banking system. Love and attention are invested in the hope of a large return in satisfaction, regard, and caring. All in all, the family is a blue-chip psychological investment.

What is more, the family gives the individual a way to deal with historical time. Donella Meadows has concluded that most of us tend to think forward in history to the expected life span of our children (about 70 years) and no further. This 70-year period is directly implicated in the world problematique and the search for paths to a sustainable society. It forms the numerator in the equation used to compute the time it takes an environmental process to double when assessing resources and population:

$$doubling\ time\ =\ 70/annual\ growth\ rate$$

Family history and family future are good benchmarks to use in conveying society's memories and projections for itself, for opening a discussion of the sustainable society. If people are persuaded to debate the future in concrete terms of what life will be like for *their* children and *their* grandchildren, they may be able to overcome some of the narrow, limited thinking that holds us back from transition to a sustainable society. To do so, however, people must see that the fate of their children is bound up with the fate of other people's children at home and abroad. We must articulate future social welfare systems for the children to come, our own and the others who will populate their world.

Population studies give us a sense of general family trends and allow us to speculate about their reasons. However, although history is usually studied on a social level, life is lived by individuals, and they are the real subjects of attempts to understand the changing face of society. Rosa Luxemburg, the European socialist of the early twentieth century, said: "It is in the tiny domestic struggles of individual people, as they grope toward self-realization, that we can most truly discern the great movements of society." Sociologist C. Wright Mills (1963) echoed this theme when he spoke of history as biography. The real trick is to show people how their family's fate (what Mills called "personal troubles") is connected to the fate of the Earth (what Mills would call "public issues"). If we can forge this link and transform personal into public concerns, we will be able to harness the motivating power of the family in transforming Spaceship Earth. (For example, if people can see how their use of energy has implications for the way their grandchildren are to live, it may increase their receptivity to conservation measures.)

Modernization and Families

Modernization is *the* contemporary historical transformation. How has it affected families? In what ways has modernization "happened to" families, and in what ways have families created it? Some say the institution of family has only *reacted* to social change in this century and has been the passive victim of modernization. This theme has dominated social analysis in this century. W. F. Ogburn, a pioneering sociologist writing early in the twentieth century, concluded that the nuclear family was inappropriate and unstable in an urban industrial society. Many have echoed that theme in the six decades since. The problem he saw and emphasized was the loss of family functions. On farms and in small businesses that once dominated the economic landscape, family members could work together—albeit in ways that were often backbreaking and spirit destroying. Modern technology promised to relieve us of that kind of work and to liberate women from the oppression of traditional family life. But modernization goes beyond that; it has stripped the family of its many productive and educational responsibilities. In this way families have become solely emotional and developmental centers rather than economically productive entities. As critic Ivan Illich and others have shown, women especially are limited by the modern nuclear family, because it provides them with the worst of two worlds: neither personal outlet nor the opportunity to contribute to the family's material needs. One promise of the sustainable society is to restore to the family functions to be performed in an energy-efficient, labor-intensive, and just manner—offering productive roles for children, encouraging purposeful interaction between parents and children, and enhancing the status of women. All this is possible if the transition to a sustainable society occurs in tandem with an end to patriarchy. A patriarchal but sustainable society would put women back in their old homemaker roles, and would thus be unacceptable to modern women.

The American nuclear family, like the energy-intensive modern economy itself, may have reached its zenith in the 1950s. Families in earlier generations were frequently broken up by death, in subsequent decades by divorce. Family sociologists like Andrew Cherlin (1981) point out that the 1950s were an oasis of stability. The potential economic payoffs of modern society blossomed, and many families did likewise: more people married; they married earlier and more permanently; had more children; had more children earlier; and lived more often in nuclear families than did people before or after that time. Cheap energy, new productive technology, and receptive world markets all gave rise to a Golden Age for the modern family. This has made it all the more difficult to accept the reality of the Dark Ages envisioned in the world problematique. After having apparently solved the fundamental material problems of the human condition, it seems all the more difficult to accept the need to wrestle with the prospect of profound scarcity and a "worthless state of existence." What is more, feminist gains of the 1960s and 1970s make many women rightfully suspicious of proposals that may appear to be reactionary—calls for a return to traditional family forms and household division of labor. The status of women has improved markedly in the two decades since Betty Friedan wrote *The Feminine Mystique* (1968), and many women worry that "ecologically sustainable lifestyle" may be a code phrase for "The Total Woman," may mean return to being barefoot and pregnant.

Theories that women and men are "naturally" locked into different and mutually exclusive roles are both simplistic and inaccurate. Many in the 1950s and 1960s correctly criticized as unjust family structures in which women were confined in rigid roles and denied choice while their husbands' only responsibility was to bring home a paycheck.

Roles within marriage have begun to change, and sociologist Jessie Bernard (1981) calls this change "the fall of the male good provider." In the monetarized market economy, men were judged on the basis of their ability to provide for their families financially. Emotional and domestic responsibilities were secondary. Cooperation between men and women in providing for their families became split. Separate? Surely. But equal? Not quite. Each sex was identified in opposition to the other, unable to share in common tasks or concerns.

Even the modern family is thoroughly patriarchal, with men controlling the action and women forced into a defensive posture in which choices often seem limited to passive aggression or withdrawal from the relationship with those same men. Bernard conveyed the hostility and resentment some feel regarding this when she wrote: "As the pampered wife in an affluent household came often to be an economic parasite, so also the good provider was often, in a way, a kind of emotional parasite" (Bernard, 1981, p. 10).

The male's role as provider flourished as women were relegated to the home exclusively. Women have always been primarily responsible for child rearing, but only in the nineteenth and twentieth centuries has it become a full-time job that virtually excludes other economically valuable activities. Using conventional economic models, the role of homemaker only makes sense when there are many children to care for. On the other hand, the role of good provider only makes sense in a family in which women are totally dependent economically. Modern observers such as Bernard foresee this role diminishing as the frequency increases with which women join the labor force and raise children. As noted earlier, by 1984 more than 60 percent of all mothers of children under age 18 were employed outside the home; by the year 2000 it could be 90 percent. But a sustainable society may require fewer wage earners *outside* the household and more work being done *inside* the household. No wonder psychologists Urie Bronfenbrenner and Ann Crouter have identified the relationship of work and family as *the* human development issue of the 1980s.

The Family of Choice

Child psychologist Bruno Bettelheim recently identified two social innovations linked to modernization that have deeply affected the modern family: the rise in the material standard of living and the availability of birth control. The increased wealth available in modern society has tended to free the nuclear family from dependence on others—kin, neighbors, and friends. Early in this century one in three New England families had a boarder in the household. Modern affluence has decreased the financial need for such arrangements for both boarder and host. As the economy expands, there is more mobility, both within and between families. Young adults are able to move away from their parents. Adults can provide food, child care, and recreation through cash purchases rather than through social exchanges. And the elderly are more likely to be able to support themselves through purchased services rather than through good will and a sense of obligation felt by their grown children. Affluence tends to increase physical and emotional distance in families and between families and their social networks. The question is, will that distance be perceived as freedom or as isolation? If isolation, the cost is likely to be impaired mental health.

Advances in contraception have made childbearing less the destiny and more the choice of women. Child *rearing* is another matter. A woman may choose whether to bear children, but most have little choice when it comes to rearing them. Highly publicized exceptions aside, society decrees that child care, particularly in the early years, is a feminine occupation—whether at home or in day care. Thus for most women, most of the time, the choice is limited to whether to give birth. Once that decision is made, assumption by women of primary responsibility for child care seems mostly ordained. Some see it as a tradition that has grown out of the different biological predispositions of males and females, and others see it as mainly the result of historical factors that have become obsolete—or at least would become so if women were liberated from patriarchal family relations.

Choice exists always in a particular social context. The movement toward greater choice for women demands that men increase their participation in "women's work." This seems the only way to increase the range of choices available to women without stacking the deck against families, and particularly children. If men stick to "men's work" only, the result will be frustrated and angry women, women who see families as oppressive and opt out of them, and families that become battlegrounds in which children, and ultimately all of society, are losers. Are men up to the challenge? The answer will go far toward determining how smoothly we make the transition to a sustainable society, if we make the transition at all.

Sexual behavior, size of families, number of women in the cash labor force, and the role of women in general are all intimately related to women's ability to control pregnancy and to influence their relationships with men. Affluence and birth control have made family arrangements more a matter of choice and less one of biological or economic necessity. The challenge of creating a sustainable society demands that individuals and institutions redefine affluence and enhance contraception. At the same time it requires that families become more economically functional in ways that respect the adults who lead them. This is a tall order. In recent history, individuals have been "released" or "liberated" from traditional family roles. The future may demand a return to more orientation to the family as a socioeconomic unit, but in a new way that emphasizes quality over quantity. At present in modernized countries, families tend to be free—free of official and unofficial pressures to be demographically responsible (i.e., to limit their childbearing to replacement levels), free to pursue their goals regardless of ecological implications. They are free to be part of the problem, however much they are potentially a key to the solution.

The Expectations of Freedom

Families are on their own. Family privacy, economic prosperity, and geographic mobility all separate parents and children from traditional sources of nurturance and feedback such as church, elders, kin, and neighbors. Isolation is contagious; we become estranged from each other, and families lose the social support of close and caring loved ones. It is increasingly difficult for family values to compete with the seductive materialism and freedom of modern commercial society. What is more, the ethic of individualism works against the cooperation and mutual sacrifices necessary for stable families. This theme emerges is a spate of analyses of modern society by Amitai Etzioni (1983) and Donald Campbell (1976), among others (e.g. Winn, 1983).

Our level of expectation is very high. The rising tide of expectations has made families vulnerable to frustration. Life's inevitable disappointments are magnified by often unrealistic standards for self-fulfillment and material aggrandizement. On the economic scene, the expectation that everyone can and should live in a single-family house—in the suburbs if possible—has led many families to become financially overcommitted and tied to ecologically dangerous patterns of transportation, land use, and household energy consumption. The result is a high level of stress, and disruption of family life as well as the life of the Earth.

Futurists like Alvin Toffler and others may be right when they predict that traditional family forms will neither cease to exist nor return to dominance. Rather, they will coexist with surrogate families and with real families at the atomistic or elemental end of the continuum so long as contemporary modernization holds sway. As modernization causes customs and institutions formerly required for economic survival to give way to chosen and voluntary ties, we face a challenge to build social welfare systems that meet people's needs for intimacy, love, and meaning. The family will exist as long as people recognize and respond to each other's needs for close lifelong bonds. Furthermore, a collapse of the technocratic modern order may mean a comeback of revamped old family forms like the clan. Collapse of modern life would mean a return to close geographic proximity, shared facilities, bartering, social recreation, and home-based food and energy production as cheap energy, petroplastics, commuting, and cash purchases decrease. Out of the recession of the 1980s in the United States have come some encouraging tales of such family- and neighborhood-oriented social reforms. And they come usually with a refreshingly improved pattern of relationships among the women and men in them. The community, our institutions, and all of society must move carefully and respectfully around families, so as not to disturb the fragile and terribly important process going on within them—creating and nurturing human beings.

Overpopulation: The Dark Side of the Family

And yet, a demographic spectre hovers over contemporary families as they create and rear human beings. Each miraculous birth sets in motion a chain of events that moves the Earth's ecosystems one step closer to crisis and disaster; because the parents, community, and society that assume responsibility for that life will do what they can to clothe, feed, house, and otherwise equip that child in the style to which local economies are accustomed. The birth of each child is a moment of joy. The birth of a hundred million children in the 1980s in a world of five billion is a sober challenge. But the possible birth of hundreds of millions in a world of more than six billion in the twenty-first century is a threat to the very integrity of the social and physical environment. Demography, not economics, is the truly dismal science of our age. We cannot escape issues of family quantity, just as we cannot neglect the issues of family quality if we hope to achieve and maintain a sustainable soceity.

We can call the family a human lifeboat that travels the social currents of the world problematique. The lifeboat metaphor is ambiguous, however. It suggests a haven, a vehicle for surviving catastrophe. The danger of the metaphor is that it may encourage some to advance their individual families in a selfish attempt to live in comfort while others peerish in a sea of diminished prospects. There is a kind of "every-man-for-himself" mentality that pervades much of the survivalist movement, in which affluent families seek a paramilitary solution by walling themselves off from society or setting off on their own to ride out the storm. Naturally, this is not the way we interpret the metaphor. In choosing the image of the family lifeboat, we see the institution of the family as a vehicle to help us negotiate today's stormy social and economic currents and bring us safely to a sustainable society.

The current economic system, like the ocean liner *Titanic*, has struck an iceberg and is taking on water. The survivalists have already cast off in their luxury cabin cruisers. Herman Kahn, Julius Simon and others tell the rest of us, "Don't worry. This ship is equipped with the most modern technology. It is unsinkable." Much of the world, if not sinking, is already listing seriously. We need to use our family lifeboats to reach shore where together, as fellow humans, we can create a sustainable way of living. This is the kind of "lifeboat ethic" to which we should aspire.

This perspective leads us to consider the significance of childbearing and child rearing in the historically new settings promised or threatened by the world problematique and the sustainable society. We can see three principal forces at work. The first is sociobiological.

Human Beings as Social Animals

Aristotle, and centuries later Spinoza, conceived of human being as "social animals." We have our biologically based predispositions, our genetically programmed agendas, but we act out these scripts through our social selves. Nature is mediated by nurture. Those sociobiologists who see our social behavior tied to our biology remind us that our cultures and personal values, our sociology and our psychology as human beings, evolved in counterpoint to our genetic development. We should not be surprised, they argue, that our social behavior in general and particularly with reference to families is rooted in our evolved biological nature.

Our genetic heritage makes some forms of social organization easier to create and maintain than others. For example, Leonard Eron's (1981) research on physical aggression suggests that males are more easily socialized into aggressive roles than are females. According to developmental psychologists such as Eleanor Maccoby, some hormonal differences appear to play a role in this. Similarly, sociobiologists argue that females are hormonally predisposed to nurturance and caregiving. In no case is social function fixed and invariant, but some patterns of social organization are more genetically plausible than others.

And what is the driving force in this evolutionary drama? It is reproduction—the successful passing along of genetic identity through one's own offspring or through the offspring of one's blood relatives. The closer the blood relationship, the more a child shares one's genes, and thus the greater the value of that offspring, and the greater the sacrifices that are genetically sensible. The greater the genetic connection the more willing one is to give one's time, resources, even one's life. Sociobiologists are often adroitly clever in interpreting the social implications of this thesis for individuals, the family, and the community.

What Robert Trivers (1974) calls "investment" tells us that domestic relations are governed by one's genetic stake in a particular offspring. Humans' reproductive strategy generally emphasizes quality, with high investment in each of a relatively small number of offspring. Sociobiologists call this a "K" strategy, and contrast it to the "r" strategy, which emphasizes many offspring, into each of which little is invested. "Few" and "many" are relative terms, of course. Mammals with eight offspring per litter are "K" types compared to insects with hundreds or thousands, but "r" types when contrasted with the human proclivity for single births. Men and women differ from each other as well; men are more on the "r" side (quantity) while women are more on the "K" side (quality).

In general, this means women tend to value individual children more than men do; because women have relatively few children while men can have as many children as they can successfully impregnate women. This fact, in the sociobiological view, shaped the history of domestic relations in many ways, and continues to influence the modern era. Men insist upon sexual loyalty from women for whom they are responsible because only in this way can they assure paternity and, thus, genetic success. Women trade this sexual loyalty for economic loyalty, their only way of assuring they will have adequate support while they are tied down by pregnancy and childbirth. Thus does their high investment in each child pay off genetically. This need not govern modern relationships, however, because of advances in contraception, infant nutrition, and cultural standards for assigning social responsibilities.

The Sociobiological Foundations for the Population Problem

Sociobiology has something to say about most matters of kinship and community life—for example why stepchildren are at special risk for mistreatment in their families and why patrimony is so resistant to bureaucratic regulation and reform attempts. It tells us to invest in social welfare systems that benefit families so that we can harness the power of genetic "investment" to motivate people. The task is to empower women to make family planning decisions on the basis of their "natural" commitment to quality over quantity in childbearing.

Females are more likely to value quality in children, males to value quantity. Evidence indicates that the birth rate would decrease 25 to 50 percent worldwide if women who wish to limit their offspring were empowered fully to do so. Males, with their quantitative perspective, account for most of the obstacles to resolving the demographic dimensions of the world problematique. The Club of Rome's phrasing—the "predicament of mankind" and "mankind at the turning point"—may have been not obliviously sexist, but right on the mark. It is man, as male, who has caused the global predicament. Men are facing a turning point in their history of domination.

The role of women and the feminine perspective in the transition to a sustainable society are considered in Chapter 7. Suffice it to say here that successful population control requires empowering women through contraception. The continued lodging with men of control over contraception is a serious obstacle. In fact, the issue of who is to properly control procreation and contraception may be one of the oldest human issues. It certainly is well documented in recorded history, from biblical times to current battles between "pro-choice" and anti-abortion forces in American politics. And it may extend backward into prehistory: in Jean Auel's novel *The Clan of the Cave Bear* (1979), prehistoric women practice contraception using herbs and other natural substances, but keep it secret from men, who they know would deny them that control.

The very existence of the world problematique derives in part from our species' success in developing a genetically sound population program. Our genetic programs tell us to "go forth and multiply." Until the last few historical moments, human population in all but a few areas has been marginal in the world's physical ecology. Early in human existence, when most of our genetic programming was done, the challenge was not to *limit* population growth, but to *sustain* it. The issue was quantity. Would enough humans survive? Now, the issue of quality has dramatically superseded the issue of quantity. By the fourteenth century, the human population was so firmly established there was no need to worry (although the Black Plague of the Middle Ages gave Europe quite a scare). Yet it was still so small in relation to the Earth's ecosystems that we could operate without fear of overpopulation, except in special, localized cases. This period has come to an end, and the issue of quantity is once again paramount. Instead of worrying that our numbers are insufficient, we must worry that we will exceed the carrying capacity of the planet. According to the Environment Fund, it took thousands of years for the human population to reach 1 billion in 1750, almost two hundred years to reach 2 billion (in about 1930), thirty years to reach 3 billion (in 1960), and fourteen years to reach 4 billion (1974).

In the 1980s we have reached 5 billion, with a projected yearly increase of 90 million. What are the engines that drive population growth?

We carry within us a genetic predisposition to breed that is precultural. Having offspring really *is* doing what comes naturally, for most of us, most of the time. What can we do now, when we need to control and even override that genetic program? Much that we value about civilization is that it allows such overcoming—caring for the physically disabled, developing eyeglasses for the nearsighted, and delivering babies through caesarean section for women not well suited to vaginal delivery. Biological might does not make right. This applies to population control as well.

Certainly, we can resort to social engineering, including reinforcements for procreatively responsible behavior. But we must capitalize upon genetic predispositions such as investment, rather than fight them. Altruistic appeals that go against manifest self-interest don't make much evolutionary sense. The result of population control measures around the world testifies to this. When social conditions impose reinforcements that reward small families and punish large ones, population growth slows and may even stop. These reinforcements may be deliberate policies or socioeconomic factors. The former includes recent Chinese efforts to provide special privileges and economic guarantees to one-child families. The latter includes the *eventual* decrease in offspring once modern societies have achieved and become accustomed to affluence, and as financial costs of childbearing have risen while payoffs have declined or remained steady. Both create mixed emotions in societies, even when their ecological "logic" is clear. A closer look at both will shed light on how the economics and social psychology of childbearing struggle with its sociobiology.

The Ups and Downs of Population Growth

U.S. Census data shed some light on the historical ups and downs of childlessness and single-childness in twentieth-century America. The data reveal substantial variations in response to the economy's ups and downs—variations resulting from the availability of contraception and abortion. For example, for women born between 1891 and 1895, 37 percent had fewer than two children. Forty-seven percent of women born between 1906 and 1919 had fewer than two children. Of women born between 1921 and 1925, only 28 percent had fewer than two children. The first group were in their prime childbearing years in the second and third decades of the twentieth century and had relatively little contraceptive control by contemporary standards.

Many in the second group reached prime childbearing years in the Great Depression of the 1930s, and the low birth rate reflects a response to economic hard times. The third group had greater contraceptive control than the others and yet produced the famous post-World War II "Baby Boom." Affluence and strongly pronatal ideology resulted in the population boom of those years, a high water mark against which we will measure population trends for the rest of the twentieth century.

Nancy Davis (1982) analyzed these data to show that age of first marriage, marital disruption, and educational attainment all exert a significant influence: a well educated woman marrying late and then divorcing is most likely to be childless or to have only one child. But these demographic characteristics operate in conjunction with—and can be overridden by—socioeconomic trends. The 1950s were special in American demographic history, in large part because a surge in affluence and pronatal ideology produced social conditions "ripe for early marriage and rapidly paced childbearing" (Davis, 1982, p. 45).

The American experience in the twentieth century is instructive because it deals with a modern society. But it is only part of the story. Modernization has no simple effect upon population. Its demographic significance depends largely upon when and where it occurs in socioeconomic time and space. When it does not produce widespread improvement in conditions of day-to-day life, it may not lower the birth rate, as was evidenced in Brazil in the 1970s.

The relationship between modernization and population is complex indeed. In most respects modernization seems to produce a population boom followed by a lowering of the birth rate. In premodernized countries, most childlessness is involuntary and due to disease, and in modernized countries most childlessness is voluntary. Thus, it appears that increased affluence decreases childlessness in developing countries but is associated with an increase in developed countries.

A "Rational" Analysis of Childbearing and Family Life

Authority, dogma, and mystery dominate in traditional societies, particularly where families are concerned. Modernization has tended to bring "rational" analysis to more and more of daily life. This usually means economic analysis, because economics is assumed to be *the* rational science of human behavior. In practice, this means assessing "costs" and "benefits" in a very narrow sense. Family life is a prime target for such analyses, with Gary Becker's 1981 book *A Treatise on the Family* being the preeminent example. Replete with mathematical equations, his book expresses all family relations as functions of psychic supply and demand.

This sort of analysis is applied by Sharon Houseknecht (1983), who discusses voluntary childlessness in terms of an economic approach labeled a "social exchange framework":

> Both *career commitment* and *child rearing* can be evaluated in terms of *economic* costs/rewards and *social* costs/rewards. In general, child rearing represents an economic cost and not a reward. Economic reward comes with *not* having children, since a greater amount of money is then available for other things. On the other hand, career commitment means that there are not only economic rewards forthcoming, but all sorts of social rewards as well. (1983, pp. 462–463)

Houseknecht concludes that "the only significant cost of remaining childless . . . is the loss of those social rewards that are typically associated with child rearing" (p. 463). It is interesting and revealing that this sort of analysis has the same narrowness of concern that characterizes economic analysis in general. It does not consider costs and benefits to the Earth's ecosystems of human activity, nor does it consider psychological or spiritual costs and benefits. The latter makes sense given the scientific and secular aspirations of economics. The former, however, is surprising. Each "career" engaged in can cost the Earth a great deal if it consumes nonrenewable energy and materials. Children are an economic benefit in households, neighborhoods, and communities that rely on human labor rather than nonrenewable energy and materials to produce food and provide utilities. This, of course, is one reason why many families in technologically primitive societies favor large families. Children provide labor for necessary work.

Conventional economic analysis is a very circumscribed tool. It may well accurately predict behavior right up until the time when the human community either voluntarily alters its collective relationship to the Earth and generates a sustainable society, or falls into that "worthless state of human existence" about which we were warned in *The Limits to Growth*. Indeed, one reason why we must adopt an ecological analysis is that it does not endorse such calculations divorced from the larger picture. Microanalysis may produce accurate results in a narrow sense, but it can easily produce a tragically defective aggregate picture. The "tragedy of the commons" (Hardin, 1969) is a good example, where rational self-interest brings down commumity well-being. Hardin's concrete example is a case of farmers who try to exploit some commonly held pasture for private gain. Their efforts unintentionally combine to overgraze and thus ruin the pasture. Proper microeconomic analysis of family life is critical when computing population and energy variables, the two issues that underlie the world problematique.

Ecologist Lester Brown considered this problem in his 1980 book *Building a Sustainable Society:*

> Until a decade or so ago, population growth reduced but did not preclude gains in per capita production of such basic commodities as forest products, seafood, and petroleum. Only as world population moved toward four billion did it begin to outpace the production of the basic commodities on which humanity depends. Now, if population growth continues as projected, a decline in material living standards the world over may be unavoidable. (1980, p. 140)

If we who live in modern societies have a goal, it is to have our cake and eat it too. Most of us have trouble recognizing too much of a good thing. If one steak is good, then how about steak every day? And our overly beefy diet brings on heart disease. If one television is desirable, why not a television in every room? And our families become estranged. If one life-preserving medical device is good, why not one for every person? And our budget for medical care become fiscally and morally untenable. If one child is good, why not as many children as one can bear? And we move closer and closer to exceeding our material limits.

How do people calculate the value of children? Conventionally, they have adopted a microeconomic approach, seeking to maximize value in light of costs and resources. But how does one assess the value of children in a modern society? This is a central issue in Garrett Hardin's (1969) classic paper "The Tragedy of the Commons." His answer is, it depends on what the social environment permits and demands. If it permits individuals to reap the benefits while passing costs on to the general public, such escalating irresponsibility means the eventual collapse of public resources. That is the tragedy of the commons.

In conventional microeconomics, people take into account their personal resources and needs in light of what they can get "for free" from social welfare systems. With unimpeded access to what they can obtain for free from the public sector, people's decisions about childbearing are intrinsically irresponsible. In the modern era there is only one responsible alternative: zero population growth at a level consistent with carrying capacity. The ghost of the demographic grim reaper Thomas Malthus sits waiting, as if to say "You can pay me now or you can pay me later." No magic technological solution will allow unlimited childbearing and population growth. The flaw identified by Hardin is that wishful thinking ignores the modern realities of population. Childbearing decisions are private no longer, because families who control sufficient "private" resources depend on a nonsustainable social order to preserve their advantage. For those who depend more directly on the welfare state, the problem is more clearly transparent, as conventional social welfare systems (the commons) are "overgrazed." In either case, there is a compelling community interest in controlling population levels.

Population Control as Social Welfare Policy

The concept of population control is difficult for those of us who define ourselves as pro-child, pro-family. On the one hand, we want to glorify (not too strong a word) childbearing, child rearing, and family life. On the other, we must identify the quantitative dimensions of childbearing—and to a lesser but still quite real degree, child rearing—as a critical part of the world problematique. Controlling population is undeniably as emotionally ambiguous as it is intellectually and technically challenging.

Imagine a discussion with friends on these issues. The statement is made that "having more than two children is socially irresponsible." A verbal storm ensues. "No!" responds a young father of two who is likely to have another child. "That's ridiculous. What matters is how well you can raise them. Limiting population is something that societies do naturally when they become developed." The discussion continues, and all the major themes are introduced: "Waste is the issue." "The poor countries need to control their population, not us." "But a child born to our way of life consumes many times more resources than a child born in a poor country." "But our society is nearly at zero population growth through natural processes, so we don't need policies that limit individual families." "But we must serve as a model." "I don't think our modeling is going to count for much in the big picture." On and on it goes.

Through it all sits a childless young woman soon, by her own declaration, to be in the childbearing time of her life. Her contributions are knowledgeable. She recognizes the demographic problem and understands the need for control. She sees the validity of the two-child family. But her face tells a different story. Finally she comes out with it. "I know I shouldn't want to; I know how unsound it is. But I think I might like to have three children just like my mother did."

No simply rational process is sufficient to encompass all that needs saying and doing. The choices are several, but they all incorporate two things: rewards for responsible, limited procreation and penalties for exceeding ecologically appropriate limits. Encouraging people to stay out of the business of creating families is one way to limit population. A pro-family solution noted earlier is to encourage single people to ally themselves with nuclear families as informal or bloodline uncles and aunts, to become part of familylike social arrangements that provide psychological and social support. In parts of China under the One Child Policy, a man who chooses to have no children can cede his right to paternity to his brother. Limiting this to men is sexist, of course, but it does illustrate a way that uncle-hood (and aunt-hood) can meet both psychic and demographic needs.

Responsible Fertility

Any realistic discussion of the number of children a family should have must acknowledge the strong—one might say primordial—feelings most of us bring to this topic. Those content with a socially responsible one or two children can afford the luxury of wholeheartedly endorsing population controls, just as those of us who don't smoke can clearly see the health menace and endorse a total ban on smoking. We naturally see the logic of rationality when it conforms to our situation and feelings. We just as naturally accept rationalizations that let us off the hook, whether we want a big family or want to smoke cigarettes. Social psychologists have produced thousands of studies that document the workings of such a "cognitive consistency model."

Is it "unnatural" to limit births within a specific family? Sociobiologist Pierce van den Berghe (1978) says yes, and he says those who do so are reacting to an unnatural environment, unnatural in the evolutionary sense. He argues that "voluntary" restrictions self imposed by individuals don't make genetic sense. Garrett Hardin presents his agreement in his critique of appeals to conscience, which he considers unsound because they place people in a double bind. The nobler sorts respond positively and against their narrow self-interest. The others exploit the good will of the "suckers." The net result is population increase and decrease in socially responsible behavior—because such behavior is at best extinguished by being unrewarded, and at worst punished, as the "responsible" people foot the public bills for the "irresponsible." Garrett Hardin asks (1982, p. 5): "When we use the word responsibility in the absence of substantial sanctions are we not trying to browbeat the free man in a commons into acting against his own interest?"

Is it "unnatural" to limit population? For the individual concerned only with genetic success, the answer is often "yes"—if social conditions permit unlimited breeding and costs can be passed on to the community. But for the community, for the collective interest as articulated and managed by public institutions, the answer is "no"—not in the modern world when the scale of human enterprise threatens the Earth's ecosystems and the quality of human existence. We need to transcend our genetic instructions to "go forth and multiply," because we have accomplished that goal beyond our ancestors' wildest dreams.

Many benefits will flow from collective action to decrease the rate of childbearing to a level consistent with available renewable energy and materials. The chief benefit will be to increase the prognosis for society as a whole. Another benefit will be a focus of attention on human quality, on bearing and rearing the best possible children. Fewer children are likely to be more highly valued children, as has been observed in China and elsewhere (the ravages of a sexist preference for boys over girls not withstanding). A third benefit is that responsible individuals will be freed of the double bind they experience when faced with appeals to conscience in a world dominated by the self-defeating tragic dynamics of the commons.

Limiting the size of specific families may make children an economic commodity, if people can sell their rights to bear them. And there are a host of other moral dilemmas: what about women who exceed their allotment of pregnancies, men who exceed their allotment of impregnations, parents who have a boy but wanted a girl, and children who are born yet are officially illicit? There are costs to any course of action so fundamental as limiting population. But we can contain these costs, and they are the lesser evil in any realistic moral calculus.

How Many People Is Enough? How Many Is Too Many?

As pointed out in Chapter 2, the Environmental Fund envisions that population will increase from the current 5 billion to somewhere between 8.5 and 13.5 billion in 2150. These projections derive from assumptions about declines in birth rates in countries where they were formerly high—assumptions that may prove invalid, either if the association between increased affluence and decreased birth rates does not hold, or if the projected increase in material affluence does not take place. Both are real possibilities.

Lester Brown of the Worldwatch Institute reports that an appropriate population balance would exist with birth and death rates stabilized at about 13 per thousand, with a life expectancy of about 70 years. Current variation among countries runs from about 6 to more than 20 per thousand in the death rate, and from about 9 to nearly 50 per thousand in the birth rate. The task of stabilizing the population still lies before us. According to the 1980 World Fertility Study, about half the world's women do not have access to contraception, but if it were available to them they would use it and birth rates would be significantly reduced. Family planning is the most fundamental family support system, because it permits women and men to balance quality and quantity within the family.

Trusting that families will choose freely to limit childbearing may be insufficient to stabilize the population, but free access to contraception is absolutely the first step. In the Soviet Union, among rural women in Uzbekistan, aggressive efforts to permit and encourage contraception have reportedly succeeded in lowering the birth rate substantially. However, even educated women there who work outside the home still bear an average of five children! This is hardly a sustainable pattern of reproduction, and it illustrates that modernization alone—at least in the simple sense of educational and economic development—may not be enough. A stable population does not happen automatically. Few things do.

Population and the drain on resources are related but are not identical, of course. Per-capita use of resources varies dramatically, depending on social class and level of modernization. A relatively poor American family typically uses less of the world's resources than an affluent American family, but it still consumes much more than a family living in subsistence on the Indian subcontinent, even if the latter family has more children. Likewise, production per capita varies. Of course, it is only realistic to speak of "production" in terms of cultivation of renewable resources such as fish, grain, and wood. With oil wells, mines, and steel mills, where "production" is really consumption of nonrenewable resources, the disparities are perhaps even more marked between the impact of small modern families and large traditional families.

Lester Brown (1980) has compared population trends, resource use, and production, and sees some disturbing trends. Between 1950 and 1973, economic growth and population growth were balanced. "Since then, however, global economic growth has fallen to less than three percent per year, and the population component of the overall growth in global demand has become dominant" (p. 142). Once again, we need to know whether the 1970s were simply a recession in growth or a critical turning point. If the former, we may have a prolonged period of economic ups and downs in which to work things out. If the latter, we may have to cope simultaneously with the problems of population growth and a net decrease in global productivity.

All this tells us that issues of human quantity and quality are not strictly separable. We cannot divorce the kind of life available to people from the number of people available to live that way of life. The image comes to mind of building a sand castle on the ocean shore. Where you build it has a lot to do with the chance it has to survive. Set up near the surf, and all your effort will go into maintaining the most rudimentary structure, responding to the demands of each new wave—not to mention the greater challenge of the incoming tide. But if your operation is far enough back, where the waves cannot reach, you can build for quality, for art, refining and elaborating creatively.

Which kind of world do we want—one in which we are struggling, perhaps hopelessly, to make global ends meet, or one in which we can concentrate on human quality, on helping each child become all that he or she can be? Perhaps I load the question, but I think uncontrolled population growth will force humanity to live with its back to the wall. With the specter of nuclear war, it already lives with a gun to its head. Isn't that enough?

The metaphor of the sand castle is also ambiguous. For individual people, families, communities, and even societies, it may be possible to build in a protected niche, away from the tide of increasing population, increasing demands on resources, and increasing discrepancies between the needs of families and the resources available to them. It may even be possible to profit financially from this rising tide. But are such efforts sound? Are they moral? Certainly, they seem to violate the criterion of justice required for a sustainable society. Discussions of population that consider only numbers without linking those numbers to life styles, ecology, historical prognosis, and justice are unsound at best, foolhardy in the ordinary case, and disastrous in a worst case scenario.

The Concept of Carrying Capacity

Until recently, it seems, much of the debate over population took place within in a context shaped primarily by faith and assumption. Most arguments projected the number of people likely to be born and responded to this number with either alarm or complacency, depending on orientation. On the one hand, Paul Ehrlich (1967) referred to the population "bomb"; on the other, Julius Simon (1975) spoke approvingly of population growth as "the ultimate resource." Lindsey Grant chooses to call those who warn against letting current trends continue the Jeremiads; those who predict that technological innovation automatically will solve the population/resource problem are labeled Cornucopians. The Jeremiads warn that we must redirect our efforts to achieve a sustainable society or face crisis and disaster. The Cornucopians promise that business as usual will somehow solve the problems before us, including population. There is a clear tautological element in Cornucopian thinking about population. It predicts that economic modernization will lead to a steady and sustainable population worldwide, as it has done in some societies. But it does not grant that current levels of population growth in those societies have already resulted in net per-capita *decreases* in affluence.

Disputes exist, of course, over the mechanics of projecting population. It is hard to know how the numbers will go—except "up"—for most countries, most of the time. The problem is that most decisions about quantity are not informed by a clear concept of quality. What kind of life is or will be available to which children? Add to these qualitative questions "for how long?" and the list of variables has grown so long it becomes intimidating.

It is encouraging, then, to see arise a movement to empirically specify the amount of population a particular ecology can sustain at different levels of economic activity. This movement seeks to learn the "carrying capacity" of an environment by considering the nature and costs of a particular life style—or mix of life styles—and the ecology. The concept is sound, but data are only just becoming available. Preliminary studies of the United States argue for reducing population and stabilizing it at 200 million or fewer to reduce environmental stress, ensure sustainability, and increase the likelihood that agricultural and other surpluses can be used to assist other societies facing shortages.

In 1972, *The Limits to Growth* indicated that with existing population trends, global carrying capacity would be exceeded within a century. *Mankind at the Turning Point* (1974) and *Groping in the Dark* (1982), assuming an unchanged global order, projected that some regions would exceed their carrying capacity in only a few decades, while others could expect to stay within their carrying capacity for decades longer, assuming they could maintain their privileged positions. This is a vital differentiation. Carrying capacity must be calculated using assumptions about the boundaries of a particular social system. It is a political and moral as well as a biological issue when it comes to human societies.

What Is Our Carrying Capacity?

What is the carrying capacity of the Earth? No one knows for sure, of course. The answer depends so much on availability of resources and patterns of use that any projection is subject to modification. For example, carrying capacity increases if consumption decreases. It increases if we slow the conversion of high-entropy materials into low-entropy waste. It increases if technological innovation permits substitution of plentiful or renewable resource for scarce or nonrenewable ones. The higher the estimated carrying capacity, however, the greater the risk of overshooting the actual carrying capacity. For example, basing agricultural projections on a period of optimal climatic conditions such as existed in the 1950s and 1960s over most of the world (as the *Global 2000* report did) is riskier than basing them on average expectable climate. The latter provides a margin for error without catastrophic agricultural shortfall.

Similarly, estimates of carrying capacity for a specific society are more or less risky depending on one's assumptions about the influence of other societies. In the case of the United States, for example, the Environmental Fund has argued that projections concerning population growth reach one conclusion if they are based primarily on birth rate, and a quite different conclusion if they take into account an open-door policy with respect to immigration.

What is more, emigration to the United States has an undetermined effect on population in the country of origin. In Mexico, for example, it appears that the potential for population growth can probably replace the numbers who emigrate. Also, as Lindsey Grant and John Tanton (1981) have shown, such emigration tends to deplete the sending nation of laborers after it has supported them through childhood, leaving it with a disproportionate number of dependent children and elderly. For these and other reasons— such as political and military responses to emigration—it is impossible to specify carrying capacity precisely. Those who seriously engage in global modeling of economic, environmental, and population trends do agree that the world is up against some tough limits to growth as conventionally defined in terms of per-capita income, energy use, and the like. This consensus forms the core of the Donella Meadows', John Richardson's, and Gerhart Bruckmann's 1982 book *Groping in the Dark.*

Few who have examined the issue of global carrying capacity believe the Earth can support even the current population of 5 billion in the style to which Americans have become accustomed. Some estimate that carrying capacity is about 7 billion, if current regional disparities in material standard of living are reduced to eliminate extremes of extravagance and desperate impoverishment. Lester Brown (1980) suggests 6 billion as a more appropriate goal, one that will provide a more secure cushion against famine and ecological catastrophe. That number requires no more dramatic reduction in population growth rates than what some nations have already achieved. We will probably reach 6 billion in about the year 2000—but not as a conclusion to population growth. It will be a momentary milepost en route to a much larger number—anywhere from 8.5 to 13.5 billion, as noted earlier.

We may be in a decisive historical period with respect to population. James Grant and John Tanton pose the issue this way:

> Along the curve of history, we are in the vicinity of the point at which human expansion forces a progressive decline in the Earth's carrying capacity, just when that capacity is needed to support the population growth which undermines it. (1981, p. 3)

James Grant poses the issue of carrying capacity in its three basic forms:

> 1. What population level would permit maximum consumption per capita under given assumptions about technology?
> 2. Under those population assumptions may we expect to achieve a harmonious and sustainable relationship between mankind and the planet? (Or "this country?" "this plain?" "this valley?").
> 3. What human population levels would permit such a sustainable relationship with the Earth without forcing the entire system to be engineered to human requirements?

The third method of formulating carrying capacity is the most conservative of the three because it leaves the greatest margin for error. For example, it can accommodate surges in population, which frequently happen. What is more, it is the least arrogant. It respects other life forms, and indeed the Earth as an integral unit on which humans coexist with other creatures. Can we expect our families to nurture gently and teach peaceful coexistence if our societies wantonly and rapaciously devour the planet and our fellow creatures?

Conclusions

We can come away from the issue of carrying capacity with several principles. First, as the world's leading consumer, the United States has a special obligation to reduce our demands for resources to a level that is domestically sustainable. At the very least, we should become self reliant so that we are no longer a negative influence upon the carrying capacities of other societies. This means we should seek a lower than maximum stable population with lower per-capita waste production. Population rarely falls below the replacement level of 2.1 children per family, but sometimes surges above that level. Our great-grandchildren need a demographic cushion. Second, other modernized societies should do the same. Third, the international community should make humane *but feasible* assumptions regarding carrying capacities of nonmodernized societies. These assumptions must reflect local conditions as well as the international availability of resources. Anyone who offers the United States as a model for development fails to recognize the limits of the Earth's ecological resources. Prospects for modernization and conventional economic expansion are radically different in a world of 5 billion than in a world of 1 billion. The 1990s are not the 1770s.

Discrepancies between have and have-not nations are not likely to disappear, particularly under current demographic conditions. But they may be reduced within an overall picture of material adequacy and global justice. This would be a morally as well as an ecologically adequate outcome. But even such a modest proposal will require enormous social and political mobilization. And at the heart of it all will be the day-to-day dynamics of population. How do we convey the vital message that our family lifeboats are roped together? Each crew must husband its own provisions, and must also recognize that if we are all to make the journey comfortably and safely we must act in a socially responsible manner. This brings us closer to the original conception of the lifeboat as articulated by Garrett Hardin. How many of us there are will go far toward determining how well we do.

This brings us back to our friends and their discussion about family size. One argued that it was not socially irresponsible for him and his wife to have third (and maybe a fourth) child because they were talented, fortunate people who could nurture and support several children. And they *are* a family with many resources. In effect, he was asserting that carrying capacity is a concept to be applied at the level of individual families through the decisions of individual parents or couples. He believed that his family could count on sufficient material resources because of technological innovation, his own personal productivity, an efficient household economy, the fact that others would have few or no children, and the assumption that the American way of life will continue. Our friend believes all this without ever actually using the language of carrying capacity. Cornucopians Julius Simon and Herbert Kahn believe it also, aggressively so.

Based on what we have learned, it is doubtful that these assumptions will stand the test of time. If not our friend's children then his grandchildren will begin to pay the price, as people in Brazil, the Sudan, and China are already doing. The ultimate well-being of families is linked to the fate of the Earth; each depends upon the other. As Lester Brown puts it: "The challenge now is to bind the family's fate to the fate of the nations—a challenge first for governments and educators, then for individual men and women" (1978, p. 158).

There are many natural links that require elaboration and expansion if we are to assure foundations for social welfare. For example, the family is the key to separation at the source of materials for recycling, and small family farms are the key to agricultural productivity in a labor-intensive, ecologically sustainable fashion. Yet dominant economic models denigrate the family as a productive entity. Indeed, modern industrial urbanization tends to strip families of their economic functions while exploiting human acquisitiveness. The next step, then, is to look at these and other obstacles to a transition to the sustainable society.

CHAPTER

4.

May 1985:
Wad Medani,
the Sudan

The Dilemma
of Human Wants
and the Reality
of Human Needs

I CAME TO THE SUDAN IN THE MIDST
*of drought and famine. Fields plowed and planted several years ago lie
barren, barely distinguishable from the desert around them. Animal car-
casses are commonplace along the road. In small villages outside the regional town of Wad Medani I see more clearly than ever before the meaning
of "basic human needs." In villages where an astute and enlightened private
development program (Foster Parent Plan International) has operated, the
social fabric is intact. Children are cared for, not abandoned. One-room huts
are clean and orderly, dirt floors and all. Families have convenient access to
drinkable water and cook on simple but efficient stoves. One family has a
cabinet with "prized possessions": a few plates, some glasses, some cere-
monial items, and a few pictures. People work at irrigated vegetable
gardens and tend goats; sometimes they earn some cash when openings in
the modern economy become available. An immunization and public health
program has succeeded in cracking the infant mortality problem. More than
anything else, this is a very concrete definition of "meeting basic needs." In
other villages that have not felt the nurturing hand of an enlightened development agency, the drought has brought social chaos. Whole village populations are taking refuge in camps and moving to the city. I think about
American shopping centers and the difference between human wants and
human needs.*

What obstacles impede the transition to a sustainable society? One that
comes to mind and stays there is our love affair with things, our pleasure
in acquiring material goods, the ease with which we become addicted to

buying and accumulating. When Ferdinand Marcos was deposed from the Philippines in 1986, the world discovered that his wife had 2,000 pairs of shoes and 500 black brassieres in her wardrobe. Most saw this as excessive (some said it was disgusting; some saw it as merely humorous). But is it not simply an exaggeration of something quite common among affluent consumers? Is not shopping a popular "recreation" for most of us? Is owning 10 pairs of shoes so very different from owning 2,000 pairs, when each of us has not more than two feet?

This is not a trivial affectation of modern life. This enjoyment of owning, having, spending, buying, and consuming is a serious threat. It threatens our relationship with the Earth and our relationship with each other, particularly in our families and in our efforts to sustain resources necessary for social welfare systems. It cannibalizes the planet, undermines the spiritual order, and leaves us scrambling to fill the social and spiritual void with possessions. It is an addiction pure and simple (although, of course, it is far from pure, and hardly simple). The transition to a sustainable society depends in part upon overcoming it.

One can predict that the human race will survive the economic crisis. We will continue as a biological presence upon Earth. We might even survive nuclear holocaust, with its almost incalculable devastation. It might be—as Thornton Wilder would say—by "the skin of our teeth," but we humans are a tenacious bunch. But can and will we survive without falling into "a state of worthless existence"? Of course, existence is intrinsically worthwhile to most of us most of the time. But for an appropriately human discussion of the sustainable society and its relation to social welfare systems, we must move beyond the gross issue of survival as a biological phenomenon. We must consider survival in cultural terms, in terms beyond mere electrical activity in the brain, respiration, and defecation.

The late Aurelio Peccei, founder of the Club of Rome, elaborated on this theme in his 1977 book *The Human Quality*. As he saw it, salvation depends upon some profound shifts in orientation, away from material addiction and toward greater attention to the social, psychological, and moral texture of life. Amidst the necessary debate about how many people, how much energy, and what kinds of materials, the central issue is human quality. What is "the good life"?

Perhaps the ancients faced the same issues we face, but only the elite few ever had to contend with too much of a good thing. Perhaps they saw the difficult challenge of disentangling quality from quantity, of escaping materialism yet not sinking into poverty. Perhaps not. Perhaps we experience new challenges in our modern age—challenges for which we are ill equipped biologically and culturally. Perhaps issues of human quality have lain dormant until now because low-power technology and traditional forms of economic organization prevented people from ever having to struggle with the problem of having too much.

Ironically, materialism has joined the Four Horsemen of the Apocalypse. As societies flee War, Famine, Pestilence, and Death, they run into the arms of a beckoning figure that promises to protect and nurture them. Instead it delivers them back into the hands of the Four Horsemen, fattened up for slaughter. That beckoning figure is Modern Affluence.

Ecologist Lester Brown, among others, sees that the seductive power of material acqusitiveness is working hand in glove with unrestrained population growth to push the Earth to the brink of disaster. Look at the world today as it experiences the ravages of modern materialism: some suffer because they are "haves," while others suffer from being "have-nots." We might recall how native Hawaiians were ravaged by diseases brought through early contacts with Europeans. Just as smallpox ran amok among the Hawaiians because they had no natural immunity, it seems that we as a species are defenseless against modern materialism. Once the natural limits of low-power technology are removed, our inherent and voracious appetite comes into play, and mass consumption reigns supreme. Generations of well-established cultural patterns often prove as insubstantial as sand castles exposed to the rising tide at the seashore. South Pacific villages who met at public gatherings each Friday evening for centuries terminated that ancient tradition within weeks of gaining television reception. Everyone wanted to stay home and watch *Dallas!* This power of the modern is captured well in a passage from Shirley Hazzard's novel *The Transit of Venus* in which the steady, conserving ethic of Depression-reared Australians surrenders without firing a shot to American-style mass materialism. This encounter seems a parable for our times and bears recounting in Hazzard's own words:

> One morning a girl whose father had been in America for Munitions came to school with nibless pens that wrote both red and blue, pencils with lights attached, a machine that would emboss a name—one's own preference—and pencil sharpeners in clear celluloid: And much else of a similar cast. Set out on a classroom table, these silenced even Miss Holster [the teacher]. The girls leaned over, picking up this and that: Can I turn it on, how do you work it, I can't get it to go back again. No one could say these objects were ugly, even the crayon with the shiny red flower, for they were spread on the varnished table like flints from an age unborn, or evidence of life on Mars. A judgement on their attractive-

ness did not arise: Their power was conclusive, and did not appeal for praise.

It was the first encounter with calculated uselessness. No one had ever wasted anything. Even the Lalique on Aunt Edie's sideboard, or Mum's Balibuntl, were utterly functional by contrast, serving an evident cause of adornment, performing the necessary, recognized role of extravagance. The material accoutrements of their lives were now seen to have been essentials—serviceable, workday—in contrast to these hard, high-colored, unblinking objects that announced, though brittle enough, the indestructibility of infinite repetition.

Having felt no lack, the girls could experience no envy. They would have to be conditioned to a new acquisitiveness.

"They would have to be conditioned to a new acquisitiveness"—and how easy it was (and is). Would that we could reverse the conditioning as easily! In 1983, newspapers reported on the deregulation of the telecommunications industry in the United States. One result, according to a Federal Communications Commission spokesman, would be competitive manufacturing and sales, making the telephone a "disposable appliance" (his words) just like any other in the modern household. Imagine advertisements for "the BIC disposable phone—make one call, then throw it away!" Indeed, a hotel in Hong Kong advertises precisely that. When a guest checks out, his or her personal phone is thrown away.

One need not stretch things at all to imagine warehouses full of telephones, each one (sold or not) representing the transformation of nonrenewable raw materials into incipient waste. When telephones were uniform and solely functional, did we know we needed to be able to choose from among the myriad alternatives we now have? Having felt no lack, did we experience any envy? Having a need only to communicate, could we have an unmet need for a designer phone? a Mickey Mouse phone? a phone in every room? Will we become better people if telephones become disposable?

The same can be said of our cars, our clothes, our dwellings, our furnishings, our recreational equipment, and our health care. The ease with which we as a species have accepted the principles and practice of modern disposable consumerism argues for some fundamental innate predilection, some vulnerability that may prove just as culturally and environmentally devastating as the native Hawaiians' susceptibility to European-borne disease.

There is an inescapable sense in which the transition to a sustainable society represents a crisis of values: "more and bigger is better" versus "small is beautiful"; and "more" rather than "enough." The former of each pair is manifest in mass modern materialism and in planned obsolescence; we observe the latter in an emphasis on frugality, a preference for quality over quantity, a wish for more harmonious relations with nature. Most of us are *capable* of both. Here as elsewhere we humans live out contradictions, often knowing that our enjoyment of extravagance is wrong for the world—if not for us personally—yet seeming powerless to resist. Listen to the central character of Paul Erdman's 1976 novel *The Crash of '79*, as he expresses his preference for the "good old days" of extravagance that preceded a hypothetical collapse of the petro-based world system.

> I liked the old days when we still had airplanes and television and dry martinis and pornography. I admit it. Sure, there are lots of Latter Day Saints around these days who claim that it was hedonists like myself who were ultimately to blame for what happened . . . us being the world in general and America in particular—because we were so hell-bent upon the pursuit of pleasure and money. . . . And the truth is the we, my generation, managed to ruin our world so completely that we have no legacy to leave them but poverty and disorder. (pp. 7–8)

Americans debated "Plutocracy or Social Democracy?" in the nineteenth century. We are, as David Potter called us in his 1954 book, the *People of Plenty*. But never before has affluence been a "problem" with such far-reaching implications for the social order, because never before has society matched the instinct for consumerism with the economic power to give that instinct its head. Unbridled materialism is the dynamic that drives modern societies into the position of being between the rock of inflated expectations and the hard place of limits to growth.

Shirley Hazzard's account of the Depression-reared Australians has its parallel in John Steinbeck's American classic *The Grapes of Wrath*. Steinbeck's tour de force on the precisely human character of the Great Depression of the 1930s in the United States focused on the travails of the Joad family, an archetypical Oklahoma clan of dirt farmers. Ground into economic collapse by the joint forces of unusually hostile weather, unsound farming practices, and the malevolent interests of what we now call agribusiness, they are evicted from their steady if subsistence agrarian life and set on a course westward to the promised land of California. En route they encounter the marshaled forces of exploitation and greed as well as glimmers of personal and institutional caring and good old-fashioned American neighborliness. They're the children of the prairie meeting both the children of darkness and the children of light.

With their arrival in California, they face still more travails, hoping that economic deliverance is discernible on the horizon. And it was. But what of the next generation of Joads, born and bred to post–World War II affluence? One might envision them in the 1960s and 1970s as newly affluent consumers come to command and expect modern material affluence. We can picture the menfolk settled around the television set, beer and pretzels in hand, in a comfortable house cluttered with disposable that and this, watching the football games after a morning out on their dirt bikes, while the womenfolk prowl the shopping plaza buying more plastic this and that and eating out at McDonald's. Whatever happened to the noble poor and the heroic proletariat?

It's a reactionary question, of course. It creates a straw man. It's just the kind of legitimate question that the affluent Right might use as a ploy to justify cutting wages and feathering the nests of the upper class. The working man has dirt bikes and K-Mart; the rich have BMWs and all the luxurious amenities advertised in *New Yorker* magazine. Neither caricature is fully accurate; both are dehumanizing. But each reflects a legitimate criticism of modern materialism as being wrong for the fate of the Earth as an ecosystem and wrong for the human spirit. What would Jesus Christ say to the pursuit of affluence, American style? What would the Buddha say to disposable plastic razors? What would Karl Marx say to the proletariat turning their backs on social justice? What would Thomas Jefferson say to suburbia?

As a matter of fact, we can know with some assurance what each of them would say. Each in his own voice would say that "mankind does not live by bread alone." Each sees essential human quality as being beyond material affluence, although each would criticize materialism in his own way.

E. F. Schumacher, the late British proponent of "economics as if people really mattered," examined the Christian and Buddhist critiques of materialism. Of the Christian perspective he concluded ". . .that the Christian, as far as the goods of this world are concerned, is called upon to *strive* to use them *just so far* as they help him to obtain salvation, and that he should *strive* to withdraw himself from them *just so far* as they hinder him" (1974, p. 129). This implies a preference for quality over quantity. Gross National Product (GNP) means little in itself, and precious little if the criteria for evaluating it are spiritual. If a rich man once had as much chance of entering Heaven as a camel has in passing through the eye of a needle, then most of us had better look for a new home for eternity. According to Christian values of human scale, simplicity, and nonviolence, modern materialism is anathema. Material "goods" are good only insofar as they help relieve physical suffering, meet basic needs so that spiritual needs can be addressed, and provide a modest vehicle for expressing human creativity.

But the Christian perspective is not thoroughly in tune with the needs of the Earth's ecology. Indeed, the splitting of Man and Nature, the putting of Man above Nature, contributes to the problem. Lynn White recognized this in his 1967 article "Historical Roots of Our Ecological Crisis" when he wrote: "Despite Darwin, we are not, in our hearts, part of the natural process. We are superior to nature, contemptuous of it, willing to use it for our slightest whim" (p. 1206). Blinding rabbits to test cosmetics. Shame on us.

In this respect, at least, Christianity was an ecological regression compared with the primitive animist impulse that emphasized the spiritual integrity of existence, the commonality of being that demanded respect for the trees, the waters, the plants, the animals—for the Earth as a whole. To quote White again, "The spirits *in* natural objects, which formerly had protected nature from man, evaporated. Man's effective monopoly on spirit in this world was confirmed, and the old inhibitions on the exploitations of nature crumbled." Elizabeth Dodson-Gray in her book *Green Paradise Lost* took up this problem and has sought to "go over against the whole Christian hierarchical ordering of the Creation and the whole cosmos" (her words). In this she stands with that small minority in the Christian tradition exemplified by St. Francis and Albert Schweitzer that has sought to retain fundamental faith in a Creator, yet has emphasized the gentle harmonizing voice of that Creator rather than the stern domineering voice that most Christians listen to in their dealings with the world and their fellow beings.

Primitive animism is more readily in keeping with emerging ecological science, although other religious traditions can accommodate to it also. The salience of the built environment and the imperiously exploitive orientation of modern technology may blind us to our fundamental dependence on the Earth as a physical environment—to our economic as well as our spiritual peril. Religion and science are bedfellows. Just as the body is temple for the soul, the Earth's oceans, rivers, lakes, forests, grasslands, and fields are the irreplaceable foundation of the economy.

Elizabeth Dodson-Gray correctly asserts that masculine-oriented hierarchical Christianity exacerbates rather than helps solve the problem. A softer approach is needed to justify and reinforce the attitude of wholeness and interdependence necessary in an ecologically sound society. The patriarchal family is a bad model for ecologically healthy relationships between humans and the rest of Earth's beings. A reformed human family emphasizing equity and responsive harmony, on the other hand, presents a good model to adopt in relation to Earth as a whole. Here again, the family can be a training ground for the world. It is little wonder that researchers studying effective families find a "spiritual orientation" to be one of their qualities (Stinnett et al., 1977).

Buddhist and Christian traditions both contain themes that *should* make the believer uncomfortable with modern materialism. Both put spiritual development first. For the Buddhist, work serves several purposes. It offers an opportunity to use and develop individual characteristics, to create a sense of fellowship in common tasks, and to achieve the sense of satisfaction that comes from producing useful objects needed to sustain life. Neither inhumane work nor indulgent leisure as an alternative to work makes spiritual sense. The principal danger lies in seeking wealth as an end unto itself, in becoming attached to objects. Simplicity and nonviolence in one's relations to the material world are essential. Schumacher renders this idea with the phrase, "amazingly small means leading to extraordinarily satisfactory results" (p. 141). In this sense, Buddhist thinking is dramatically opposed to conventional modern consumerism.

Buddhism teaches that material goods are only a means for achieving human well-being. Consuming for its own sake has no value. Rather, one is encouraged to *minimize* consumption, to let go of objects unless they further spiritual goals. Contrast this with our culture, in which we are urged to view conspicuous consumption as a patriotic duty, a sacred trust. Each quarterly report on consumer spending is awaited eagerly, and if such spending declines we are accused of losing faith in the economy. If we do not purchase all that our income permits, we are viewed with suspicion, as cultural heretics or economic traitors.

In *An Immodest Agenda: Rebuilding America Before the 21st Century,* Amitai Etzioni castigates the 80 percent of the population identified by survey researcher Daniel Yankelovich who believe that needs of the self take precedence over work and the needs of others. Of course, the very existence of social welfare systems derives from a sense of responsibility for social relations. But such social responsibility is not necessarily or ethically linked to increasing material productivity in the conventional terms embraced by Etzioni, who denigrates concern for "quality of life" and personal fulfillment because they stand in the way of industrial development. While he rejects an orientation that is "indifferent to wealth," we can see that such an attitude is vital for a sustainable society, one that can live lightly upon the Earth and in tune with basic human needs.

In this sense Etzioni links consumerism, the work ethic, and cultural patriotism. It is this linkage that we must break, replacing it with a middle way that combines passionate commitment to a humane social environment with rejection of materialism as an end rather than a very limited means. Certainly refocusing time and energy away from materialism toward social welfare systems and productive family relations is one way to break the consumer habit. Cynthia Hollander's "My Turn" column in Newsweek, titled "Thanks for the Recession," is worth noting. Confronted with an economic crisis when her husband lost his job, she and her family found that "you can lower your standard of living and be happy. . . . I can't say that money is not important. It is. But how I spend my time is equally important." Once adequacy is achieved, the key is to do things that require the investment of time and human energy rather than cash and petro-energy.

It may be symbolic that the Buddhist is told to plant a tree every few years and nurture it until it is well established. Given the threat of deforestation in much of the world, this alone lends credibility to the Buddhist ethic. The positive symbolism of planting trees to celebrate the birth of children and the social benefits of nurturing those trees as a family activity make forestation a model enterprise for families, one that social welfare systems can profitably encourage. Living off nonrenewable energy is parasitic and does violence to the Earth. Planting trees is a modest gesture of repayment. Doing so as a statement of family commitment to the future of the Earth is ecologically wise and spiritually elegant.

Both Christian and Buddhist principles condemn modern materialism. But the Christian can easily become the Puritanical, with its distrust of simple worldly pleasures like dancing and making love. The Buddhist is tempted to become so unworldly, so immaterial in the search for spiritual development, that active concern for the physical world atrophies. Schumacher did much to outline the needed "middle way" in economic thinking and technology when he urged us to commit ourselves to "a technology more productive and powerful than the decayed technology of the ancient East, but at the same time nonviolent and immensely cheaper and simpler than the labor-saving technology of the modern West" (p. 144).

Religion puts spirit first. This can offer a compelling alternative to material consumption *if* it avoids the pitfall of reinforcing human acquisitiveness, aggressiveness, and imperiousness in the name of humankind's unique position in the cosmos. Whether it be Islam, Judaism, or Zoroastrianism, religion can provide important resources for the transition to a sustainable society.

Of course Christian and Buddhist spiritual principles are just that, principles. When Stalin was advised to consider the Pope's views in making decisions about the shaping of Europe at the end of World War II, he asked, "How many divisions does he command?" The power of modern materialism in the Christian West and its appeal in the Buddhist East suggest that the credence and wisdom of these principles is not enough alone. But it is something. Single-minded pursuit of wealth is silly at best and sinful at worst.

But How Do We Proceed?

Progress is slow. Duane Elgin's book *Voluntary Simplicity* (1978) presents evidence that some of us are turning away from the dominant materialist code that "more is better" and embracing a way of life more in keeping with both Christian and Buddhist principles. In volunteering for a more materially simple life, such individuals seek a more spiritually, psychologically, and socially enriched existence that stands as a demonstration of hope. By living the credo "enough is always plenty and less is often more," they provide concrete reassurance to those who fear that the alternative to modern mass materialism is a subsistence-level life that is brutish, nasty, and short. On the contrary: it is graceful, enriched, and sustainable. The world needs such living demonstrations to show that people can *live* their beliefs and values, not die or kill for them.

Thomas Jefferson originated much of the language of modern political and social discourse, particularly for those who sympathize with American-style democracy. He saw what was needed to preserve and nurture human character in a manner that would support a politically, morally, and culturally sound way of life. He saw that when people were divorced from the land, they became estranged from their essential humanness. Such estrangement made them ripe for being led astray down unwise political paths. Looking at modern materialism, he would perceive its falseness and its cultural, spiritual, and political dangers.

In his radical ideology, Karl Marx foresaw a postrevolutionary society in which economic struggle would give way to the socialist good life—a communal existence marked by balance, by being in tune, and in which human beings would live economically justly with each other and in harmony with the planet. His vision may have been politically naive and may have been overcome by struggles in later years as he contended with the violently oppressive forces of capitalist materialism in its nineteenth-century form, but that vision remained. Its human validity certainly did.

Ironically, we may have adopted the materialist part of Marx's equation without the justice part, and now are threatened with the worst of both worlds. Certainly the oppressive regime based in Moscow seems to have done so. It recalls Aldous Huxley's novel *Ape and Essence,* a post–nuclear holocaust parable in which all the worst chickens of the modern age have come home to roost. A character worthy of Dostoyevsky's Grand Inquisitor sums it up this way: You have taken the worst of the East (its disregard for individual autonomy) and combined it with the worst of the West (its acquisitive materialism) and created worldwide terror and a soulless existence. Perhaps that is what the Club of Rome's leaders had in mind when they spoke of "a worthless state of existence." It certainly isn't what Jesus, Buddha, Jefferson or Marx had in mind.

In seeking a transition to a sustainable society, we must disentangle human wants from human needs. How much do people really need? How much should they want? Can we meet our genuine material needs in ways that increase our psychological, social, and spiritual well-being without cannibalizing the planet and degrading our spirits? Almost any effort to answer these questions begins with two assertions. First, most individuals in most modern societies have bloated conceptions of their material needs that interfere with their ability to seek fulfillment of their highest human purposes, their psychological and spiritual wants. Second, in addition to being unwise psychologically and spiritually, our present course will prove disastrous for the well-being of the planet.

But how do we find good answers to the many questions posed by affluence? We begin by recognizing the economic context in which human needs arise and are met, or are not met. Consider the complex human issues surrounding poverty and unemployment in the modern era.

Glen Elder's study, *The Children of the Great Depression,* describes the impact of the Great Depression of the 1930s on families in the United States by focusing on two groups of children, one group born in 1920 and 1921, the other born in 1928 and 1929. The study included middle-class and working-class families, some of whom were hit hard by the Depression, others who escaped relatively unscathed.

In families in which the father lost his job or most of his income and the marital relationship was weak, the mother often led the way in blaming him for "his" economic failure. Girls were encouraged by the dominance of their mothers and boys were disillusioned by their fathers' failure, with the result that girls had fewer personality and emotional problems than boys did. These factors intensified if the children were young rather than adolescents when the Depression came, because they were more dependent on their parents and were exposed to the new situation for a longer period of time in the home. On the other hand, the pressures of economic deprivation tended to strengthen families in which a strong marital bond existed. As always, the state of family did much to determine whether individuals sank or swam. The real measure of worth is the psychological, social, and spiritual wealth of families.

Note that these findings describe families with a pre-Depression record of relative stability. Parents were married and had an adequate work history. These were not the underclass, not the hard-core unemployed, nor were they single-parent households. For them, economic deprivation was an *event,* not a permanent condition. This is significant, and cautions against simple generalizations about other groups such as the single-parent families that have constituted the core of the chronically poor since 1980 in the United States.

As if all this complexity were not enough, we must remember that the Great Depression was followed by the economic "boom" of World War II and the 1950s. Per-capita real income increased by 62 percent between 1946 and 1970. Some "victims" of the Depression were ready to benefit from that opportunity, while others were not. What is more, one response to the Depression was the creation and expansion of a massive social welfare system in the United States that included unemployment insurance and Social Security. Ironically, many now consider these very systems to be part of today's problems because they foster family disintegration and discourage initiative.

A child is more at risk during economic or social disaster than in less troubled times. Whether troubled times will damage a child depends on whether those troubles are transmitted to him or her. Elder's study makes this clear. Families who did not directly lose income did not show the negative effects that deprived families did; some occupations were more affected than were others. Some communities suffered more than average, some much less. And individual temperament played a role: some people treated the stress as a challenge; others responded by withdrawing. Developmental psychologists have begun to speak of "stress-resistant" children, whose personal and social resources help them cope with very difficult life circumstances.

Because much of a family's energy and time go into making a good life for its children, we cannot understand the psychology and ecology of affluence without examining the needs of children. What does it mean to be a child? In the modern sense, it is to be shielded from the *direct* demands of economic, political, and sexual forces. Children have a claim on those who bear them, and they have a right to receive support from their families and the communities regardless of their economic value in conventional accounting terms. Usually, families want to provide this support and will do so if at all possible. But when they cannot provide for their children, society recognizes some responsibility to pick up the tab. This deeply held principle gives moral force to public efforts to eliminate poverty. And it heightens our concern when poverty increases in the lives of children, as it has in the United States in the 1980s.

Similarly, children are not fair game for political activity. They cannot vote, are not legally responsible, and are not pawns to be used by competing political forces in the society. More broadly, children are expected to relate to adults on a direct person-to-person basis, not in the organized bureaucratic way that adults must relate, at least some of the time.

Finally, children are not supposed to be sex objects. In their behavior, their interests, their attitudes, and their bodies, they are explicitly asexual. To be sure, children can be and usually are very attuned to physical contact and affection, but not genitally oriented sexuality. One of the worst crimes is to sexually violate a child. As David Finkelhor's excellent book *Child Sexual Abuse* (1984) makes clear, children are not in a position, developmentally or socially, to give informed consent for sexual involvement with adults.

If the child is shielded from economic, political, and sexual forces, what then is childhood all about? Play! Children have a license to play, and in so doing they explore the world. This play is distinguished from adult work in that it doesn't depend upon formal organizations, and from adult social life in that it isn't the basis for courtship. Children are shielded so that they can play, and this play is fundamentally human, as Jacob Bronowski (1974) so correctly recognized when he spoke of the human being's "long childhood" as a key to the ascent of man.

The second fundamental purpose of childhood is development of basic competence. Children must become adept at language, body control, morality, reasoning, emotional expressiveness, and interpersonal relations. Unless they do, they are a problem—for their families, for our society, and for themselves.

What do they need to develop basic human competence? The basic ingredients are parents and other adults who have time, interest, and love enough. Access to basic health services, food and shelter, and continuity of care are crucial. In the psychological domain, the key is that the child be in relationships that are emotionally validating and developmentally challenging. The child needs to hear the message: "Yes. You are worthwhile. I care enough to listen to you, to talk with you, to help you, to care for you, to teach you." Play and development of competence go together. For the child they are the main items on life's agenda. They are how the family socializes the child. For the community, protecting them is an important part of the social contract.

Children are a good starting point for elucidating basic human needs because they appreciate human essentials—love, play, and security. Of course, their fantasies and their experience in their families influence their interpretation of the essentials, but they generally have a good, if often unarticulated, grasp of what is important. Furthermore, those who care for children likewise learn to appreciate what's really important. This may be one reason why women, who are usually primary caregivers, tend to have a better grasp of social reality than do men. Children put economic needs in a useful light, particularly when the issue is defining and assessing the impact of poverty.

Is Poverty the Alternative to Affluence?

Few of us would choose poverty except for didactic purposes, and most would agree with Sophie Tucker's classic statement: "I've been rich and I've been poor, and rich is better." Often, naive or disingenuous critics of the limits-to-growth thesis ask, "Would you have everyone live in poverty?" They see modern materialism as the only alternative to comprehensive impoverishment. The distinction is false, of course. It is no panacea, and it is a menace to material adequacy.

A generation of research on the harm of socioeconomic deprivation has on human development in the United States associates the ups and downs of the American economy with the incidence of breakdowns in human quality—suicide, domestic violence, and illness, for example. At first glance, the inference seems simple: provide more money and jobs. But a more penetrating analysis challenges such a simplistic response. As revisionist economists such as Orio Giarini have amply demonstrated, the fault is in the economy's ecological and cultural foundations, not in some easily fixed quirk in business cycles or a simple cash transfer program. What is more, harmful influences do not result directly from low income *per se* (i.e., from a certain number of dollars), but from an economic context that is inherently stressful and becoming more so. It is inherently stressful because it is ever more apparently unstable and because monetarized activities have displaced nonmonetarized ones. More and more people are more and more dependent on the institutions of the cash economy and more vulnerable to its ups and downs.

The penetration of family life by the cash economy jeopardizes many important family functions. It is at best irrelevant, and at worst inimical, to meeting many basic human needs. Poverty is primarily a social concern, however, and only secondarily an economic concept. It is a state of social being in which life is denuded of essentials. The modern economy can actually *increase* poverty by destroying the foundation for nonmonetarized ways of meeting basic needs. In Brazil, for example, the "economic miracle" of the 1960s and 1970s did not lower the high rate of infant mortality, and it decreased real income among the rural populace who formed the bulk of the population.

The modern economy can decrease quality of life by disturbing relationships that meet basic human needs for children and parents. Moreover, it actually can increase the negative implications of low income for families. Where more and more cash is required for basic daily needs, the human costs of being cash poor increase. For example, many families are disrupted by the issue of spending money for adolescents. Spending by teenagers rose 50 percent between 1975 and 1980, a period during which the number of youth declined 6.6 percent. Do teenagers *feel* richer?

In the long run, of course, dependence on cash and the economic institutions related to it will increase the stressfulness of life by generating new needs and thus increasing the size and speed of the socioeconomic treadmill. As a UN report so eloquently puts it: "We have not inherited the Earth from our fathers, we are borrowing it from our children." And living with those debts is likely to be very stressful for our children and their children forever after. For example, many young Americans now recognize that they are paying for a Social Security system that will become increasingly less solvent in decades to come, even as it becomes a bigger and bigger drain on their pocketbooks today.

It appears that we humans have a special vulnerability to modern materialism. My first-hand experience with societies other than our own reinforces the reports of other observers on this score. Fast-food restaurants, video games, and plastic gadgets are found everywhere in the world. The penetrating power of modern materialism is astounding. Few if any societies seem to have—or even want—the armor needed to deflect it. Airports, modern hotels, and shopping centers all over the world are characterized by their sameness, and are harbingers of a worldwide trend in declining cultural diversity. The overarching course of "cultural development" around the world seems to be toward homogenization based on the lowest common denominator of mass materialism. It moves in this direction rather than preserving human cultural diversity—diversity that can serve as a hedge against evolutionary social dead ends much as genetic diversity does in the realm of biology.

The modern way seems destined to become the way of the world in the short run. Conditions will permit this if the dominant world economic order continues. "Conditions" include the intentional efforts of multinational corporations whose very slogans (e.g., "it's a small world") extol this trend. They include the collusion of local governments and people whose eagerness to become part of the modern picture usually overwhelms their understanding of and commitment to worthwhile themes in their own traditions. By and large, the victory of modern materialism seems assured until physical limits to growth enact their catastrophic global restraining order and we reach that "state of worthless existence" feared by the Club of Rome. Or, we wise up. Even if we avoid collapse by stopping short of the upper limits to growth, we face the prospect of an ambiguous cultural landscape dominated by the fruits of affluence—or rather the pits, hulls, and skins—and the wreckage of older social systems.

In socioeconomically and ecologically sane and safe times and places, the family is the headquarters for human development. When the environment comes unglued and society is awash with stress and disruption, adults and children huddle together in their families to try to weather the storm. When families become unglued, we have reached a period of crisis for social welfare systems. As we saw in Chapter 3, the contemporary economic war in Brazil resembles the civil war that ravaged the Soviet Union during the 1920s; both left millions of children without families, to become a social menace. The family is probably the most reliable and durable vehicle for human survival under extreme environmental stress. When it goes down, individuals go down. Recall the Joads. They survived poverty as individuals in and through their family.

An Economic Prospectus

Is the takeover of modern materialism assured? Have we no resistance? Are we totally vulnerable? The answers to these questions seem clear: yes, no, and yes. But there are encouraging signs that for all our gullibility, for all our apparent eagerness to buy into materialism, it sticks in our throats, and its victory is not complete. People are not satisfied by modern materialism, and that is cause for hope.

Maybe "man does not live by bread alone" is more than wishful thinking or sentiment. Maybe it is based on some very sound thinking, and reveals a profound insight into both human nature and the way of the world. Psychological technicians such as B. F. Skinner tell us that we must abandon classic conceptions of humanity and move "beyond freedom and dignity." They argue that we need only a set of scientific principles and techniques of behavior modification. Many of us are dubious, and hearken back to what Joseph Wood Krutch said almost sixty years ago in his book *The Modern Temper:*

> Science has always promised two things not necessarily related—an increase first in our powers, second in our happiness or wisdom, and we have come to realize that it is the first and less important of the two promises which it has most abundantly kept. (p. 43)

Techniques for modifying behavior are essential, and this is science's strong suit. But values to motivate and direct the mechanisms of social guidance and control are required too.

We should be willing to accept new cultural vehicles—but not at the expense of classical conceptions of human purpose. A generation of research on the "quality of life" encourages this view. Ironically, the classic philosophical search for "the good life" has been supplanted by the efforts of social scientists to measure "quality of life," just as philosophers have retreated to logic and linguistics. There is a science of the good life in the making.

As psychologist Donald Campbell has noted, as early as 1798 Sir John Sinclair described statistics in the following terms when he introduced them in his *Statistical Account of Scotland:* "The idea I answer to the term [statistics] is an inquiry into the state of the country, for the purpose of ascertaining the quantum of happiness." As Angus Campbell's 1981 volume *The Sense of Well-Being in America* makes clear, we are still searching for a way to measure happiness. But we have made some progress, and that progress tells us that basic human needs are not satisfied very well by modern materialism. In fact, despite rising material affluence in the United States since World War II, large-scale surveys report no increase—and in some cases even a decline—in the proportion of people reporting themselves to be "very happy." And the decline is most evident among the more affluent.

The role of affluence in defining human quality of life is complex and often contradictory; it often bears only a weak direct relationship and has a negative effect. As affluence increases, it becomes an ever more ambiguous indicator of quality, sometimes creating and exacerbating as many problems as it solves or reduces. The affluence that permits a diverse diet tends to result in excessive ingestion of animal fats, for example. The industrial economy that reduces backbreaking labor substitutes the risk of carcinogens. The increase in electrical consumption that reduces physical exercise generates the need for weight reduction and physical fitness centers. No, GNP is hardly a good measure of quality of life.

Beyond GNP

The most primitive efforts to move beyond GNP and systematically assess quality of life focus on public health and economy. They measure infant mortality, life expectancy, educational attainment, employment, per-capita income, and material possessions such as telephones, radios, cars, and washing machines. This is the stuff of which most international and regional comparisons are made. The statistics function well some of the time in describing gross differences among some human communities and socioeco-nomic systems. However, they seem to imply a simple one-to-one correspon-dence between modernization and the meeting of basic human needs. Such a direct relationship is called "linear" in mathematical terms. But is the relationship linear? Anyone with a spiritual conception of human existence wants the answer to be "no," and the evidence is comfortingly in agreement. In this case, at least, social science meets philosophy on common ground.

GNP measures the price of goods and services entering the social system rather than the current stock of goods available for use. It thus measures "throughput" of things rather than use of things. It values waste but not conservation. It devalues the way human beings really live at their best because it emphasizes "having" rather than "being." Ideal events, from the point of view of GNP, are those that accelerate the transformation of resources into priced goods; anything that lasts a long time or is outside the cash economy is a drag. In conventional economic terms, families are a drag unless they consume products. Conventional economic measures such as GNP do not represent humankind well.

Several analyses testify to this. Robert Heilbroner's *Business Civiliza-tion in Decline* (1978) arose from the recognition that "economic success does not guarantee social harmony" or personal satisfaction. William Leiss (1980) followed this analytic path to fruition in *The Limits to Satisfaction*. He examined the several ways in which the materialist ethos is flawed, and in so doing revealed much about the anxiety, ambiguity, and dissatisfactions in modern societies. Leiss understands that most of the satisfaction inhering in material commodities is social. The satisfaction derives from what they convey: one's social status or prestige; one's monetary worth; one's awareness of fashion; one's good taste. Yet these impressions must be constantly reaffirmed through replenishment with ever more expensive commodities that show one still has what it takes. Thus, satisfaction does not increase in any reliable and sustainable fashion.

Like all addictions, the materialist addiction provides only a temporary "high" followed by an adjustment and a new threshold for stimulation. Yet despite what Leiss, Campbell, and others say about the hopelessness of material aggrandizement, few of us really seem to believe them. "Psychology applies to other people," we seem to say. Even here we are living out a psychological concept, what David Elkind (1980) has called a "personal fable"—the irrational belief that the regular rules of day-to-day reality do not apply. Consumer junkies, like all junkies, always think they can handle it. Who among us does not take for granted, or at least become accustomed to, each new level of material success, each new increment in material consumption, each new possession?

Materialism is bad psychology, as demonstrated by Tibor Scitovsky's *The Joyless Economy* (1981) and Fred Hirsch's *Social Limitations to Growth*. But it is also bad sociology. Modernization disrupts traditional social sources of meaning in human experience. Stuart Ewen's *Captains of Consciousness: Advertising and the Social Roots of the Consumer Culture* (1983) and Marshall Sahlins' *Culture and Practical Reason* (1982) make this clear. Increases in the national GNP or in per-capita real income do not produce increases in happiness or personal satisfaction: thus they fail the statistical test applied by Sir John Sinclair as he sought to develop ways to ascertain "the quantum of happiness."

What is more, by disrupting traditional sources of meaning, modernization creates a void. Human nature abhors a psychological vacuum. Thus, we rush to fill the void with things. Pursuit of things and attachment to wealth are probably the natural expression of our need for meaning in a world increasingly stripped of traditional significance. Erich Fromm developed this theme in *To Have or To Be* (1955), in which he argued that people once defined themselves by *being* something in relation to others, while now they are more likely to define themselves by *having*. No matter what it is, we must have something to be someone. This is particularly true for women trapped in stereotypical sex roles. Consigned to the role of consumer, they need to have more things to feel more worthwhile. This stimulates the economy, and buying things thus becomes what John Kenneth Galbraith calls a "convenient social virtue."

Often the fullest picture of reality comes not from social science, but from fiction, where the rough edges of incomplete factual information can be smoothed by the visionary imagination. Some of the best thoughts on the essential falseness of gross materialism as a human social psychology are found in Austin Tappan Wright's utopian novel *Islandia*, published in 1942. It describes a fully sustainable society in which pursuit of human quality totally informs and guides decisions about quantity. The economic and social unit is the family farm. The family unit is the basis for decision making, and all decisions are made with an eye to harmonizing traditions established by past generations with needs of generations yet to come. Family members make extended visits to other farms and meet annually for their only political event, a congress of landowners. Islanders have no contact with other countries and little "modern technology." They are educated in one-room schoolhouses and have but one national university. Individual work pace and family integrity are valued over speed and gross output. *Formal* social services are all but nonexistent; like the state in Marx's vision, they wither away because they are not needed. Informal networks provide routine help to individuals and families faced with acute problems. *Islandia* presents an alternative to our superficial materialist modern society. But, it does so through a social organization that offers enough material technology to permit the dignity of economic adequacy for all. Human quality is paramount.

The two characters in the following excerpt are discussing how Islandia would change were it to become "modern" as John, the contemporary American, understands the term.

> Dorn: Why should I change?
> John: Progress!
> Dorn: Speed, is that progress? Anyhow, why progress? Why not enjoy what one has? Men have never exhausted present pleasures.
> John: With us, progress means giving pleasures to those who haven't got them.
> Dorn: But doesn't progress create the very situation it seeks to cure— always changing the social adjustment so that someone is squeezed out? Decide on an indispensable minimum. See that

> everyone gets that, and until everyone has it, don't let anyone have
> any more. Don't let anyone ever have any more until they have
> cultivated fully what they have.
>
> *John:* To be unhappy is a sign we aren't stagnating.
>
> *Dorn:* Nor are we. "Happy" wasn't the right word. We are quite as
> unhappy as you are. Things are too beautiful; those we love die;
> it hurts to grow old or be sick. Progress won't change any of these
> things, except that medicine will mitigate the last. We cultivate
> medicine, and we are quite as far along as you are there. Railroads
> and all that merely stir up a puddle, putting nothing new in and
> taking nothing out. (Wright, 1942, pp. 84–85)

E. F. Schumacher, the "small-is-beautiful" economist, offered a useful insight into the misleading character of strictly quantitative economic analyses. He noted that all the debate about economic indicators among the immensely rich 25 percent of the world's population pales into insignificance when one considers the rest of the world, which is immeasurably poor. This much is obvious, using any sort of qualitative standards of affluence. That many who are relatively rich monetarily and materially do not *feel* rich is part of the problem. And this problem highlights the fact that poverty is primarily a social, rather than a narrowly economic, concept. It's not how much money you have, but how well you are able to recognize and meet basic needs.

When considering cash income, we must resist the temptation to simply count dollars. Instead, we should consider how frequently families receive incomes that permit them to achieve qualitatively different styles and standards of living. This is the thinking behind a series of budgets generated by the U.S. Bureau of Labor Standards. Best known is the poverty budget, which defines the minimal financial needs of a family (about $12,000 for an urban family of four in 1988). Less well known but of equal or greater importance are the low, intermediate, and high budgets. We may call these "struggling," "comfortable," and "affluent," as they rest on corresponding assumptions about life style—principally the level of disposable income once basic needs are met. For 1988, these budgets for an urban family of four were about $25,000, $35,000, and $50,000, respectively. They and the poverty figure provide focal points for discussions of political economy, not average income or per-capita income. Looked at this way, it is easy to see that "satisfaction" and "meaningfulness" transcend income—particularly if the social and psychological costs of earning income sufficient for a comfortable life style increase. Indeed, because material goods depend upon social interpretation for their meaning, they are *always* a risky psychic investment.

They are foolish at best; tragic at worst. Survey data tells us this much about human values and needs.

Over and over again researchers ask what makes people happy and what worries them most. They find "family life" at the top of the list on both counts. In his 1976 report, Angus Campbell and his colleagues investigated the correlates of satisfaction using the question, "In general, how satisfied or dissatisfied would you say you are with your life as a whole these days?" Others have taken much the same approach and found that six areas of life are important to people: satisfaction with self, family, standard of living, fun, housing, and government.

In his 1981 book, Angus Campbell studied the effect upon well-being of conditions such as being successfully married, employed, and educated, and having friends. He considers that these measures both fulfill social expectations and maintain intimate and supportive relationships. We might subsume them all under the rubric of being socially integrated, being socially well endowed, and generally being in tune with the social environment. The main themes are social interconnectedness, physical well-being, and purposefulness. Family plays a large role in sustaining all of these.

Modern materialism plays an ambiguous role. First, once basic needs are met, materialism often plays a subversive role in families. It robs them of productive functions and tempts family members to rely on material alternatives to the investment of time and energy in each other. Second, it puts pressure on people to define their worth in financial terms, and thus undermines the family by defining children as costs, causing parents to devalue nonpaid productive labor such as child care, and causing wage earners to devalue homemakers because they participate in the cash economy only as consumers. Third, while materialism permits improvement in physical well-being by raising the standard of living, it typically does so in a gross and often self-defeating way. An individual may have more money, but less access to "free" resources such as clean air and water or to neighbors willing to provide supplementary child care. Modernization "giveth with one hand and taketh away with another" when it comes to meeting basic needs. Until now, most people have believed that the giving outweighed the taking away. Increasingly, however, some are wondering whether the balance may have shifted. An analysis of basic needs may provide the rosetta stone for deciphering the meaning of this fundamental challenge to human quality.

Basic Human Needs

What are basic human needs? Who would presume to answer? Many have labored to compile a list. Some make short lists of key words such as "belonging," "being," "loving," "having"; others rely upon evocative phrases such as "havinng control over one's life." Some draw out the implications of key concepts. All seek to combine acknowledgment of human beings as physiological creatures with a respect for the finer qualities of human existence.

For most Western-style thinkers and social scientists, Abraham Maslow's (1951) needs hierarchy is the be-all (and often the end-all) of efforts to define human quality. His hierarchy begins with survival needs and extends upward through social esteem to personal fulfillment. Leiss (1979) notes that such a list is flawed because it does not place these needs in their social and ecological context. He argues that for a discussion of human needs to be useful, it must move from abstract to concrete analyses of how needs and economy are related in day-to-day practice. The way we define and meet survival needs for clothing and shelter affects the planet, for example, if we deforest vast areas in doing so (and thus violate key values). Similarly, if we seek to satisfy our need for actualization through energy-intensive activities, we may disrupt the regenerative capacity of field and stream. The raw power of industrial society makes our needs and the ways we go about meeting them into very important factors in the planetary ecology.

Leiss is right on the mark. Current forms of economic organization affect what human needs are. It is only marginally helpful to speak of "basic human needs" that have no social context. The alternatives are two: to accept the context's validity by simply cataloging the needs of those within it (we might call this the "people's-choice" approach), or to critique the context itself, thus permitting a specification of human needs based on a better social context. Better in what sense? Better in that it is more in tune with the realities of human psychology *and* the global environment. We might call this the "knowing-what's-good-for-you" choice.

Modern societies are unrealistic on both counts. They falsely assume that ever greater affluence leads to ever greater satisfaction and meaning. It may not; it certainly cannot do so indefinitely. Also, they operate on economic principles that allow people to choose to do violence to the Earth's natural systems and threaten the very long-term existence of human cultures—often without being directly confronted with the ultimate consequences of their life styles.

In a saner economic system, humans could live more lightly upon the Earth *and* invest time and effort into activities that *are* satisfying, that *do* convey a sense of meaningfulness. This means, among other things, an expanded emphasis on family life as a focal point for social existence. Further, it means a restructuring of economic activity to create a social context in which the family is the natural focal point for human needs—not just one of several competing sets of human needs created by the materialist institutions of workplace and commercial recreation.

This conception is tied closely to a definition of human development as the creation of social maps of the world, maps that reflect experience, intelligence, and insight, and then provide guidance on how to live in the world. Human beings are meaning-seeking organisms. If we establish a false environment, we generate false needs and doom individuals to developmental dead ends, because people will do all they can to achieve what society defines as meaningful. There is madness in the message of modern life.

Modernization has promised to enhance human development by minimizing physical threats and by extending the power of the individual to discover, sustain, or alter the environment. But it has unleashed forces that threaten to alter this environment negatively, that neutralize human development by establishing "needs" that undermine the family and create unfulfillable economic expectations. This economic order and its cultural baggage are major obstacles in the transition to a sustainable society. In *Islandia,* the *need* for social welfare systems was diminished, yet welfare was increased by a "small-is-beautiful" social organization. We face a mirror image: the need for powerful social welfare systems grows while the forces generating that need erode the foundation for sustaining those systems.

CHAPTER

5.

November 1982:

Ft. Wayne, Indiana

The Tragedy of
Conventional Economic Thinking:
Does Everything
Have a Price?

I HAVE COME TO THE AMERICAN
*heartland to speak to the staff and supporters of Ft. Wayne's Mental Health
Center at a seminar titled "Today's Adversity: Tomorrow's Strength." The
issue is this community's economy and its relation to the mental health of
its citizens. Most of the nation has been wallowing in the morass of recession, but cities like Ft. Wayne have been experiencing Depression-like unemployment rates. Major industrial plants have closed or drastically cut
back, causing unemployment directly and indirectly. Ft. Wayne recently received a serious blow, when International Harvester announced it would
close its truck/bus body production plant. The direct cost is some 2,200
jobs; the eventual total is several times that because of the ripple effect. I'm
here to review social science research on human consequences of unemployment. My special focus is the impact on family life.*

*During the moderator's opening remarks, I look out over an audience of
worried faces. They are not the people the television news shows each
night waiting in line at the unemployment insurance office, but they are
worried nonetheless; some out of compassion, some because their friends or
spouses have been affected, some because they fear they may be next. My
thoughts turn to my first undergraduate course in economics nearly two decades ago.*

*It was called "Economics 101: Introduction to Economics." The instruc-
tor, discussing unemployment, says, "it is a necessary part of the economic
system as a way of controlling prices, demands, and production." He rolls
onward into the classical capitalist economics of unemployment, its functions and benefits in combating inflation. I am on scholarship, attending a*

private college where nearly everyone else takes affluence and employment for granted. The instructor's words make sense to them. But my father was unemployed during one of the "minor economic dislocations" of the 1950s, and I can't forget the human cost of that period in my family's life. Finally I speak up, asking in effect: where are the real people in this lecture on unemployment? What kind of discipline is economics that it views such human disasters as "normal, even beneficial"?

The Meaning of Economic Development

We can begin the discussion of the relationship between economics and social welfare systems with two books: Frederick Jackson Turner's *The Frontier in American History*, originally published in 1897 and issued in the early 1960s, and Walter Rostow's *Stages of Economic Growth*, published in 1962. Turner considered the official end of the frontier in 1890 (declared so by the U.S. Census Bureau) a pivotal event in American history. The physical frontier, he argued, had made the American character democratic and optimistic, but significant changes in the post-Frontier era were changing that. His thesis would have special metaphorical appeal for America in the 1980s, as we face the closing of the unlimited economic growth "frontier." Rostow analyzed stages of economic growth and development in societies around the world. He saw some as having completed the sequence, while others were just starting as the 1960s passed into history.

I read both books in 1963. Two decades later, when Walter Rostow came to lecture at my university, I attended, with anticipation. But his "line" seemed alien and out of step with the new economics of development articulated by E. F. Schumacher (*Small is Beautiful: Economics As If People Really Mattered*), Kenneth Boulding (*Evolutionary Economics*), Herbert Daly (*Steady State Economics*), and Orio Giarini (*Dialogue on Wealth and Welfare: An Alternative View of the World Capital Formation*). Rostow sounded somewhat anachronistic, and oblivious to the ecological realities with which economic policy and practice must come to terms.

Some checking in the university library revealed intriguing historical coincidences. Rostow published *Stages of Economic Growth* in 1962. In 1972, while he was publishing a second edition with commentary from an evaluative conference, Meadows and colleagues were publishing their report to the Club of Rome, *The Limits to Growth*. After another decade, the tenth anniversary of *The Limits to Growth* was marked by a conference hosted by the Smithsonian Institution in Washington, D.C. In the wake of that 1982 meeting Rostow's lecture sounded like an unfortunate plea for "business as usual—only better." All of this prompted a rereading of *Stages of Economic Growth* as a counterpoint to "ecological economics."

In 1972, Rostow responded to questions that had been raised since publication of the first edition, but he left the core text intact. Like evolutionary economist Kenneth Boulding, who defines economic development as "the rate of increase of human know-how" and "the evolution of human artifacts," Rostow begins by defining economic growth as the "degree of efficient absorption of technologies" (p. xiii) rather than simply as an increase in Gross National Product. That certainly was an encouraging start, because in a sustainable society, alternatives to GNP as a yardstick for assessing change will be necessary. In that 1972 preface, Rostow made several other statements that are interesting for what they say about economics in general and his book in particular.

First, he asserts the book is "both a scientific effort and a tract for the times" (p. xiv). To what extent is his analysis limited to specific times and places? To what extent is it universal? Rostow believes it is the latter. He said in 1972 that the 1960s produced numerous examples of societies that have successfully combined rapid economic growth and social progress congruent with national cultures "in an environment of political independence." This is an affirmation of his belief in the universality, the scientific objectivity of his approach.

In the 1972 preface, Rostow described his purpose in writing the book: ". . . to raise a number of questions that men, societies, and governments would have to answer as they turned to explore new frontiers . . ." (p. xiv). Of course he was part of John F. Kennedy's brightest and best, so the new frontier metaphor was more political courtesy than it was an allusion to Frederick Jackson Turner. But Turner is the more relevant allusion. The end of cheap energy, like the end of cheap land that Turner described, was the closing of a frontier.

Rostow identifies five stages in economic growth: "The Traditional Society," "The Preconditions for Take-Off," "The Take-Off," "The Drive to Maturity," and "The Age of High Mass-Consumption." The traditional society is dominated by subsistence living for the masses based on low-power technology and labor-intensive agriculture. Small elite classes wring their luxuries out of the sweat of the masses. "But the central fact about the traditional society was that a ceiling existed on the level of attainable output per head" (p. 4). Traditional society has had the longest tenure, of course. But at moments in historical time things change, and there may appear the preconditions for take-off.

In Rostow's view the essence of these preconditions is a shift in ideology, values, and purpose.

> The idea spreads not merely that economic progress is possible, but that economic progress is a necessary condition for some other purpose judged to be good: be it national dignity, private profit, the general welfare, or a better life for the children. (p. 6)

For my purposes, it is significant that the demand for social welfare systems may motivate economic development in Rostow's scheme. The engines of this shift in economic ideology include new and exemplary enterprises, social policy initiatives by elites, the infusion of a new world view that redefines human goals, and technological breakthroughs. The point is that new economic possibilities come to the fore in the form of a glimpsed new economic order. (Recall that the *technical* expertise for the Industrial Revolution existed in the early centuries A.D., but was not harnessed for lack of an appropriate world view.)

In the take-off stage, the economic parts created and developed earlier become a whole greater than the sum of those parts, and an economic chain reaction starts.

> The take-off is the interval when the old blocks and resistances to steady growth are finally overcome. The forces making for economic progress, which yielded limited bursts and enclaves of modern activity, expand and come to dominate the society. Growth becomes its normal condition. (p. 7)

This is a period of rapid change, in which old patterns are disrupted, modified, and replaced by the institutions and facilities of the new order. As this process becomes the norm, the society enters the drive to maturity:

> After take-off there follows a long interval of sustained if fluctuating progress, as the now regularly growing economy drives to extend modern technology over the whole front of its economic activity. . . . This is the stage in which an economy demonstrates that it has the technological and entrepreneurial skills to produce not everything, but anything it chooses to produce. (pp. 9–10)

One can imagine a visual display. Computer graphics would show "modern economy" in vivid color spreading over the screen until the entire map was covered. The net result of the drive to maturity is to empower economic institutions to an unprecedented degree. What then? To what use do societies put their economic machines? Rostow calls their answer to this question the age of high mass consumption.

In the age of high mass consumption, the industrial infrastructure is so effective and efficient that what by any *historical* criterion would be called "luxury" becomes a mass phenomenon. The economic system shifts away from building the physical plant to managing the production of consumer goods and services.

> As societies achieved maturity in the Twentieth Century two things happened: real income per head rose to a point where large numbers of persons gained a command over consumption which transcended basic food, shelter, and clothing and the structure of the working force changed in ways which increased not only the proportion of urban to total population, but also the proportion of the population working in offices or in skilled factory jobs. (p. 10)

These are the five stages of economic growth as Rostow sees them. The rest of his book deals with two sorts of questions. The first are technical questions concerning the *historical* validity of his model. Did it really happen this way? Where and when did it happen first? Why? Most of the 1972 commentary dealt with these questions. The other questions concern the future. What will societies do after they reach and experience the age of high mass consumption? When will societies still in the first four stages achieve the fifth? Our interests lie in that second set of questions—and in the apparent *lack* of interest shown in them by conventional economic thinking.

What did Rostow see for the future? With the benefit of 1980s hindsight on a 1960s vision based in large measure on 1950s data, we see that his view is a humanly rich image, but fatally flawed. He recognized that economic growth is not automatic, but acknowledged only social and political limits to growth, not physical and ecological limits. As history this is understandable, for until recently the principal issues were social and political, and discounted ecology.

Rostow has something to say about the fate of both the current haves and have-nots of the world. For the have-not nations he sees economic fulfillment (i.e., reaching the stage of high mass consumption)—if they can use technology to increase agricultural productivity; if they have adequate external capital assistance; and if their elites can manage rapid population growth, which comes when modern medicine lowers death rates before affluence stimulates effective contraception. This last condition is crucial. Of these elites he says:

> It is they who must overcome the difficulties posed by the rapid
> diffusion of modern medicine, and ensure that the humane decision to
> save lives does not lead to an inhumane society. (p. 144)

This was seen in the 1960s, when world population was three billion. What
of the 1980s, as population reached five billion?

All in all, Rostow seems optimistic about the outcome. He discusses a
variety of issues connected with agricultural productivity, capital availability, and population control, and foresees successful movement to a state of
worldwide high mass consumption.

> Billions of human beings must live in a world, if we preserve it, over the
> century or so until the age of high mass-consumption becomes universal.
> (pp. 166–167)

And again:

> The end of all of this is not compound interest forever, it is the adventure
> of seeing what man can do when the pressure of scarcity is lifted from
> him. (p. 166)

The End of Scarcity

But is scarcity on its way out? Or will it stage a comeback in the world's
successful economies and continue to hold sway in the rest of the world?
Rostow foresaw the modern problem as one of dealing with life beyond
scarcity, and asked

> what to do when the increase in real income itself loses its charm?
> Babies, boredom, three day weekends, the moon, or the creation of new
> inner, human frontiers in substitution for the imperatives of scarcity?
> (p. 16)

As we move through the 1980s, public rhetoric has taken a very
different turn. Affluence is still the main difference between the American
way of life and life in the "undeveloped" world, of course. Schumacher's
characterization of the world as 25 percent immensely rich and 75 percent
immensely poor holds true. But a new theme has entered public discourse
in the United States, "the new scarcity," and it figures ever more prominently
in dialogs on political economy where one sees conventional thinking at its
best.

In 1982, former Colorado Governor Richard Lamm presented his views
in a piece entitled "The Economic Pie Isn't Growing, But More Americans

Need Slices." He cited declining real income and increasingly fierce competition for public funds:

> Very quietly the United States has seen its economy falter and then slide backward. Median family income in 1970 was $20,939 and by 1980 has risen only $84, to $21,023.00. Family income was actually less in 1980 than it was in 1973. All wage increases and benefits since 1975 have been wiped out by inflation, and in 1980 the average American saw a 5.5 percent loss in real income. The economic pie, sad but true, is not growing.

The supposed prosperity of "the Reagan years" that have followed have hardly brought an end to scarcity, with one in four American children living in poverty.

The voices raised to deplore the new scarcity are numerous and diverse. One that has sounded loudly and influentially in political circles is that of business policy analyst Robert Reich. In his 1983 book *The Next American Frontier,* he chronicles the decline in American productivity. He sees as the villain increasingly anachronistic management approaches to industrial production, but his solution is the same that others offer: "Get America moving again through more production!" His formula is slightly different; he sees the rise of industrialism in the Third World and financial manipulation instead of productive activity as the roots of the problem. He asks us to recognize that modern nations such as the United States cannot compete with developing nations in enterprises requiring mass production and unsophisticated workers. Modern societies must shift their attention toward expertise-intensive enterprises, he argues. What is more, the United States must discourage "paper entrepreneurialism"—the skillful manipulation of rules and numbers in which nothing real is produced, yet which can generate a profit for the manipulator. Otherwise, Reich argues, wealth will be increasingly scarce in the United States and other modern societies.

Lamm wants more growth to solve this problem. Reich wants a shift to more productive enterprises suited to a modernized economy to solve it. But what exactly *is* the problem that needs solving? Put simply, it is that productivity is declining and real income is no longer increasing—that families are not experiencing a net increase in their ability to purchase goods and services in the marketplace. This is scarcity?

Lamm acknowledges that "yesterday's luxuries have become today's necessities," but his political orientation and acceptance of conventional economic perspective prevent him from seeing a path out of the current economic crisis into a sustainable society. The best that Reich and others can do is devise a more efficient unsustainable society. The conventional economic perspective can do nothing but urge "more growth," either indiscriminately or in a more responsible way that seeks income redistribution to reduce poverty and perhaps tries to reduce damage to the social and physical environment. But no matter how innovative efforts are to "reindustrialize America," they will falter if they are unsound. And they are.

One searches for adequate metaphors. What is the problem faced by a person who cries out in hunger because there are no potato chips, Twinkies, or candy in the cupboard, only bread, fruit, and cheese? Such a person feels hungry, of course. But at what cost should that hunger be met? A heroin addict feels an undeniable craving, but do societies legitimize the economics of drug trafficking and its spin-off crimes? Some do, of course. Perhaps there is our metaphor for modern economics, founded as they are upon the corrupting dynamics of an addiction.

Economics, the Beautiful Science?

The beauty of conventional economics is its ability to define all human activity in monetary terms. But it's a sinister beauty indeed. We enjoy the fruits of conventional economies in a modern society. We attend films. We eat fruit grown half a continent away. We travel. We have credit. Can we eat all this cake without depriving others of their bread? Are we confident that our children's children will enjoy life and not fall into the "worthless state of existence" now experienced by many hundreds of millions of the world's already impoverished?

It seems not, if conventional economics continues to reign supreme. So long as the dominant economic perspective does not discriminate between cash-money (monetarized) costs and real costs, no path will lead away from a radical worldwide deterioration. Examples abound of how pervasive and deeply embedded the conventional economic perspective is in our thinking about social reality.

Let us begin with Rostow himself. He simply projects into the future the process of economic modernization that facilitated modernization in some nations in the eighteenth, nineteenth, and twentieth centuries. The task as he sees it is to hold things together politically, "over the century or so until the age of high mass-consumption becomes universal" (pp. 166–167). And just how is that to happen?

Rostow is in the mainstream when he urges stimulation of Western-style economic "development" for all the world's people. The 1980s may come to be known as the decade when economic development in conventional terms became a bad word, however. The historically unusual and unusually fortuitous circumstances of the post–World War II era are now coming to an end. The "economic miracles" of the postwar era are turning belly up. In Brazil, for example, the years of "miraculous" growth rates in monetarized GNP have come to an end. Default on the 100+-billion-dollar foreign debt that financed the miracle is a practical fact of life, even while legal fictions deny it. The Mexican oil bubble has burst. Nigeria has proclaimed a grudging austerity. The dynamic economies of the Pacific basin are living on borrowed time. And what has been the net effect of economic development in these and other societies?

The evidence in the case of Brazil is abundant and compelling. The economic miracle meant the dramatic expansion of the modernized economic sector from a minuscule to a significant segment, embracing perhaps 20 percent of the total population. But it was accomplished by a net *decrease* in real income and social welfare for the bulk of the rural population. The 80 percent living outside the modern sector became poorer than they were before the miracle. In many areas the infant mortality rate actually increased, and stands nationwide at nearly 100 per 1,000! In contrast to a nation like Sweden, where deaths of children under five account for about 1 percent of all deaths, in Brazil they account for nearly 50 percent of all deaths—a figure more medieval than modern. Sylvia Hewlett's book *The Cruel Dilemmas of Development* explores this, and lays responsibility for it with models of economic development used in Brazil. The social chaos there exemplifies the ever more apparent flaws in conventional economic thinking about development.

Of course it is risky and somewhat unfair to lump together all economists and economies under the label "conventional economic thinking." But it is necessary for the purpose of posing "ecological transformational economics" as an alternative. There *is* diversity within the economic community, of course. Many who criticize "conventional economics" are themselves economists. The names Nicholas Georgescu-Roegen, Bruce Hamin, Herbert Daly, Orio Giarini, Kenneth Boulding, and E. F. Schumacher come quickly to mind. For evidence of the diversity in economic circles, one can consult *The Crisis in Economic Theory*, edited by Daniel Bell and Irving Kristol—or for harsh criticism *of* economists *by* an economist, Lester Thurow's *Dangerous Currents*.

Some say the science of economics is neutral. Our problems are not the fault of economics or economists, it is argued. The culprit is the politically-

and profit-motivated use to which self-interested individuals and groups put economics. Perhaps. But perhaps not.

As the modern equivalent of sixteenth-century clergy, economists are no more nor less to blame for economic conditions, for the economic war that rages between the forces of wealth and the forces of basic need, than were theologians for the religious wars in sixteenth-century Europe that led to the suffering and deaths of thousands. We can only understand the meaning of an economic model in context. There is no economy that is not political. Economics has nothing like the doctrine of separation of church and state that served to dampen religious wars. Unlike religion, which can be partially hidden away from public life, economics is intrinsically and inevitably in the public domain. Despite the "God Is Dead" movement, there is no real spiritual analog to *The Limits to Growth*.

The essence of the problem is how conventional economics approaches reality through the costs, price, and value. Major problems in these three areas are becoming apparent as monetarized accounting gets further and further out of line with actual transactions among people, in families, and between people and the physical environment.

Of course, economists are not totally blind to this problem. They have developed the concept of "externality" to identify costs that stand outside production, marketing, and sales. Externality is a central issue in Hardin's concept of the tragedy of the commons, where each person seeks to push as much of the cost of doing business onto the general public as conditions will permit. Externality becomes primarily a political issue then, for it exists to the degree that communities tolerate it. Sound economics acknowledges its political roots and limits as it does its environmental ties. In a sustainable society economic analysis insists upon a method of accounting for costs that includes an appreciation for future generations.

Future generations cannot "bid" for resources directly. Families must manifest their concern for the future. Another facet of externality is that the planet's other beings are also unable to bid in the economic process. In Dr. Seuss's book *The Lorax,* the Lorax appears before a profit-seeking, polluting businessman to declare: "I am the Lorax, I speak for the trees!" But the Lorax is economically invisible. He can influence the economic life of the community only through the political process. Who speaks for the Lorax?

An economist friend writes: "We must force firms into accounting for *all* their actions by altering the legal, political, and social environment that firms operate in so that they must price resources at their true value." Amen. But this hardly exonerates economics, because it will proceed with its analyses regardless of whether costs are internalized. Giarini argues that this approach was perhaps acceptable in the past, when human impact on the life of the planet was relatively small; but it has become ever more misleading as human impact has grown. Conventional economics seems ready to talk price even when price is an ecological fiction.

Is Economics an Endangered Species?

With ecology on one side and politics on the other, conventional economics has an ever more precarious hold on reality, because it operates as if the other two weren't there. Political economics? Yes. Ecological economics? Yes. But economics on its own? No. Enter the efforts of systems dynamics analysts such as Jay Forrester. His approach does incorporate the interplay of economics, ecology, and politics (not to mention demography). By constructing complex models that characterize the *real* world, systems dynamics is often at loggerheads with economics, which minimizes such complexity through grand assumptions. But "assuming X" and acting "as if Y" doesn't serve us well anymore. The results are misleading at best. Witness the case of GNP.

Gross National Product is the sum total of monetarized *transactions* for goods and services. Some note that a more sensible approach would focus on the *stock* of goods, not the flow. But when the scale of human economic activity was relatively small, GNP made pretty good sense. It was essentially correct to assume that increases in monetarized goods and services occurred without offsetting decreases in nonmonetarized goods and services. Certainly, there were many individual decreases in the nonmonetarized sector. One cannot read Charles Dickens' nineteenth-century accounts of economic modernization without seeing some of the costs—as the green commons was enclosed and rent charged, as taxes increased beyond the bartering of produce and labor, as communities were torn asunder by industrialization, and as symbiosis with the land was displaced by calculations concerning alternative uses. But all in all, things in the nonmonetarized side of the equation absorbed the costs of increasing the monetarized side. For modernized societies such as the United States, the turning point has come with the transformation of household economies, as the nonmonetarized family economy has been monetarized—with a vengeance.

It appears that family economies previously were approximately balanced between the monetarized and the nonmonetarized, because households were labor intensive rather than capital intensive. Food preparation, childbearing and child rearing, health care, recreation, cleaning, and repair were very labor intensive. The big change has been to substitute capital-intensive technologies in all these domains of family life. Rostow defines the drive to maturity for the socioeconomic system as a whole as "the period when society has effectively applied the range of [its] modern technology to the bulk of its resources." This includes its children. The *cash* cost of bearing and rearing children has skyrocketed. Most childbirth occurs in hospitals, and the event has become a financial spectacle. Outfitting and training a child through adolescence requires big bucks. From 1975 to 1980, for example, spending by teenagers increased 50 percent, at a time when the number of teenagers was decreasing by nearly 7 percent.

Thus far, this line of reasoning only brings us to the threshold of the new home economics. At this point the microeconomists of family life and household management arrive upon the scene. They begin to examine the economic productivity of family members. They speak of the "opportunity costs" of child rearing: what income does a person forego by spending time and laboring in the home as a homemaker and child rearer? A 1980 estimate figured the cost at about $40,000 for a woman with clerical or blue-collar skills and about $80,000 for a woman with a graduate education. The "direct costs" of raising children stood at about $100,000 for 18 years for a middle-class family, according to recent Department of Agriculture and Labor calculations. This focus on opportunity costs does result in greater appreciation for the productivity of women, particularly those maintaining households. But that's the *only* good thing about it; in the long run it's dangerous because it reinforces the idea that everything and everyone is for sale. That's bad news for today's children, and for their children's children.

Some Jobs Are More Equal Than Others

Monetarized exchanges form the basis for these calculations, of course. The key variable is the entrance of mothers into the labor force outside the home. This mass entrance is the dominant issue in family economics today. However, if we consider merely costs, price, and value, we cannot see the economic implications for families of the transition to a sustainable society. Data on the monetary income of mothers—25 percent of family income on average in the United States—do not tell the whole story.

The introduction of capital- and energy-intensive technology into the family economy has real costs that transcend monetary transactions. From a strictly monetary point of view, a net gain occurs when a family member substitutes purchased energy-intensive goods for a formerly labor-intensive activity—if cost is less than cash income earned during that time. Imagine that a family pays eight dollars per meal for highly processed "convenience" foods because members are employed outside the home and have no time to cook a five-dollar meal from scratch. Conventional economic accounting asks only, "How much did the family earn for that time?" If the answer is "ten dollars," then the family has a net gain. These kinds of substitutions and this kind of cost-benefit accounting run the gamut of household activities and extend beyond to the neighborhood, for example walking versus driving to shop.

The point is that such calculations are flawed. Every substitution of energy- and material-intensive goods for human labor has costs that extend far beyond the dollar price in the monetary economy. If such goods rely on nonrenewable energy and materials and are used by masses of people, the costs involved are historically significant. Each such substitution is a moral issue. Conventional economics is blind to all this, or at least approaches it with only one eye open. It has an invalid conception of cost, an artificial idea of price, and an incomplete concept of value.

This is not to say that economics and economists have no way of dealing with these problems. To the contrary, most economists seem to believe that anything and everything is possible, if we will only arrange the flow of dollars correctly. Want to cut down on the use of oil? Charge more for it. Want to increase the amount of oil available? Pay more for it. Want to reduce employment of women outside the home? Pay them less. Want to increase the number of women running households full time? Pay them to do it. No one would disagree that adjustments in the flow of dollars can have a significant, even dramatic influence on human behavior. Everyone and everything has a price, right?

Right—within limits. What are those limits? That is precisely the issue before us. What are the limits to conventional economic analysis? The physical and social environments impose limits upon economics, and we are bumping up against them with ever-increasing frequency and significance as we move through the latter part of the twentieth century. We ignore those limits at peril of our social selves.

Family Economics and the Meaning of Productivity

Family economics is at the cutting edge of efforts to illuminate the dynamics of the transition to a sustainable society. Other institutions determine much of what goes on in families, of course, but it is within families that the ecological drama of consumption and waste is played out. That's why discussions of rising and falling family income are difficult to interpret. Do more dollars mean less waste and consumption, or more? Conventional economics doesn't recognize the difference between the "more" and the "less" of this question, and that's its problem. The task is yet more complicated because one of the main variables in the equation has many cultural connotations. That variable is, of course, the role of mothers in the monetarized labor force outside the home—"working mothers," to use a term that is a model of redundancy. No answer will succeed if it simply asks mothers to absorb the burdens alone. Where is the justice in allowing fathers to work outside the home at energy- and capital-intensive activities, while expecting women to perform labor-intensive work in the home? A just solution is to base all aspects of work and play on renewable energy and material, to enhance dignified human labor.

We need an economics that will rationalize and account for such a transformation to sustainable society, an economics that will put social welfare systems in harmony with planetary systems. Conventional economics just isn't it. Rostow's vision of the future as "the end of scarcity" is brought to fruition with the more recent analyses of Cornucopians Julius Simon and Herbert Kahn, who seem to believe that everything really does have a price, and that we can overcome *all* physical and social limits if we pay someone enough. These approaches rely on flawed fundamental assumptions about economic life, technology, and the Earth's ecology.

One such assumption concerns productivity. Conventional approaches assume that economic development arises from shifting financial resources toward those who will spend or lend it more "productively" and away from those who will put it to less "productive" uses. As Rostow points out, this is "one of the oldest and most fundamental notions in economics" ((pp. 45–47).

What Is Productivity?

And what are the criteria for judging productivity? Here's the rub, of course. Conventional economics was built and continues to rest upon a foundation of assumptions about prices, costs, and values that is a tragic flaw in the classic sense. As Aristotle tells us in his *Poetics*, a tragic flaw is a characteristic that simultaneously makes for nobility, success, and worth and creates the conditions for inevitable defeat. Oedipus was a tragic figure;

the very ambition and courage that permitted his success led ultimately to his downfall.

Conventional economics has just such a tragic flaw. Many a wag refers to economics as "the dismal science." There is growing recognition that it might be better labeled "the immaterial science," because it operates as if its conceptual and symbolic transactions were grounded firmly in the world, when in fact they may not be. Revisionist economists Nicholas Georgescu-Roegen and Kenneth Boulding, among others, have identified and explored this tragic flaw.

Conventional economics sees the economic process as a closed system, independent of the material systems of the Earth. It admits no limits to what adjustments in the flow of dollars can achieve, as if everything really does have a price. (This leaves aside its often unrealistic social and psychological assumptions). As Georgescu-Roegen put it, "the patent fact that between the economic process and the material environment there exists a continuous mutual influence which is history-making carries no weight with the standard economist" (p. 50). Human economic activity can change the physical and social probabilities of future possibilities. Thus, we cannot presume that what were valid economic assumptions, models, and theories in the past will be valid in the future.

In fact, *human activity cannot produce anything material at all.* All we do, all we can do, is transform and eventually degrade materials. Our economically "productive" activity transforms one state of matter into another by capturing and focusing energy. Of course, some transformed matter is beautiful and clever. Some is ugly and stupid. But all of our "products" are really just tranformations. This transformed matter is, *for a period of time,* useful to us in economic terms. Then it becomes waste. This is the key to understanding conventional economics as an immaterial science: the thing we always "produce" is waste. At issue is only the length of time between initial transformation and eventual degradation into waste, and the duration and magnitude of the environmental impact of this process.

Conventional economics does not recognize the material base of "production" as temporary. It ignores entropy and proceeds as if metal and wood, oil and solar energy, polyester and cotton, and machines and people may be manipulated equally through adjustments in the flow of dollars. One with even the most passing acquaintance with Earth's ecology can see the absurdity of this. Some costs do not translate into dollars.

"Everything has a price" is the standard economic paradigm, which evolved during the seventeenth century when the scale of human civilization in relation to nonrenewable resources made it a rough approximation of reality. It is dangerously unrealistic today.

Standard economics assumes that the production/consumption process is real apart from its material aspects. It assumes that all is in order because the books balance. I am reminded of a joke heard some years ago. A group of professors is marooned on a desert island. A case of canned food washes ashore, but they have no tools for opening the cans. What to do? Each offers a suggestion based on his academic background. The physicist suggests a complex series of pulleys to create sufficient force per square inch to open the ends of the cans. The biologist suggests growing an algae that will eat through the metal. The lawyer suggests they sue the maker of the cans. Finally, the economist announces he has the solution. The group is all ears as he speaks: "First, assume we have a can opener . . ."

Unfair? Not when we look at the assumptions conventional economics makes about the world. We are on a global spaceship, left to our own devices to feed, clothe, and shelter ourselves and to build satisfying and meaningful relationships, *permanently*. Each year there are more and more of us, many with the barest minimum of food, clothing, and shelter. At a gathering to discuss this quandary, a conventional economist from one of the luxury suites might announce he has a solution. "First," he says, "assume we are *not* on a spaceship left to our own devices to feed, clothe, and shelter ourselves. Assume instead that we have an infinite source of canned food. . . . Then offer to pay top dollar for a can opener . . ."

The news from television, newspapers, and magazines suggests that conventional economics is more like astrology or alchemy than it is like other sciences—very accurate and complex, but basically invalid. The stock market goes up and down, and "analysts" explain why in daily readings. The "Crash of 1987" brought this home to even the most trusting, and the "Fall of 1988" made the point to the rest. The stock market itself bears only the most passing connection to the material realities of life. The only "scientific" thing about it is that those with inside information can do better than chance, while those without it are gambling (or worse). That's why regulatory efforts are so difficult. In the 1984 annual report of Twentieth Century Fund, executive director M. J. Rossant put it this way: "Economists and economic policy makers have distinguished themselves only by the inaccuracy of their forecasts and by the wrongheadedness of their advice." Many observers enjoyed a hearty chuckle at the report some years back that the small stock portfolio of the American Economics Association did *worse* than it would have if investment decisions had been made by rolling dice.

Are Lee Iacocca and William Shakespeare Identical Twins?

In 1982, George Stigler won the Nobel Prize for economics. He opposes governmental regulation and the ethos of those who seek to control the economy for political purposes. He dismisses those who argue that semiannual automobile model changes are wasteful, because he believes the market is the best arbiter of economic choices. Stigler suggests, tongue in cheek perhaps, that if we reject automobile style changes, why not books and newspapers? Why not continue with Shakespeare instead of reading Tennessee Williams? Why have today's news when the newspapers of 1900 were plenty good enough? A man of such intellect and wit must see the human difference between cars and plays—as a person, at least, if not as an economist. Conventional economics really doesn't see the difference, of course. It *really doesn't,* and it often seems proud of that fact.

Stigler objects to the common casting of economics as the dismal science: "I resent the phrase, for only young children should get angry at a corpus of knowledge that prevents hopeless but costly endeavors." Endeavors such as what? Semiannual automobile model changes that serve only fashion and accelerate the transformation of low-entropy materials into high-entropy waste? Would that conventional economics *were* such a dismal science when it comes to preventing ecologically "hopeless but costly endeavors," rather than being a pollyannaish "science" of basically false assumptions about the material world.

Contrast Stigler with Nicholas Georgescu-Roegen on automobiles:

> Every time we produce a Cadillac, we irrevocably destroy an amount of low entropy that could otherwise be used for producing a plow or a spade. In other words, every time we produce a Cadillac, we do it at the cost of decreasing the number of human lives in the future.

And again, on fashion:

> We must also get rid of fashion. . . . It is indeed a disease of the mind to throw away a coat or a piece of furniture while it can still perform its specific service. To get a "new" car every year and to refashion the house every other is a bioeconomic crime. (p. 74)

Conventional economics dismisses such thinking as romantic, utopian, visionary, fuzzy, or worse. Conventional economics offers the much more ethereal concept of the "guiding hands" of the marketplace—"everything has a price," and "if we offer to pay for it, it will be provided." It's a socially suicidal vision at worst and wishful thinking at best.

Is "Economic Man" a Family Man?

Conventional economics lives in an ecological fantasy world. The irony is that most conventional economists see themselves—and are seen by most outsiders—as hard-nosed realists. There has long been criticism of the concept of "Economic Man" as a valid representation of the human being. In conventional economics, Economic Man is an "information processor" who makes rational decisions concerning investment of labor and capital. This Economic Man is, of course, very masculine as opposed to being generically human, as we shall see in Chapter 7. To his credit, Rostow goes beyond a simplistic concept of Economic Man and echoes the early ideas of Karl Marx. This passage is from *Stages of Economic Growth:*

> In the stages-of-growth sequence man is viewed as a more complex unit. He seeks, not merely economic advantage, but also power, leisure, adventure, continuity of experience and security; he is concerned with his family, the familiar values of his regional and national culture, and a bit of fun down at the local tavern. And beyond these diverse homey attachments man is capable of being moved by a sense of connection with human beings everywhere, who, he recognizes, share his essentially paradoxical condition. In short, net human behavior is seen not as an act of maximization, but as an act of balancing alternative and often conflicting human objectives in the face of the range of choices men perceive to be open to them. (p. 149)

Reading this again after twenty years, I remember Rostow's appeal. His Economic Man may be male, but at least it's human! He may not go far enough, but he does show an appreciation for human quality that most conventional economics lack. Behavioral psychologist B. F. Skinner's "Psychological Man" as presented in *Verbal Behavior* and *Beyond Freedom and Dignity* is much the same one-dimensional information processing entity as classical Economic Man. Both are correct in detail but tragically incomplete in the whole. Neither is really a family man. A mature view of human behavior recognizes multiple sources of motivation, some unconscious, some rooted in biology, and some culturally conditioned. Any simple economic model is psychologically naive.

Rostow transcends the psychological impoverishment of conventional economics, and he does consider the family as a central factor in the future of socioeconomic life. In societies just beginning to move through the stages of growth, he believes dealing with the quantitative aspects of family life is important.

Among societies already in or just reaching the age of high mass consumption, he also recognizes family as critical. He sees scarcity as permanently removed in societies that have reached that stage, and the population turning to other matters. Attention shifts from supply to demand and "welfare in the widest sense" (p. 73). Indeed, much of the public agenda is dominated by discussions of social welfare systems. Automobiles, the technology of entertainment, and household gadgets, as well as employee benefit packages, medical specialization, and social security—these are the issues in the age of high mass consumption. And family.

> Americans have behaved as if, having been born into a system that provided economic security and high mass-consumption, they placed a lower valuation on acquiring additional increments of real income in the conventional form as opposed to the advantages and values of an enlarged family. (p. 31)

Birth rates and family orientation were indeed high in the economically buoyant 1950s, the source of data upon which Rostow based his conclusion. Today, we can agree that concern with and valuation of family remain high, although family size has shrunk. Rostow's view is not great family history; the 1950s were an aberration in a century-long trend, as Andrew Cherlin's analysis makes clear. The divorce rate has been rising and family size decreasing since 1900. But it's not only as *family* history that Rostow's analysis falters. It falters as economic history as well.

The debate over limits to growth is historical in its essence. The historical questions are these: Is conventional economic thinking limited in its historical validity? Will the near future, until the year 2010, be a simple extension of the recent past from 1950 until 1970? Is the current period (1970-1990) typical of the long-term trend (1900-2010)? To answer these questions we must turn to Orio Giarini's *Dialogue on Wealth and Welfare* (1981). In it he examines the essential features of monetarized and nonmonetarized sections of the human economy, and their relationship.

The Need for an Economic History That Is Historical

Rostow's analysis may be called economic history, but it is strangely nonhistorical in its approach to relating the human population to the material Earth. He seems to assume the relationship is constant and will not change. Giarini, on the other hand, begins and ends with this relationship.

First, Giarini argues, the modern economic system required a technological and cultural base that would permit the Industrial Revolution. He cites a report in the *New Scientist* (noted earlier) that the *technical* knowledge necessary for the Industrial Revolution was available during the fourth century under the Roman Empire—but the cultural underpinnings were not yet in place. In this respect he supports Rostow's thesis about the preconditions for take-off.

Second, Giarini argues, modern conventional economics is very much historically bound to conditions in the seventeenth and eighteenth centuries. Key assumptions then were that money could accurately reflect value, that monetary cost was a good measure of real cost (as in the cost of the "free" materials of the Earth), that market forces are sufficient to regulate economic activity, and that "production" is intrinsically good. The standard economic model then was a rough approximation of reality—much as a child's early concepts of the world are functional so long as he or she is limited to a supervised playpen. By offering this developmental perspective Giarini is doing for ecological economics what Piaget and Vygotsky did for child psychology.

Giarini argues that the match between the standard economic model and reality has become less and less perfect ever since. In the present period between 1970 and 1990, the model's flaws are becoming obvious, as human activity increases to the point at which assumptions of "free" and "unlimited" materials, production, and waste disposal are shown to be false. Standard economic thinking has become anachronistic. Such thinking is not only imprecise, but wrong, because it produces "scientific" conclusions that run counter to humanity's best interest. This begins to explain why the world seems so economically puzzling and mysterious so much of the time, particularly for those who rightly seek to put social welfare systems at the center of their analyses. This is evident in food production, the quality of the physical environment, and the social consequences of capital investment strategies. Why is there hunger? Why are the air and water filled with toxins and carcinogens? Why is life such a rat race for so many of us?

Giarini argues for a new economic model that will *accurately* describe and analyze the new conditions we face. In it, economics and ecology return to their natural relationship, the former a subsidiary of the latter. At the heart of the model is a better estimation of total value, one that includes both monetarized and nonmonetarized economic costs and benefits. In such a model, the meaning and relationships of labor and capital must be rethought and recalculated, with everything that implies for industrialization and urbanization.

We began with Walter Rostow's analysis of the stages of economic growth. His very strength as an economic historian proves to be his greatest weakness as an analyst of the human condition. Ironically, his work founders because he doesn't recognize the historical discontinutiy between the ecological/economic relationships of the past and those of the future. History is propelling us toward the ever greater need for an ecological, transformational economics, one that recognizes that human activity produces nothing material. It only transforms energy and existing material into new forms, which exist for a shorter or longer period and then become waste—which itself may be transformed further if will and technology permit. Conventional economics is flawed in its assumption that adjustments of cash flows ("price") have unlimited power to incorporate these transformations. These limits once were of only marginal physical significance, although their social, psychological, and spiritual significance has long been recognized. Now, with human activity increased to the point that it is physically significant to the Earth's ecosystems, limits of conventional economics are becoming ever more apparent. What were once hypothetical limits have become actual. This is manifest in the world's cities and factories, as we shall see next, where efforts to integrate social welfare and conventional economic models founder.

CHAPTER

6.

January 1984:

Taishan,

People's Republic of China

Industrialization
and
Urbanization

Viewed from the air, china's cities resemble green doughnuts. The urban centers are surrounded by greenbelts producing food—particularly vegetables and rice. A natural and mutual interdependence is at work here. Food is transported a relatively short distance to reach the concentrated urban population. The city provides cash income, organic wastes for fertilizer, services of many kinds, and a market for labor not needed in or suited to the countryside. There is little of the long-distance food transportation we depend upon in the United States, where the average molecule of food travels more than 1,200 miles before being eaten.

Other modernizing societies have failed the test of stabilizing the countryside, providing a living standard for the rural population that compares well with that in the city, and preventing an unmanageable flow of people from the country into the cities. Unlike Brazil, which reversed its rural/urban mix during the 1970s (from 35 to 65 percent urban in 10 years), China remains 80 percent rural. But the agrarian and spartan collective policies of the past appear to be changing. Recent years have seen a new national commitment to modernization, which translates as mass industrialization and consumer goods. Accompanying this change has been a "new responsibility system" that favors individual initiative in economic matters and includes new pressures and rewards for agricultural and manufacturing production at almost any cost. This new wave is changing the face of China. Driving into Guangzhou (Canton), a returning visitor observes in horror that land only two years before devoted to vegetable growing is now a field of high-rise apartment buildings. The green doughnut is being split by new corridors of urbanization. China is experiencing a massive physical, social, and economic redefinition.

All this is on my mind as I walk the streets of Taishan, a smallish city in southern China. New construction is rampant—some of it nibbling away at the food-producing greenbelt. Small shops, factories, and television antennas are sprouting everywhere. Motorbikes have begun to swim in the stream of bicycles. Neon signs reminiscent of Hong Kong are appearing. In the bustling market, the traditional items—vegetables, livestock, household crafts—are being joined or even displaced by brightly colored polyester clothes, plastic containers, cassette tape decks, and other accoutrements of modern life. One booth is even selling plastic shopping bags printed with all-too-familiar messages: "Souvenir of Niagara Falls." "London Bridge." "Welcome to Disney"!

I'm hearing a new song: "How ya gonna keep them down on the farm, after they've seen Disney?" (doo wah doo wah)

If Henry Ford was the perfect symbol for industrialization in the first half of the twentieth century, then Walt Disney, Inc., serves that function for the second half. Ford focused on basic mass industrial production and consumption. Disney, Inc. focuses on plastic sensations, on high-tech environmental manipulation, and on information. Many analysts of the American economy recommend just this for our future; two good examples are Robert Reich (*The Next American Frontier*) and Alvin Toffler (*The Third Wave*).

In 1982, Disney, Inc., opened EPCOT Center—a partner for the Disneyworld complex itself near Orlando, Florida. EPCOT is a vision of the postindustrial order, the "information society" that Disney has been working on for decades. In a way it succeeds. Disneyworld–EPCOT Center is the modern industrial order drawn out to its logical but absurd conclusion. It is environmentally imperious and energy intensive. It lives off the basic enterprises of others. It provides social and physical arrangements that are comfortable but deceiving. And it manifests a vision of the future as bigger, better, and more—with little or no appreciation of human needs and global resources. Henry Ford, move over. Walt Disney, Inc., is coming through.

The nineteenth-century English poet Coleridge told us that appreciation of art requires a "willing suspension of disbelief." A visit to Disneyworld–EPCOT Center, though enjoyable, requires a willing suspension of *belief*—belief in the world problematique. If those concerned about the fate of the Earth become increasingly curmudgeonly as they rant and rave about shopping centers, amusement parks, and so on, it is because they find it ever harder to suspend their belief that crisis looms, socially and physically, on our planet. We *all* ought to worry about our grandchildren, born and unborn, and their prospects for a materially and socially sustainable existence. When I look beyond my family to the larger human family, I worry about the children I met in China, the Sudan, and Brazil who are already refugees of economic war. What will industrialization and urbanization mean for Chun Chien Wu Hamad, and Edney Marciell Cardoso, as well as my own Joshua and Joanna?

Putting "more and more energy and machinery at the disposal of each worker and consumer" (to use Harlan Cleveland's and Tom Wilson's phrase)—this is the essence of industrialization and urbanization stripped of ideological content. The Europeans evolved this strategy over three centuries of trial and error, increasingly in partnership with North America, Japan, and the Soviet Union. The "western model of development" that emerged emphasizes the melding of social and physical technology in large, complex industrial systems (of which international conglomerate corporations are the most mature incarnation, and monster cities and mechanized farms the most visible symbols). This was not accomplished without a great deal of disruption, suffering, and injustice for families. The result was a general increase in energy and machinery available to the average worker and consumer, and unprecedented luxury for the elites. Even the "losers" in modern industrialized societies have access to more energy and machinery than their peers in other places and times, no matter that they are too demoralized to make good use of it. We must question the future value and viability of this urban industrial order, both in newly modernizing societies and in the societies that gave birth to it. We must wonder about its effects on our children and their children to follow.

In this chapter we apply the abstract economics of the last chapter to the concrete environment—the physical expression of modernization in factories, farms, and cities. This is necessary so we may move beyond the limitations of economics as the immaterial science of "production" to more socially sensible principles of an economics of transformation. Industrialization and urbanization show us how and where transformation occurs. Technological sophistication has risen with urbanization. Indeed, in his book *Ecological Economics*, Kenneth Boulding goes so far as to *define* civilization as "cities drawing their food from the surrounding countryside" (p. 127)— a process still evident in China and elsewhere, where mass transportation of processed food has not yet obscured the fundamental dynamics of land use. With some exceptions, cities provided the critical mass for cultural evolution to move into high gear and produce scientific and artistic progress.

City, Factory and Farm

The grand outline of the intertwined history of industrialization and urbanization is well known. Industrialization creates and employs physical and social technologies that permit significant increases in output per worker. This means ever more transformation of materials and energy into products for human consumption. All aspects of human activity have come under the dominance of this basic shift.

Even agriculture becomes industrial. By using technologies that cost money, it serves to maximize output per worker. Costs rise, but it "frees" people from the land. They are then available for other industrial purposes, like working in city factories where transformation of materials and energy occurs most intensively. However, if there is to be even the semblance of justice in industrialization and urbanization, it must arise out of high-yield agriculture. Without high yields there is no food surplus for feeding city dwellers. Without a surplus, either urbanization halts or cities impoverish the countryside by extorting food from subsistence farmers. This dynamic operates today. In Brazil, efforts to supply the cities with both food and grain alcohol-based fuel threaten subsistence farmers in the rural areas. People in the countryside are "freed" from the land, but most have no economically tenable place in the cities. The overriding trend is to alter agriculture in pursuit of urbanization, but to do so without any morally sensible alternative for families displaced in the process. They are left to reenact the suffering chronicled by Charles Dickens as he watched the industrialization of England in the nineteenth century. Displaced Europeans in the eighteenth and nineteenth centuries could emigrate to the new world. But today's displaced families have nowhere to go, and no real prospect for successful transition to the kind of mass industrial society that was once feasible but has become improbable. Sylvia Hewlett calls this one of the "cruel dilemmas" of development, and she is right on the mark.

As agriculture becomes more industrialized, cities grow rapidly. More city dwellers means a higher output of food required, and further industrialization of agriculture means that more farm workers are released to join the urban ranks. Under optimal circumstances (mainly in the past) this was a self-reinforcing cycle of greater output and greater demand working hand in hand, with physical waste being dumped in the countryside (rivers, fields, the atmosphere) and the social waste of uprooted and demoralized children and adults being fed into the cities (to live in slums). Physical and social environments were stressed, but relatively small populations and relatively low power technologies allowed the luxury of a sloppy and inefficient transition. Coal, tannic acid, and cotton are, after all, environmentally minor league when contrasted with plutonium, PCB, and polyester.

This process in the originally modernized societies of Europe was often turbulent. It did, of course, give birth to the hard-nosed ideology of Communism. To permit industrialized agriculture, people were forced off the land. Industrial work was nasty and brutish in many cases, and life expectancy short. Quality of life for families in cities was usually low, with its poor sanitation and housing and employment insecurity. The labor of children was often brutally exploited. Charles Dickens, Upton Sinclair, and others cut their literary teeth on all this. Indeed, from the perspective of families and communities, Dickens was a better historian than most of his contemporaries (and many of ours as well), because they looked at the big picture (industrial progress) while he documented the essential details (children and their parents struggling to survive physically and morally).

Industrialization and urbanization have many complex consequences for the physical environment that eventually affect the social environment. Soil erosion is one such problem. Production of methane and carbon dioxide is another. Atmospheric scientists believe that significant increases of these gases can affect climate. At very high levels they can produce a global increase in temperature sufficient to melt glacial ice at the polar caps and raise the level of the world's oceans enough to flood coastal cities. This may eventually reshape patterns of human settlement. Natural factors producing these gases and their levels in the atmosphere are giving way to factors deriving from human activity.

Three human sources influence these gases. First, of course, is the burning of hydrocarbon fuels. Second is the increased activity of gas-producing termites in wood debris resulting from the widespread clearing of forests. Third is the agribusiness of cattle-fattening—an important activity in industrial food production. The massive concentrations of excrement produce large quantities of methane. Methane was reported to be increasing by about 2 percent annually in the early 1980s. Industrialization and urbanization in the twentieth century are beginning to have global environmental impact in both the physical and social domains. As Herman Daly puts it: "Until recently the economy of man was 'peanuts' in the total economy of nature" (1980, p. 245). This has changed. We are now the big kid on the environmental block.

China: Progress At What Cost?

That the environmental significance of modernization is linked to scale is clear. A review of available evidence concerning China illustrates the staggering physical dimensions of modernization in a nation of more than a billion people. Even in this predominantly rural and marginally industrialized nation, the entire environment already seems engineered for human purposes. Every animal and plant serves the needs for human consumption. For example, songbirds are caught for eating; after harvesting crops the fields are cleaned so that stalks and leaves can be burned for fuel; and every hillside is a potential site for terraced farming. This was true even before efforts during the last three decades to upgrade the productivity of farms, factories, and power-generation facilities to increase material comforts for a population that has doubled since 1950.

According to Victor Smil's report, most of the need for fuel for 800 million rural Chinese has been met by environmentally cannibalistic practices—e.g., burning wood beyond renewable levels and using vegetable matter that could function as fertilizer. I was struck by this when I visited there. It seems every available bit of biomass is accounted for. The forest floor is literally swept clean; pine needles, leaves, and branches are collected for use as fuel to boil the water, which is unfit for drinking otherwise.

Smil reports that agricultural development has worked hand in hand with fuel needs to deforest huge areas. In Helongjiang Province, supplier of 50 percent of the country's timber, forested areas have been decreasing by about 2 percent per year. Other areas show the same declines in the past two decades, although reforestation efforts are ongoing, with an annual tree-planting campaign that requires even white-collar workers to meet a quota.

The process of environmental degradation has traded a 70-percent increase in grain production since 1950 (counterbalanced by population increase) for soil erosion, chemical pollution of lakes from fertilizer, and other consequences of large-scale agriculture. Smil reports a 30-percent *loss* of farmland to these forces since 1960. What is more, Chinese agencies and communities have not implemented reclamation and irrigation projects thus far. Irrigation canals effectively deliver only about 45 percent of the water entering the system, and Orville Schell reports that under the new individual responsibility system no incentive exists for collective action to upgrade them. Thus, some of these facilities are deteriorating rapidly. Only about one-third of the saplings planted in reforestation programs since the 1950s actually survived. Despite a massive tree-planting month each year, the impoverished soil and predatory fuel needs of the population slow progress in reforestation. The costs of modernization have been staggering, even for a society accustomed to dealing with massive challenges.

The Modern Economy: Who's In Charge?

Modernization proceeds through families. Making economics concrete means working out the implications of changes in the techniques, organization, and side effects of transformation ("production") for families. The motive to provide for one's family is strong, so strong that harnessing it runs the engines of the larger economy. People work to provide for their dependents. How and when they work affects the care children need and receive. Pre- or nonindustrial agriculture restricts the variation in patterns of day-to-day life. Subsistence farming consumes labor at a rapid rate. Modernization dramatically increases the variation in what people do and brings new challenges to family life.

For example, the modern era permits and thus demands expansion of the "day" into the night. Shift work is possible with electric illumination. Nearly one-quarter of the American work force serves on evening or night shifts. Thirty-three percent of children age 14 or younger have at least one parent thus employed, according to U.S. Census data. A shift worker's physiological functioning is impaired, particularly if he or she works long hours and changes shifts frequently. Shift work is necessary from the perspective of conventional economic thinking. Modern industrial plants have large capital investments to pay off, and they must run at *their* capacity—regardless of the needs of the human beings who serve them.

Harriet Presser's research tells us that shift work often means sacrificing children or spouse. Evening shifts take their greatest toll on parent-child relationships. Shifts that run overnight undermine spousal relationships. But more production boosts GNP, directly through work on the job and indirectly through enterprises that develop to provide child care, processed foods, and so on to the families involved. And because traditional household work by women is invisible in GNP, moving them to what male economic models define as "real" work shows up not as an economic trade-off, but only as a sign of economic growth. As such, it may be totally bogus from the perspective of the wealth of families.

Modern transportation permits and thus demands expansion of the size of the family's economic environment. Work and home can be separated geographically and then linked together by commuting. The same is true for school and home, and marketing and home. The costs are enormous, but conventional economics treats the trade-offs as "growth" because they add to GNP. It is a special irony that walking to work is now a luxury few can afford. Doesn't this tell us something about modernization?

Modern machinery permits (and has thus required) a diminution of "productive" enterprises in the family. Industrialization "frees" the family from its historic role as producer and recasts it solely as consumer (to use these terms in their conventional sense). Conventional economics registers more gain in GNP as families pay others to grow, transport, and prepare their food, clothing, shelter, and entertainment. Women, particularly, are changed in this process. Traditional household work and child care are no longer simply taken for granted, but are actually discounted as costs to be borne by the family because they represent nonparticipation in the cash labor force outside the home.

All these aspects of modernization seem to have a relentless internal logic. Once they become feasible, they seem to become inevitable. We have opened a Pandora's Box, and old ways seem powerless before the onslaught of power, speed, efficiency, and quantity over quality.

"Time is money." Money is the essence of modern industrialism—the standard of value and the primary criterion by which to organize and judge human endeavors. It even takes precedence over increasing the energy and machinery at the disposal of each worker and consumer. As such it is worth exploring. For help in understanding this we can turn to Orio Giarini's insightful *Dialogue on Wealth and Welfare* (1981).

What Does It Mean To Be Rich?

Giarini maintains that economics "is the discipline of the industrialization process and specifically of the Industrial Revolution, which started in Europe more than two centuries ago" (p. 4). As he sees it, the basic concepts of economics evolved from industrial modes of production. Economics is no longer concerned with the direct productive work of which a person is capable (the prehistoric world) or the indirect productive work of making tools (the preindustrial world). Instead it measures the creation of capital to finance machines with high productivity per unit that reduce the need for human labor. Capital, not labor, is the backbone of the industrial society.

Industrial society focuses on the marshaling and management of money to organize energy and machinery. Industrial organizations create jobs, of course. Their purpose is not to create work, but to produce things to be sold in the monetarized economy and thereby generate more money. Each element in the system seems to assume that someone else will provide the jobs. Let Jack do it. We see the "normal" level of unemployment rising around the world as more and more economies become modern. In the United States, political rhetoric seems ready to accept an unemployment rate higher than 7 percent as "normal," when the standard was less than 5 percent only a decade or so ago. But families need jobs, regardless of the total amount of capital around them, regardless of GNP, regardless of conventional measures of economic development.

As industrialism progresses, the capital cost of the average job site increases. These average costs can hide great discrepancies across and within industries and plants. A nuclear power plant costs hundreds of thousands of dollars per job site, while a bakery may cost tens of thousands and a small pottery studio only hundreds. Use of the term "production" is almost unavoidable in our discussion, particularly when summarizing analyses presented by others. These job sites are engaged not in production, of course, but in transformation. The full social and physical costs of these transformations must account for their impact on families—in the realms of child care, commuting, health care, food preparation, and simply peace of mind.

In an industrial society, the household is a work site. The cost of equipping it increases steadily as more technology enters upon the scene and expectations concerning size and furnishings rise. All these household items have a rationale. All deliver benefits. All save time, at least if we examine each item alone in comparison with the technique it replaced.

Where Does The Time Go?

Time- and labor-saving household items are paradoxical, however. If we have saved so much time, why do so many of us feel so hurried and harried? Social critic Ivan Illich argues that in the modern household, false labor is generated that consumes time and energy but offers little of the satisfaction and social interaction we found in the past when technology required more *genuine* work. Baking bread is more satisfying than driving through crowded streets to a supermarket, waiting in an anonymous line to buy a loaf of bread, and then transporting it back home. Illich is probably right. Modern urban families seem starved for time in contrast to their traditional agrarian cousins, who may labor longer, but do so in ways more in harmony with natural human rhythms. Leisure time decreased by 25% in the last decade according to a recent survey.

Perhaps television best represents the modern paradox of time. It is virtually omnipresent. It is always available and can consume enormous amounts of time. In the average American household, the television is turned on more than seven hours each day. Many people have insufficient time to take care of business because each day they commit nearly 25 percent of their waking hours to television. Is television as psychically satisfying and socially facilitating as radio, reading, games, conversation, sewing, or home repair? Probably not. Television is a "time sink"—we can pour our time into it in quantities easily disproportionate to what we receive from it. By and large, not enough quality programming exists to fill the hours of broadcast time. And the proliferation of cable channels (to perhaps 100, if the boasts of its boosters are fulfilled) promises to exacerbate the problem.

Television is now a cultural force with immense economic significance throughout the world. It displaces other activities, some of which have larger social and cultural payoffs. As mentioned earlier, in one South Pacific community television viewing has replaced the traditional evening get-together chaired by the village elders. Now there's no time for meetings. Television absorbs time freed by labor-saving devices. It promotes the capital-intensive urban and industrial way of life. And what is more, enough of the programming is genuinely good that few of us (I include myself) would forego it totally, difficult as we find it to watch selectively, sensitive to its costs and risks. No wonder Marie Winn calls it "the plug-in drug."

Owning or having easy access to television means we open ourselves to being exploited by it. Like most fruits of industry, it offers much that is genuinely attractive—however negative its consequences. Most of us are at a competitive disadvantage in relation to the modern industrial order; we are vulnerable to being manipulated to accept its growing costs in return for its actual and promised benefits. Just as individuals are vulnerable, so too are whole societies.

Is World Trade a Global Shell Game or a Chain Letter?

The global nature of the current economic order allows enterprises to exploit discrepancies among societies in labor and physical resources more efficiently than was ever before possible. Within the confines of conventional economic models, it is often cheaper to produce something in one area and ship it to another than to "produce" the item locally. Trade depends upon such differences—first among individuals and families, then among clans, next among villages and towns within a region, then among regions, and finally throughout the world. Trade creates new markets, and their existence reinforces specialized economic enterprise. If transportation costs are relatively low, it *appears* to make sense to stop growing food for just one area and concentrate on trading it for manufactured products. It makes eminent good sense in principle and when confined to an ecologically sensible scale—e.g., the "green doughnuts" mentioned earlier. But does it really make any ecological sense for someone in Chicago to wear a shirt made in China when the hometown mill could do the job? Does it make any sense to transport rice grown in the United States to China because Chinese labor is cheaper than American when used in factories and American agribusiness can grow rice cheaply by substituting chemical fertilizer and machinery for labor? Why should flowers from Hawaii fly on jumbo jets to New York every day? How will we explain to our children's children that we consumed their petroleum birthright moving food and manufactured goods around the world, when we could have been managing with local exchanges for most products, for most people, most of the time?

Emigration of factory jobs from the relatively affluent labor force of the United States to other countries is already well known. Emigration of clerical jobs made possible by advances in data processing provides an example that may portend the future. Keypunching has been farmed out to countries with lower labor costs, such as Korea, since the 1960s. But the new technology of microprocessors now allows direct transmission of data without "hard copy" (paper). Satellite Data Corporation of New York uses this technology to do data entry work in Barbados at a labor cost of $1.50 per hour (versus between $4 and $12 in the United States). Interestingly, the managers view their operation as a factory, not an office.

This throwback to an earlier era of industrial organization may not be the only such case. Many observers claim that the explosion of computer-assisted word processing and information management will permit, even demand, a return to a still older economic form, the cottage industry. If that happens, it will do much to revitalize the competitive advantage of the family as an economic unit. Or it may permit a pernicious and exploitive piecework system to take hold and grow. It's an interesting prospect for the sustainable society. The new technology of microprocessors that makes small, relatively inexpensive computers possible may be our last best hope for the future of Spaceship Earth and the family lifeboat. Or it may simply provide a more powerful way to conduct business as usual. It may offer a way to restore dignity to the family as an economic enterprise. Or, it may just lead to more intrusion of conventional economics into family life.

If one group can sell something at a lower price in the same market as another group and still make a profit (whatever its criteria for adequate profit), then it has a comparative advantage. The current crisis in comparative advantage for some industrialized nations is minor compared to the emerging issues raised by the world problematique. Like most conventional economic notions, comparative advantage disregards material costs and benefits beyond the monetary short term, because it confines itself to price as the criterion for assessing advantage.

Transformational economics views such a formulation with suspicion and doubt, of course. If we consider full costs and benefits to the physical and social environment in the long run, the terms of the equation shift. Conventional economic *and political* thinking cannot accommodate the changed equation, even when such thinking recognizes its validity. The inescapable conclusion is that most of the conventional economics behind "free trade" is bogus. This should become clearer as more countries realize that the maxim of the modern international economy ("export more; import less") cannot offer a stable global economy. It's like a chain letter: there must be losers (importers) if there are to be winners (exporters). In the long run, the effect is likely to be some combination of impoverished losers, squandered precious nonrenewable resources, and economic instability for families, communities, and nations.

Why are the roads filled with trucks transporting goods? Why are freight trains traveling the rails? Why do cargo ships and tankers crisscross the oceans? Why do air freighters roar off runways around the world? Why is the volume of world trade measured in the trillions of dollars? The answers only make sense in conventional economic terms. The present volume of world trade is far in excess of what transformational economics tells us is appropriate to a sustainable world.

In a sustainable system, trade would be limited to two domains. The first is ideas, technology, and artistic creations and the people necessary to communicate them. The second is material goods required to meet basic human needs or dramatically to enhance human experience for which no good alternatives are available locally. Most world trade today fails to meet either criterion.

All trade implies costs as well as benefits. It costs the physical environment a great deal to sustain the required transport, regardless of the cash price. We often hear complaints about government subsidies that increase exports by lowering their cash price, and about trade barriers in the form of cash duties raised by governments to decrease imports. But these manipulations of cash price ignore the real cost of trade: future generations unknowingly subsidizing current patterns of consumption. And these costs, even if minimized through use of (for example) solar power, do not tell the whole story.

It also costs the social environment a great deal to adjust to disruption of local patterns. Local factories may close because they can no longer compete with foreign factories. Families face challenging adjustments which may include changes in composition of the household, income, place of residence, and ability to offer continuity to the next generation. Even the winners face significant challenges—the need for new forms of income distribution, child care arrangements, and attitudes about family roles.

Against these costs stand the benefits: the filling of gaps between local needs and resources, invigorating cross-cultural exchanges, and increased material resources for newly industrializing societies. We must not dismiss or disregard these benefits. Visiting small factories in rural China and seeing first hand how recent economic changes have permitted people to purchase key items such as bicycles, wrist watches, and radios demonstrated for me the human significance of basic material accumulation. But neither must we downplay the ecological costs of trade. At present, beyond accumulating essential capital, meeting local needs, and stimulating cultural exchange, trade mainly serves other masters: private profit, nationalist and imperialist politics, and the disease of modern materialist excess.

One key point bears repeating. The goal of the industrial process is not to create or sustain work. It is to achieve the highest possible *monetary* return on the investment of capital. In early periods of industrialization, physical transformation of materials and energy into goods was the major monetary cost—just as in preindustrial subsistence agriculture, human labor was the principal cost. In classical industrial economics, investments in anything other than physical facilities (e.g. health insurance for employees, pollution controls, etc.) are "nonproductive." They are treated as a kind of necessary evil, to be minimized if possible and tolerated only as a cost of doing business.

But labor means more than economic factoring. Labor means jobs, and a job means an opportunity to work. People need jobs for psychic income as well as cash income. With the trend toward more and more excess workers, prospects for psychological impoverishment increase.

Orio Giarini argues that "a product is usable not because it exists but because it is available and it works" (p. 25). This is "utilization value," and it includes goods and services that are free (available at no monetary cost) and priced (available from the market at monetary costs). This is critical to understanding industrialization and urbanization, because the historical thrust of both is to reduce the scope of "free" goods and services. Industrialization does this in two ways—one direct, the other indirect.

The industrial order reduces the "free" and increases the "priced" directly by creating physical conditions in which one must now purchase what was once free. Thus, families need ever larger cash incomes to maintain the same standard of living. For example, if swimming free in a nearby river becomes impossible because the water is polluted, the family may have to pay cash to swim in a pool. Either would meet the family's recreational need, but the pool creates a financial need (and increases GNP) while adding little or nothing to the family's real standard of living. In fact, if the pool is highly chlorinated and less pleasant than the river, actual quality of the recreational experience may decrease. As Giarini sees it, industrialization frequently has this paradoxical result of giving with one hand and taking away with the other. However, every time priced experiences supplant free experiences, GNP increases. This affects families in everything from child care (replacing "free" home care with priced day care) to transportation (replacing free walking with priced driving).

A more complete accounting is needed, one that includes *both* monetarized and nonmonetarized costs and benefits of economic enterprise. Often, what appears to be an economic advance is actually only the substitution of priced for free exchanges—the transformation of nonmonetarized into monetarized resources. GNP goes up, but the real standard of living remains the same or even declines.

Money Changes Everything

Monetarization is also an indirect consequence of industrialization, however. As more and more of daily living is monetarized directly (and the cost of living thus increases), there is an almost inevitable tendency to view activities of the nonmonetarized economy as potentially "monetarizable" (to use an awkward word). Thus, a wilderness area is viewed by potential "developers" (a bizarre term) with eyes that ring up dollar signs. Where a hiker sees beautiful vistas, the developer see marketable views from a condominium. Where a naturalist sees a forest, the developer sees board feet of lumber.

The same is true of families. Where parents see their children, marketing specialists see potential consumers. Where children see their parents, employers see workers. Except through political channels that preserve wilderness as part of the nonmonetarized sector, hikers cannot outbid those who would convert vistas into views. Similarly, parents need the supportive intervention of political power to resist pressures to cash in on children through television advertising and the creation of monetarized needs, and to protect the time and flexibility they must have to meet their children's needs.

Monetarization threatens families and their necessary support systems. Workers are depersonalized by mechanistic social models most compatible with industrialization, which require that decisions be made as if capital and labor are interchangeable. Human feelings only enter the economic equation if they directly affect performance. One result is that what one can do takes precedence over who one is. Families are intrinsically and primarily concerned with who you are (my brother, your son, his daughter, her sister). As such, they offer a necessary balance to the dominant industrial orientation of what you can do.

But industrialization makes many demands of families. It usually demands increased mobility, which puts stress on children and parents alike, requiring that they repeatedly dissolve attachments to neighborhood and community. Traditional forms of social control and nurturance may become obsolete, further monetarizing family life by replacing nonmonetarized exchange of social support with priced services. This trend may reach silly proportions, as when affluent families buy services that shop for one's clothes and one's children's toys.

Industrialization provokes families into seeing the costs and benefits of family life from a monetarized perspective. For example, the direct costs of bearing and rearing children increase. A parent must pay money for access to the goods and services of the childbirth system, the processed food system, the technological recreation system, the day care system, the health care system, and the educational system. Budgets are often published indicating the cost of raising a middle-class child through adolescence is in the hundreds of thousands of dollars. A big item in such budgets is the income "lost" by caregivers. Economists call them "opportunity costs" because they refer to the lost opportunities that a child costs the parent (usually the mother).

Public and professional concern with "working women" testifies to the indirect power of monetarization. Women have always worked, of course, and are not now exchanging roles; they are adding to and expanding their roles and their work. What is new is the massive entry by women—particularly married mothers of young children—into the officially monetarized work force. This opportunity is a mixed blessing. Many mothers work for income to provide the margin of affluence they and their families need, or at least believe they need. Others work to avoid poverty. Some from both groups would work outside the home in any case because they prefer it. Women earn on average about 60 percent of what men earn, and supply about 25 percent of total family cash income. And they need this income mainly because the cash price of daily living has increased.

Living in an industrial society puts a cash premium on recreational leisure, which costs money because it increasingly relies on technological games or on access to priced experiences. It increases the amount spent on food; families often eat at restaurants (spending one-third to one-half of their food budget, according to 1983 figures) or eat highly processed and expensive food at home. Transportation, too, increases in price, because communities have evolved or have been created to discourage walking. And monetarization puts a cash price on self-esteem; one of its consequences is a tendency to associate personal value with financial value.

Implications for Family Life

Money—the need for it and its use to measure worth—corrodes many traditional social forms. Most obvious is the role of full-time child rearer and homemaker. Those who do not earn a cash income lose economic credence. They come to be viewed—and may come to view themselves—as "economic parasites." They are haunted by the fact that they could earn cash income in the time they now spend at home. As family size shrinks this problem becomes bigger.

Volunteer work, too, takes on a new meaning. When chosen instead of employment in the cash labor force, it is seen as a sacrifice or a rip-off, depending on your point of view. Done in addition to paid employment, it is often seen as marginal and expendable in an individual's or family's "time budget." In any case, one consequence of monetarization may well be shortage of labor for volunteer services of all kinds. The United States has come to recognize this in recent years and to rethink voluntarism.

Monetarization can have positive consequences. It may give women greater social leverage, because the dollar value of their unpaid work has been highlighted by analyses of opportunity costs. Testifying to this are movements to extend pension benefits to homemakers, and divorce decrees that legally recognize financial equity built up by homemakers in family assets. Indeed, if monetarization brings about better appreciation for the realities of households as microeconomies, it will have done women a real service. But this service may be counterbalanced or even outweighed by its disservices.

Monetarization may relieve some family pressures when people are able to succeed financially. But it creates others by influencing family members to participate in the *highly* monetarized world outside the household. For example, it creates a need for money by adolescents to permit their full participation in increasingly expensive peer activities. This in turn may produce family conflict: the parents feel pressured to provide money; the teenagers feel let down when they don't receive enough.

In the United States, adolescents have always been active in household work ("chores"), but since World War II they have entered the monetarized part-time work force in dramatically higher numbers. According to Laurence Steinberg, by the time they graduate from high school nearly 80 percent of American adolescents will have had some formal paid work experience. But that experience does little to enhance development of character and social growth. Rather, it tends to be geared only to making money, and overrepresents the worst part of modern industrial urban life. For example, nearly 35 percent of jobs for adolescents are in food service, mainly fast food service involving repetitive tasks that teach very little of value. According to Steinberg's research, adolescents who work part time at such jobs become more negative about work, more involved in drug use, and less involved in the socially invaluable but nonmonetarized world of community- and school-based extracurricular activities and family. In short, work for cash in the form most available to adolescents decreases their appreciation for values and attitudes needed to enhance a sustainable society, emphasizing instead money and materialism. Do we want to reinforce the belief that "time is money" or that "the best things in life are free"?

This pattern exists too among young mothers who work for money in increasing numbers and worry about the "opportunity costs" of family life. Industrialization and urbanization continually force one question into our minds: "Can I afford the price of doing X?" For both adolescents and parents, that "X" includes social activities of intrinsic value, such as time with family and friends. These difficulties derive from the increasingly monetarized nature of life; which results from industrialization and its cousin, urbanization. In industrial society, monetarization is our most important product.

Monetarization and Materialism: A Powerful Pair

The tide of monetarization has given new significance to what we earlier speculated was an innate human impulse to materialism. The preindustrial world masked this drive for most of the people most of the time. But the modern industrial and urban world shows us for what we are. In an earlier era, our time had a low price tag, so we could afford to invest heavily in each object we possessed. When you can only have one wooden bowl, it makes sense to have a very finely crafted one. You can "afford" to take two weeks to make it. But when the market value of your time can be priced high, the cost of a two-week investment in a bowl is prohibitive. Who can afford such quality? Who ever could?

Modern urbanites—particularly the most successful ones—can hardly afford to do *anything* for themselves anymore. Their time is too valuable to "waste" cooking, cleaning, taking care of children, and doing all the rest of the things that make the world go round. I asked a class of undergraduate women at an Ivy League university how they planned to balance career and home. "Get a maid!" was the consensus reply. Aristotle asked, "Who will watch the watchers?"—but the question in modern industrial society is, "Who will care for the caregivers' children?"

I recall a newcomer to computers who wrote a program that would play a card game with itself. He delightedly reported that the program could play three hundred rounds per minute. Very efficient; but what's the point? The same misguided logic is to be found in much of industrialized urban life.

Luckily for us as a species, there are some counterbalancing forces. Money—unlike other objects—has few or no qualitative aspects. That is, one dollar is as good as another, putting aside for the moment cross-national speculation in currencies. The technical beauty of money and its humanistic ugliness are one and the same: it is purely quantitative. Anyone with any sense and sanity will see the futility of approaching money as intrinsically valuable, as being anywhere besides near the bottom of his or her hierarchy of needs. But in a fully monetarized society, people are led to believe that anything and everything has a price. And it's only a small step (if a false one) to move from that principle to saying everything and anything is for sale, that money can buy anything—including substitutes for high quality parent-child relations.

When policy makers in the Soviet Union gave up on large-scale efforts to establish paid replacements for parents as caregivers, they did so recognizing that "you can't pay a woman to do what a mother will do for free." That's true, and it applies to fathers as well. But monetarization is always seducing or coercing us into believing that we *can* substitute money for time, for attention, for interaction, for investment of self—that we really can have our cake and eat it too when it comes to human relations in general and family relations in particular. The root of this evil is industrialization, and its progress tells a great deal about the dynamics of capital in human affairs. This returns us to Giarini's concept of "utilization value"—the worth of a good or service for the duration of its life span regardless of where it came from and whether it has a cash price.

Can We Eat the Forbidden Fruit in Moderation?

Utilization value gives us a conceptual tool for assessing industrialization's net worth and for determining when its undeniably real benefits begin to be outweighed by its equally demonstrable costs. It permits us to do more than simply accept industrialization unconditionally or reject it absolutely. The latter seems unlikely. Once having tasted them, who can really imagine *completely* foregoing the fruits of the industrial order? But the former is not satisfactory either, for it supposes a dynamic of growth in absolute and per-capita resource transformation of unlimited—and thus impossible—scope.

It is difficult to criticize the modern industrial order without inviting the kind of jingoistic patriotism faced by those who criticized the Vietnam War ("America: love it or leave it") or police brutality ("Next time you have an emergency, call a hippie"). One can hear the voice (and see the bumper stickers): "The modern industrial order: love it or leave it"; "My pollution, right or wrong"; "Next time you need some money, ask a tree." This attitude recalls the 1930s, when people welcomed Mussolini because he made the trains run on time, when people tolerated Nazism because it was a bulwark against Communism. Just as Nazism "sold out" to Communism by signing a nonaggression pact in 1939, so the modern industrial order seems to be selling out on its promise to eradicate poverty (if we just pay the price in social and physical environment degradation). Industrialization is actually *increasing* impoverishment in some areas and in many ways. And the future offers more rather than less impoverishment for more rather than fewer people, if recent trends continue.

We need a way of judging and saying "enough!" when conditions warrant—without having to cave in to the extremes of "love it or leave it" or "throw out the baby with the bath water." Utilization value promises us that. It can warn us when an enterprise or even a whole socioeconomic order has exceeded its proper limits. It does so in a way that GNP and other strictly monetarized measures cannot. Giarini put it this way:

> The fundamental change occurs when economic activity measured in terms of value added, starts giving signs that this increased activity is counterbalanced by its negative effects in the overall non-monetarized sources of wealth. It is the moment when we observe the "production" of deducted values: the utilization value that starts diminishing. It is the moment at which *real* zero or negative growth starts even if the GNP indices are still positive. (1980, pp. 31–33)

Historically the industrialized economy, by considering only priced values, has been incomplete. Will present and future conditions make this model worse than incomplete—make it invalid? The answer as I see it is "yes." Conventional industrial economics is doomed, or the best of the human enterprise is doomed. Either it goes or we go.

Just How Gross Is the Gross National Product?

Gross National Product is the single most publicly visible manifestation of the industrial economy. It reveals the gross dynamics of the monetarized economy, but never the value of the nonmonetarized economy—and now it hides the costs to the nonmonetarized sector. GNP does not refer to utilization value, but to cash transactions. Thus, it reflects as "value" money spent to treat illnesses (even if they result from industrial growth), to replace consumer goods (even of the planned-obsolescence variety, even if they were never actually used), to cope with toxic wastes (even if they were a by-product of "production"). GNP reflects as "value" money spent to purchase military equipment (which usually makes no direct contribution to human welfare), money spent for processed food (which could be prepared better and more nutritionally at home), and money spent in other nonproductive areas. Increases in GNP makes some sense in an environment where costs of economic activity are minuscule and the nonmonetarized economy is unaffected. But it becomes less and less sensible as these conditions diminish. The gap between changes in GNP and changes in total utilization value grows, and industrial economics becomes more and more an exercise in deception.

As Giarini notes:

- A car that lasts for 200,000 miles has twice the utilization value of a car that lasts for 100,000 miles, despite the fact that (if initial purchase price is the same) buying two of the latter makes twice the contribution to GNP.

- A cotton bed sheet that lasts through 50 washings has at least 50 times the utilization value of a plastic disposable sheet. It has more even than that, because the cotton sheet will serve as a cleaning rag when retired from active service, while the disposable sheet becomes waste almost immediately—even though the price of its replacement contributes to GNP.
- The water in a polluted lake has negative utilization value (for drinking or swimming), although the price of protecting people from it contributes to GNP.

Giarini's hypothetical examples find dramatic confirmation in actual events. The 1980s have seen growing public action aimed at management of toxic wastes—"the dark side of industrial society," as the New York Times editorially described it. Environmental Protection Agency records indicate the existence of some 12,000 hazardous sites—418 of which are so bad that even the agency's director (a self-avowed enemy of most of the environmentalist movements, and an apologist for business interests according to many accounts) described them as "ticking time bombs." A congressional report indicates that more than one ton of toxic waste per person in the United States must be dealt with each year.

The costs of even a minimal cleanup of these sites are staggering, including a federal government "superfund" of $11.6 billion supplemented by hundreds of millions in state and local appropriations. These monies appear as part of GNP when spent to purchase goods and services necessary to undertake the cleanup. Add to this the money spent on health care to respond to effects of these hazards, and we have a classic illustration that GNP is a false measure of value. Indeed, more and more GNPs in modern societies increase to attempt to ameliorate deducted values. That these activities appear as "products" in the national accounting scheme is misleading at best—and increasingly, it is just plain wrong. Our accounting of what is a cost and what a benefit is sadly out of order.

GNP Drives Environmental Deterioration

This is bad enough in already modernized societies, where the slippage is becoming evident "at the margins," as conventional economists are fond of saying. But the greatest human dangers of industrialism are most evident in nonindustrialized societies that aspire to the modern model. They try to monetarize their economy by displacing subsistence activities designed to meet basic human needs. Often, they replace domestically oriented agricultural activities with those that appeal to foreign markets, and thus tap into imported capital. The increase in foreign commerce forges a link with modern highly monetarized economies. For example, in the wake of its new "responsibility system" to encourage private economic initiative, China reports dramatic increases in productivity for all segments of its economy. But rarely if ever do these reports include the mounting costs behind these increases—costs that include ever more reliance on petrol-energy, greater use of chemical fertilizers, and worse and more kinds of pollution. China's ideology proclaims commitment to social justice and to improving quality of life for the rural masses, so one hopes remedial efforts will take place.

In contrast, in most modernizing societies the economy serves a small but politically powerful group of elites. Household and community food needs receive low priority. Cash crops and capital-intensive agriculture displace rural society, and stimulating export to secure foreign exchange is the name of the game. Stimulating a modern economic elite in the current historical context usually causes collapse of the basic agricultural subsistence economy in the countryside. This produces rising unemployment and a grotesque rush to the big cities, where a few get lucky but for most life offers little more than survival.

This displacement is a matter of growing concern as land available for food production declines in amount and quality due to population pressures and urbanization. In the United States alone, three million acres of land per year are converted from agricultural to nonagricultural uses, according to a federally funded study. Farmers who wish to stay in business believe that they must enter the monetarized economy to purchase chemical fertilizer and capital-intensive machinery. Currently modernizing societies operate under very different circumstances than did those that modernized in the last two centuries. On the positive side, they can leapfrog over earlier technologies to the current state of the art, including computers and genetic engineering. But they must find resources and markets and adjust their rural/urban balance in a vastly more competitive and increasingly scarcity-dominated international environment. What is more, in what ways are these societies supposed to catch up? Pollution? Security? Appliances? Military power? Waste? Family breakup? Physical and mental health?

Are these societies moving in the right directions? Are we, in our already modernized societies? Our goal, remember, is a more *sustainable* human community based on competent social welfare systems, just and satisfying employment, reliance on the nonmonetarized economy to meet many needs, and a political climate that encourages cultural evolution and human dignity. When visiting a community we should first ask for answers to these three questions: What's the infant mortality rate? How many children are homeless? How many young people are on the street as prostitutes? Each answer critically reflects how well the community is doing to provide support for its families.

How well are the world's modernizing societies doing in this regard? We can start by noting that *where* they are facing this challenge has much to do with how they are doing. Where they are doing it is in cities.

Big Cities Are the Wave of the Future

By the early 1980s, the world was about 40 percent urban, according to geographer Gary Shannon. In areas like Central America, however, rural areas are nearing or have reached population saturation, at 39 farm workers per square kilometer of cultivated land versus 10 in the United States. Thus, population increase in Central America and similarly saturated regions mainly reflects urban growth, as people migrate from saturated rural areas where 54 percent live in "extreme poverty" (according to a U.N. study) to urban areas where "only" 27 percent live in "extreme poverty." The Environmental Fund estimates that urban and rural population in Central America will be equal at about 18 million each by 1995. Population will double by 2025, to about 45 million urban and 22 million rural. This has happened already in Brazil, where a mid-1980s population of approximately 140 million contained an urban:rural ratio of about 2:1. China, on the other hand, has a 4:1 *rural-to-urban* ratio, and is working hard to upgrade life in the countryside. And it did well in decreasing the infant mortality rate (at least until the recent flare-up of female infanticide linked to the One Child Policy), in drastically reducing the number of homeless children, and in nearly eliminating youthful prostitution. But China is unusual in this, has paid many social and ethical costs to accomplish it, and may be in jeopardy in the coming decades.

The modern era is characterized by growth of cities as much as by any other single phenomenon. Geographers estimate that at the beginning of the nineteenth century, the world was about 3 percent urban. By 1980 the figure was 40 percent, and by 2000 the estimated figure is 50 percent. Among the world's 23 or so regions, East Africa is least urban (12 percent), while 86 percent of Australia–New Zealand is urban. The pace of urbanization is now greatest for less modernized and industrialized societies. Geographer Gary

Shannon estimates that by the year 2000 there will be 6 times as many cities with populations greater than 1 million as there were in 1950. What is more, the less developed regions' share of these cities will have grown from 32 to 64 percent. We see a similar trend regarding "megacities" of 5 million or more inhabitants. In 1950, there were only 6 (all but 1 were in the industrialized modernized regions). By 1980, there were 26 (11 in modernized regions). The projection for the year 2000 is 59 (only 16 of which will be in currently "developed" regions)!

What about these cities as environments for families? By and large, they are difficult to the point of being destructive. Mexico City, for example has more than 18 million people, and about 1,000 peasants migrate each day from the countryside. Pollution, congestion, unemployment, inadequate water supply, and poor sanitation grow correspondingly. Some foresee 30 to 40 million in Mexico City by the year 2000, as efforts to discourage further immigration from the countryside falter. This social quagmire is caused by inappropriate industrialization and failure to stabilize and increase quality of life in the Mexican countryside. Mexico City's story is repeated in Lagos, Nigeria; in Bangkok, Thailand; in Cairo, Egypt; in Calcutta, India. These and other magnet cities in modernizing societies are staggering under the double whammy of increasing population and decreasing resources.

Urbanization is not the invention of industrialization, of course. The Mayan civilization of the pre-Columbian era is one notable example of a society with substantial urban settlement. Preindustrial cities have existed in many areas of the world. They were quite different from modern cities in at least four respects, however. First, they represented a relatively small proportion of their society's population, which was necessarily concentrated in the rural agricultural sector. Second, they were small by today's standards—numbering in the tens of thousands rather than the millions. Third, they depended on low-power transportation, which prevented them from growing disproportionately to their agricultural base. Fourth, they depended upon a political system which used force against the nearby agricultural region to extract food for the urban population.

With industrialism, cities changed in all four ways. They became larger, accounted for a larger proportion of the population, depended on more technologically sophisticated transport, and relied upon trade, not coercion, for food. In the twentieth century, urbanization has a decisive influence on societies around the world. In modernized societies, cities live off the fruits of industrialization. They provide a wide range of goods and services to rural areas in return for food. The monetarized economy permits this, and it relies upon industrial activity across the society. Agriculture is necessary for life to continue, but industry is the engine that drives the economy. Mechanized transport permits new urban forms as well as shifts in rural life away from subsistence farming and toward cash-crop farming on a larger scale.

Industrialization of agriculture permitted (and thus demanded) increased food production with fewer workers. Industrialization of other forms of production required concentration of workers in urban centers. The two worked hand in hand. But early in the twentieth century, urbanization still bore a strong relationship to natural geography—rivers, bays, lakes, and other physical features that have always generated urban settlements. In the United States, growth of the old ("Snowbelt") cities was linked to the rise of the modern industrial order. As the century progressed, those cities were eclipsed by new ("Sunbelt") cities that grew quickly in the special, *historically artificial* conditions of the post–World War II boom. They were built on energy-intensive technologies that sought to override naturally occurring limits of climate and geography, most notably availability of water. Houston is a prime example. There, megagrowth has drained underground aquifers and left caverns into which the city is sinking by as much as a foot every five years. These new cities were born in the automotive era. Some have little or no "downtown" and few sidewalks in residential areas, so geared to the automobile are they. The Sunbelt cities rose as the Snowbelt cities declined, but they may be very short lived as the unusual (even freakish) conditions in which they grew dissipate. They may be left stranded by the tide of economic/ecological history. And unlike many of their Snowbelt counterparts, they lack much of the physical and social infrastructure they need to move from boom to sustainability. In 1979, many in the Sunbelt cities were crowing about their presumed futures. By 1987, the tide seemed to have turned. The Corporation for Enterprise Development, a business group, issued a "report card" on "providing jobs and economic opportunity, vitality of businesses, capacity for expansion and state policies fostering business growth." Only California among the Sunbelt states received an "A," while five Snowbelt states did.

Even short-sighted conventional economic analyses miss important evidence. Others see more clearly the madness. For example, a 1982 *New York Times* article ran under the headline "Jammed Freeways Lead Sunbelt to Mass Transit." The lead (dateline, Houston) does a good job of telling the story:

> They grew with wild abandon, metastasizing into the deserts and
> swamps around them. They are the great new cities of the South and
> West, whose very urban existence and give-me-elbow-room style of life
> has depended upon the ubiquitous automobile. Traffic congestion? Build
> another freeway. Now they are beginning to choke on their cars and
> tangled freeways. (p. 8)

One response is a return to older forms of urban transit now being renewed as some Sunbelt cities turn to a more historically normal pattern of development. Houston, Atlanta, Miami, and Los Angeles all have plans for new mass transit.

But automobile-based urbanization in these cities may interfere with operation of rail-type mass transit. America's older cities were rail-based, and thus naturally conformed to the needed pattern of a concentrated downtown and corridors of development—however much post–World War II automobile-based growth diluted those pure forms. A study supported by the federal government reported that of 30 major American cities without rail systems already operating or under construction, only 4 had the right configuration for adequate passenger volume: Houston, Los Angeles, Seattle, and Honolulu. Mass transportation prospects for other cities are uncertain. Light rails, buses, and automobiles must do most of the job now. But foot and bicycle should play a role as those cities seek more sustainable patterns. They should augment mass transit. In an ecologically sound city, they can complement conventional transportation.

Suburbia is peculiar to the industrial era, a phenomenon of major proportions. According to U.S. Census data, its economic implications are quite significant. Average (median) household income in cities was 74 percent of that in suburbs in 1980 (versus 80 percent in 1970). In some older cities the discrepancy was even greater (e.g., 58 percent in Baltimore). Suburbs are not conducive to sustainable patterns for families because they drastically limit possibilities of efficiently integrating home and work. They particularly oppress women, as Betty Friedan's The Feminine Mystique showed us a generation ago, and they deprive youth of the socially rich environment needed for sound social development, as Ed Wynne showed us in his book Growing Up Suburban.

Suburbanization began with railroads. People could live in small communities outside cities and yet be transported to the city to work. This pattern was supplanted in large part by the automobile, which permitted greater flexibility in scheduling and location. The railroad needs concentrations of suburbanites in a well-defined corridor of communities; the automobile encourages suburban sprawl. But both are part of the larger phenomenon of urbanization seen from the perspective of ecology of land and water. Where they differ is in their significance for transition to sustainability. The railroad-based suburb is much better placed and arranged for such a transition. It is likely to supply more of the infrastructure for community self-reliance, and it offers an effective alternative to the energy-intensive and wasteful automobile. Sunbelt cities may be quite vulnerable in this respect. And many of the burgeoning cities in the Third World offer the worst of all worlds—the sprawl of suburbs without personal affluence to compensate for social impoverishment.

Overall, older cities in modern industrialized societies are reasonably sound in their social, economic, and physical environments. They make sense. This is not true of many cities in the modernizing world (nor of new automobile-based cities in already modernized societies). In unmodernized societies, urbanization has proceeded rapidly without an industrial order to sustain it. Many people have left the agricultural sector, either because they have been displaced or because they hope to find better opportunities in the cities. Just as Sunbelt cities in the United States have grown in response to a historical fluke, many cities in modernizing nonindustrial societies are "unnatural" (using the conventional Western industrial model as the norm). First, they don't conform to land and water resource patterns. Second, they do not have—nor are they likely to develop—the typical urban infrastructure of services. Third, many lack sustainable industrial activity. They are simply holding pens for family disintegration or staging areas for emigration, rather than birthplaces for social welfare systems.

The Value of Cities in a Sustainable Society

In Giarini's terms, the rationale for urbanization must be found in maintaining or increasing utilization value while sustaining society's stock of useful resources. Cities fulfill this mission when they offer opportunities for ecologically sane work, when they manifest a sense of community that engenders human psychological satisfaction and meaningfulness, and when they maximize true benefits of collective residence while minimizing its true costs. But urbanization, in both industrial and modernizing nonindustrial societies, often means a net *decrease* in sustainability on the societal level and in family support systems at the individual level. Much of what we call urban development is antithetical to the needs of families, serving instead the monetary and political needs of the modern economic system.

We can recognize potential benefits of urbanization (economies of scale in services, culture, and work) but see the following costs:

Land use: Urbanization inevitably shifts land use patterns away from agriculture toward industrial, commercial, transportation, and residential uses. Obviously, sustainability suffers when we transform agriculturally prime land instead of agriculturally marginal land. Settlements are usually in close proximity to prime land because its agriculture could support a growing population. Urbanization thus tends to remove prime rather than marginal land from agriculture. This is one variable in the equation relating urbanization to sustainability. A second is the use of the land itself. Urban agriculture can make a real contribution to sustainability and can play an important role in determining overall impact of urbanization. Many cities have ignored this potential. Few can afford to do so in the future.

Ecological balance: Urbanization puts pressure on the entire ecology. The impulse to engineer the environment to meet human needs affects the habitats of many other species. It affects the regenerative capacities of natural water systems. It influences the balances of nature in many ways, particularly as urban areas increase and agricultural areas decline. The influence can be direct (raising the temperature and carbon dioxide content of the air) and indirect (opening up large new areas to termite infestation because of deforestation).

Human organization: Social science has yet to demonstrate any absolute, general effects of urbanization on psychological development and family functioning. Yet we continue to be suspicious of urbanization, and now of suburbanization. The principal cost envisioned is a loss of social identity, with a resulting decline in responsible interaction. This is seen as a problem in modern industrialized cities—where the pressing issues are neighborhood integrity and human scale—and in modernizing cities as well, where traditional rural patterns such as mutual child care responsibility are breaking down. This concern extends even to urban architecture. Does it enhance meaningful day-to-day interaction, or limit social intercourse? This is the real issue, of course. Does urban life create stress and diminish social resources? How frequently does it do so? These questions remain unanswered.

Ecological empathy: I share with many others the fear that urban life desensitizes us to the natural environment. E. F. Schumacher echoed the theologian/philosopher de Jouvenal on this matter: "As the world is ruled from towns where men are cut off from any form of life other than human, the feeling of belonging to an ecosystem is not revived" (1980, p. 147).

Interpersonal empathy is critical in preserving and enhancing the quality of the social environment. Ecological empathy serves the same function with the natural environments of field, forest, stream, lake, and ocean. Urbanization threatens this empathetic orientation. Children, particularly, need the countryside to develop a sense of kinship with nature.

When the elements are combined, what implications do industrialization and urbanization have for sustainability, for the wealth of families, and for social welfare systems? There are two. On one hand, industrialization and urbanization increase the demands on families. They increase the stakes; they increase the potential payoffs for success and the potential costs of failures. These costs and benefits increase because of the variety available to the city family—if they can afford it.

On the other hand, however, city life for those without access to its monetarized resources tends to produce a state of desperate impoverishment—what is now being called "the underclass." More money is required of the city dweller than of the rural resident to achieve the same utilization value—e.g., dollar costs of child rearing are higher in urban areas, according to the U.S. Department of Agriculture. This means the urban family must have a wider range of competence to "produce" the kind of people who can succeed in that environment. School success, once optional, has become essential. In the United States high school graduation is considered essential for full economic personhood. Fifty years ago less than half of all youth graduated.

All this is true for individual families in *smoothly running* modern industrial cities. But most cities are ecologically vulnerable; they are not sustainable if they continue to operate on the energy, waste, and land-use principles that are their foundation. The necessary transition challenges many political and economic sacred cows. For example, we—as a world system and particularly as the modernized world—need higher rather than lower prices on basic resources, most notably nonrenewable ones. To drive the engines of the modern industrial order toward sustainability, we need to make ecologically sensible policies and practices profitable. We can achieve this only if monetary costs of initial transformations ("production" using natural resources) are higher than costs of subsequent "productive" transformations (recycling, conversion to other uses, repair). Without a shift to higher prices for basic resources—prices that more accurately reflect choices we are already making for our great-grandchildren—industrial and urban policies are hopeless delusions.

The transition to sustainability will mean a shift to more labor intensive, less energy intensive approaches that bolster the family as an economic unit—with the goal of minimizing waste through recycling and other measures, and becoming more efficient in renewable domains such as growing food. In all such efforts toward change families must play a central role. Just as the family farm is the key to agricultural production in modernized and modernizing societies alike, so the family household is crucial in sustainable urban living—e.g., in recycling programs that rely on conscientious activity at the "point of use." And who is to lead the way in this necessary social and economic reformation? For this leadership we must listen to the feminine voice.

CHAPTER

7.

December 1974:

Mexico City, Mexico

The Feminine Voice
and the Foundations
of Social Welfare

I'VE COME TO MEXICO CITY TO SEE
the museums and the architecture. The city seems dominated by monuments to glorious death. What do you say of a people who seem to glorify
slaughter? My own do, at Gettysburg, where thousands died in moments
and tens of thousands in hours, and at the Somme, where in the first day's
combat 60,000 lives were forfeited. I want to hate and dismiss that kind of
wrong-headed ennobling of butchery, but something male in me balks,
Somehow I can almost hear "The Battle Hymn of the Republic," and my
disgust for the slaughter is tempered by grudging respect for "the cause"
and the courage. A female friend tells me that when she visits Gettysburg
she feels only a unity in shared communal sorrow.

In Mexico many monuments recognize that male impulse to slaughter
and be slaughtered. I've been out to the Inca pyramids. Much slaughter. I've
been to the National Cathedral, where the conquering Spanish forced Mon-
tezuma's Incas to dismantle their own temple and use the brick to build a
Christian one—with incidental and purposeful slaughter. I've seen government buildings decorated with wonderful murals, many of which deal in
beautiful detail with slaughter—while soldiers stand guard over the sight-
seers, with loaded weapons, alert for terrorists, reminding us that slaughter
is always imminent.

And I've been to another most remarkable monument to slaughter and
maleness. Beautiful Chapultepec Park in Mexico City is dominated by a
steep hill—once a citadel—on which now stand the gardens and palace of
Maximilian, the nineteenth-century French Emperor of Mexico. At the foot
of the hill stand white pillars, monuments to the young military school
cadets who leapt to their deaths in 1848 rather than surrender to the invad-
ing United States army. These white phallic pillars eloquently affirm the

male character—here in Mexico where the macho mystique is blatant, of course, but elsewhere around the world as well—in Gettysburg, at Thermopylae, at Masada. Somehow I must respect it, but I hate it too, and I fear what it means for the future in a world that desperately needs not bravado but nurturance.

Another Mexico exists in the shadow of the monuments to slaughter. Women, often with young children, sit on the sidewalk selling (little sacks of peanuts are a favorite) or begging; they are called "the Marias." There are no grand stone monuments to them in the parks, but I do meet one in the flesh through friends who live in a "typical" village thirty miles away. They introduce me to the wife of a nearby young family—the daughter, it turns out, of a sidewalk "Maria." Her mother had taken her children to the city to join other rural poor starting up the ladder. She first begged to collect enough capital to begin selling peanuts. From their sale she was able to start her children in school, to get them on the modern track. Her mission has succeeded, it would seem. Her daughter is married to a clerk and her son works as a mechanic. Considering where they started, they have arrived. But the only monuments to entrepreneurial women such as this are the lives of their children.

I am reminded of a cartoon I saw years ago: Two men sit at a bar. One has just ordered a round of drinks on a payday stopover on the way home. His money is spread before him on the counter. He says to his drinking buddy: "I ask you, my friend, what does she do with my money? I'll tell you. She blows it all on food and clothes for the kids!"

It is difficult to write anything that contrasts females and males, women and men, feminine and masculine without running the risk of stepping on someone's toes. "We all have too much at stake," a female friend reminds me. The long history of invidious comparisons casting women as second class, deviant, inferior, and less worthy makes this comprehensible. Even arguments of feminine superiority are suspect in many quarters— particularly when they seem to play into the hands of traditionally sexist themes. Witness, for example, the negative reaction to sociologist Alice Rossi's 1977 argument that females are sociobiologically superior as parental caregivers. But there are grounds for what Ashley Montague called "the natural superiority of women." If imitation is the sincerest form of flattery, then maybe men are unconsciously aware of their cosmically inferior position. Montague noted that men use feminine terms to refer to their creative work. In his book *The Male Machine*, Charles Ferguson airs his suspicion that expressions men use to describe their accomplishments (e.g., "that's my baby," or "my brain child") are really an elaborate defense mechanism to cope with the fact that women are intrinisically superior by virtue of their capacity to bear children. But any such argument opens one to criticism. We all have too much at stake—particularly in the modern world, where traditionally feminine contributions (such as bearing and rearing children) are often devalued.

This chapter is open to such criticism, because it argues that one key to sustaining the transition to a sustainable society is to replace with feminine concepts of power, value, and social interaction the masculine forms and themes that dominate public life in our patriarchal societies.

Females are the superior organism for the modern era. This is true biologically, of course. The sex ratio at conception is thought to be about 130 males to 100 females, but declines prenatally because of a higher rate of spontaneous abortions for male (often biologically defective) embryos. Some 75 percent of 190 known congenital abnormalities affect males more than females. In the United States, the ratio at birth is 106 males to 100 females; after age 65 it is 85:100; and average life expectancy for females is nearly eight years greater than for males. What is more, females appear to be more resistant to many modern illnesses (such as cardiovascular disease). The modern era in nations like the United States has benefited women by reducing the number who die in childbirth from more than 600 per 100,000 births in 1930 to about 10 per 100,000 in 1986. Given half a chance, women outlive men. This and women's biological superiority suggest that femininity is the logical guiding force for the future as humankind wrestles with the world problematique. Traditional masculinity is on its way out—or at least it ought to be. Yet this is a risky proposition to advance.

It is a risky message because two opposite themes dominate contemporary rhetoric. First, there is the reactionary view that women and their feminine ways should retreat from the public scene. Second, there is the progressive view that women should shed their feminine ways and act directly within the existing institutional and cultural framework established by men, of men, and for men. Neither view works toward the necessary transition to a sustainable society. The feminine perspective on work and family is a better foundation for a sustainable society than is the masculine. Moreover, masculine threats to women are threats to sustainability. Having laid these cards on the table let us examine them.

Women and feminine concepts are the key because

- typical socialization of females generates an ideology of caring and interdependence
- the special relation of women to childbearing generates an orientation to family that supports the movements needed for social welfare systems
- economic traditions of women better equip them for the demands of steady-state economies and thus the sustainable society.

As sociologist Elise Boulding puts it, "the ingenuity of women may be the most precious resource the human race has left" (1980, p. 59).

An Ideology of Caring and Interdependence

Carol Gilligan has written a landmark volume entitled *In a Different Voice* that considers the psychology underlying characteristically feminine concepts of caring and interdependence. She contrasts feminine and masculine concepts of morality, power, and aggression (allowing that no perfect correlation exists between being biologically female and developing a feminine orientation). From the feminine perspective, moral issues arise from conflicting *responsibilities*. In the masculine view, moral issues are defined as conflicts of *rights*. The former implies resolving moral dilemmas by seeking to increase awareness of needs; the latter implies a process of logical analysis without regard to "feelings."

Psychologist David McClelland reports that while men display strength through assertion and aggression, women display it through nurturance. For most men, taking what you deserve indicates personal power; for most women, personal power means giving what is needed. Women tend to see aggression as a problem born of fractured relationships. The appropriate response then is to try to mend and strengthen these relationships, "by avoiding isolation and preventing aggression rather than by seeking rules to limit its extent" (Gilligan, 1981, p. 43). It is a moral imperative to care, to assume responsibility for troubled relationships. Social welfare systems demand this orientation more than any moral calculus of rights and cost-benefit analysis. This may have political dimensions. But it also places an enormous burden on the shoulders of the world's women, who must provide a disproportionate share of the caring and healing required. Jesus may have died for our sins, but Mary lived through them. And this can become psychologically overwhelming without public and institutionalized support.

Many of the clearest speakers for the injunction to care have been politically active women who have contested the masculine element in society. A nineteenth-century American suffragette put it this way:

-172-

The male element is a destructive force, stern, selfish, aggrandizing, loving war, violence, conquest, acquisition, breeding in the material and moral world alike discord, disease and death. See what a record of blood and cruelty the pages of history reveal! Through what slavery and slaughter and sacrifice, through what inquisitions and imprisonments, pains and persecution, black codes and gloomy creeds, the soul of humanity has struggled for centuries, while mercy has veiled her face and all hearts have been dead alike to love and hope! The male element has held high carnival thus far, it has fairly run riot from the beginning, overpowering the feminine element everywhere, crushing out the diviner qualities in human nature. (quoted in the *Washington Spectator,* March 1, 1983, p. 3)

Even some men recognize the destructive force of masculinity. And it is the image of rape that dominates these insights. Writing about the distinctly male character of gang rape, essayist Roger Rosenblatt offered this perspective on the "male element":

Gang rape is war. It is the war of men against women for reasons easy to guess at, or for no reasons whatever, for the sheer mindless display of physical mastery of the stronger over the weaker. . . . That is male terrain, the masculine jungle. And no man can glimpse it, even at a distance, without fury and bewilderment at his monstrous capabilities. (1983, p. 98)

Rape is the lingua franca of the masculine-dominated world. Militarism is the brother of rape. The presence of soldiers means rape and prostitution for women in appalling numbers. The militarization of Africa in the 1970s brought an upsurge of rapes and other assaults against women, and of course skyrocketing mortality rates for children. Escalation of United States military involvement in Central America in the 1980s meant the reappearance of a strain of venereal disease last seen in Vietnam.

The economic analogs are clear in the conventional language of economic development as "man's domination over Mother Nature." "Virgin" forests and land being "violated" leave little doubt about the symbolism, images, and parallels relating the physical to the social environment. Former Secretary of Agriculture (now agribusinessman) Orville Freeman, in the 1976 film *Controlling Interest,* speaks of the various freedoms essential if development and profit are to proceed hand in hand. One he mentions is "the freedom of economic intercourse." In conventional approaches to economic development, one discerns more rape, incest, seduction, and molestation of minors than union between consenting adults. The male element, in its many forms, is at work in the world. This is the male element's worst side, of course.

Also characteristically male is the emphasis on separation, rights, and rules; on rationalizing social relations; on abstract principles over people. This stands in contrast to the feminine orientation, which emphasizes the social web, the interdependence of self and others. Carol Gilligan believes these contrasting patterns arise in part from the different positions of females and males in relation to the world. Others argue that what Gilligan calls the feminine perspective is really just the voice of those who are physically dominated, regardless of gender. Gilligan thinks these different positions have some basis in the biology of childbearing and temperament—that they have a sociobiological component. But they are implemented through contrasting social experiences for girls and boys. The main theme in female development is attachment, while for males it is separation. Both themes exist for each gender, of course, but we downplay separation (and thus individual self) for females while we downplay attachment (and thus social identity) for males. The result is that intimacy is a threat to masculine personalities, and feminine personalities fear separation. In a patriarchial world suffused with masculine domination, accentuating the feminine voice is a necessary corrective en route to a sustainable society.

The fullest human development occurs for the individual when she acknowledges self as worthy of separate value and he sees the social web as a source of meaningful psychic stability. Modernization institutionalizes the masculine mode and suppresses public expression of the feminine. This is critically unfortunate, because now more than ever before we need an ideology of caring and interdependence to manage the transition to a sustainable society. There is little reason to fear that the masculine element will be overwhelmed. Quite to the contrary, we should fear instead homogeneous masculinization of the population in modern societies, as the economic institutions of cash income, costs, and price penetrate more spheres of life—making women more masculine in orientation yet encouraging no corresponding feminization among men.

As women's lives have become modernized, they have been denigrated by the dominant masculine ideology of "hardball" politics and economics—just when we need "soft" energy paths and a material economy that lives lightly and gently upon the Earth. The ideology and politics of modernization have worked against women and the feminine perspective in most of the world, much of the time. Irene Tinker sees it this way:

"[D]evelopment" has been viewed as the panacea for the economic ills of all less developed countries: create a modern infrastructure and the economy will take off, providing a better life for everyone. Yet in virtually all countries and among all classes, women have lost ground relative to men; development, by widening the gap between incomes of men and women, has not helped improve women's lives, but rather has had an adverse effect upon them. (1976, p. 22)

Part and parcel of this has been the institutionalizing of Economic Man as the conceptual underpinning of efforts to stimulate and assess development. Economic Man is masculine in that he has only one primary role: rational self interest and profit, directly or indirectly in monetary terms. Ordinarily, women must perform two roles. They bear and rear children, and carry out economic activities that meet basic family needs. Conventional efforts to stimulate and assess development usually operate on the simplistic notion of Economic Man (and are typically conceived of and directed by men). They thus stimulate male enterprises (often to the detriment of both family and community economies) and assess those economies in narrowly misleading terms. As we have seen before, conventional economics defines development as growth in GNP, and GNP contains the sexist assumption that the only real work is done in the cash labor force outside the home. Who can fail to see the absurdity and injustice of asking the mothers of the world if they work? Apparently many do.

As the insightful analyses of theologian Elizabeth Dodson-Gray reveal, the single-minded concept of rights as characteristic of men contributes mightily to the world problematique. Masculine "rights" to dominate women and children parallel human "rights" to dominate the land, the forests, the rivers, lakes and oceans, and all creatures great and small. We are missing an adequate appreciation for the multiple responsibilities of self and other, home and community, present and future, human-built and natural. The world needs greater recognition of the rights of the self for those of the feminine persuasion and greater recognition of the multiple responsibilities of those who begin from the masculine perspective. Feminine personalities are often paralyzed by the injunction not to hurt others, but rather to sacrifice self. Masculine personalities often run amok in the social and physical world by serving the interest of self.

Carol Gilligan calls for an integration of feminine concepts into the dominant (male) ideology. This, she believes, will create a more powerful and responsible ethic.

[T]he concept of rights changes women's conceptions of self, allowing them to see themselves as stronger and to consider directly their own needs. When assertion no longer seems dangerous, the concept of relationship changes from a bond of continuing dependence to a dynamic of interdependence. Then the notion of care expands from the paralyzing injunction not to hurt others to an injunction to act responsibly toward self and others and thus to sustain connection. A consciousness of the dynamics of human relationships then becomes central to moral understanding, joining the heart and the eye in an ethic that ties the activity of thought to the activity of care. (p. 149)

This sounds promising. Indeed, the women's movement in modern societies promised just that. It arose out of a critique of male power and the costs of a lopsided patriarchy. It began with the recognition that masculine personalities are lost in a social and emotional wilderness, and promised that the feminine approach would bring what Suzanne Gordon has called "a life that balanced love, friendships, and work" (1983, p. 143).

But has feminism delivered on that promise? Gordon, for one, worries that women in the world of work are under enormous pressure to change themselves rather than change the world. She cites several leading "advice books" that tell women to exploit their feminine interpersonal skills for personal gain, while suppressing their feminine orientation to affiliation and intimate social connectedness. She summarizes the advice this way:

In other words, the recognition that we all need intimacy is not a strength but a weakness, a holdover from childhood that must be shed by women seeking to take their places in the adult world. These friendships are inappropriate and sticking together must give way to looking out for number one, say the corporate Machiavellis. (1983, p. 146)

This is disturbing, to say the least. It implies that the humanizing insights of feminism are bankrupted when women adopt masculine models of power and influence. It should warn us not to underestimate the power of situations to shape values and behavior. The task is only partly one of empowering women in the world—women must not simply recapitulate the masculine models that now stand as a barrier to a sustainable society. They must reorder institutions to reflect the feminine voice.

Finding a way to integrate the feminine orientation to change the system poses a profound challenge. Simply placing those who are attuned to the feminine in the system will not succeed. As always, we must use our values to shape our choices about social systems, recalling Winston Churchill's warning that "we shape our surroundings and then our surroundings shape us." Environmental psychologists call this the "principle of progressive conformity."

Of course this principle can work for, as well as against, the shift toward feminine orientation. It can be a hope as well as a warning. When we create settings that elicit empathy, intimacy, connectedness, and caring— for example, when we arrange for men to play an active role in the birth of their children—we use the principle to our collective advantage. We also use the principle when we set up groups that elicit and reinforce emotional well-being—e.g., in participative work teams on the job. Even the small accoutrements of organization can play a role. For example, a university committee for rural women has, not a "chairman," but a "caretaker". Symbolic structure is important in shaping consciousness. Social welfare systems must be attuned to that fact.

Family Orientation

Family orientation is a crucial resource for the transition to a sustainable society. Properly motivated and supported, families can help to accomplish that transition. Recycling, conservation, producing goods and energy—all are appropriate to family-level enterprise.

Children are the currency of family life, the focal point for exchanges among kin. The interests of a sustainable society are served by a qualitative, not quantitative, orientation to children. This means intensifying parental investment in few rather than many children.

Family sociobiologist Robert Trivers suggests the concept of "investment" as a key to understanding masculine and feminine orientations. The underlying issue in family life is genetic success. Men and women have necessarily different strategies to that end. The limiting factor for male genetic success is the total number of impregnated women. The limiting factor for females is the number of children born and raised (and delaying onset of childbearing into the mid-30s highlights this). Seen from this sociobiological perspective, women have a greater personal investment in each child. This leads to the hypothesis that women will be receptive to social arrangements that protect and nurture this investment and limit its costs. Strong families seem to be the answer to the implicit female question: how can I increase the chances of success for my children?

But in many parts of the world, women who seek to make wise reproductive investments face socioeconomic and psychological conditions that discourage small families. Rae Blumberg's persuasive cross-cultural research indicates that fertility depends largely on the social status of women, which in turn is derived from their economic power. With a few notable exceptions, men virtually monopolize power in two of the three principal domains of human communities—namely, power of force and political power. Only in the area of property do women ordinarily have a powerful or dominant position. Blumberg's research shows that differences in economic power of women account for a substantial amount (about one-third) of the variation in fertility rates among societies. Economic power is more influential than the other two domains. She concludes that empowering women economically and educationally is a wise strategy for limiting population growth. We considered this theme in Chapter 3, and return to it here because it takes on added significance as we consider ways to enhance the feminine perspective.

Until women have economic power—or have it restored to them where modernization has stripped them of traditional influence—they will opt for large families as a compensatory investment (regardless of the long-term costs to sustainability). Why? Because in a position of economic powerlessness, more children have few direct costs and several demonstrable benefits for a woman (status in her kin network, help around the house when they are growing up, and help in crises and old age) which she does not view as likely to come from other sources.

> Even though for the woman's nation, her high fertility may be a greater burden than benefit, family planners will have a hard time convincing her (or her husband) that two children are the ideal number when she has objective grounds for knowing her welfare would be adversely affected if she had fewer than five or six children. (Blumberg, 1976, p.18)

It's the tragedy of the commons in full force.

We must promote human quality by creating social arrangements that offer good psychological, economic, and social returns on a small number of children. A UNICEF study predicts that if infant mortality were cut by half in developing countries, it would motivate a reduction of 12 million births per year. Why? Mothers would be more confident about concentrating their parental investment in fewer children. But once the odds of physical survival change, there still remains the issue of whether parents will reap psychological rewards for their efforts, whether children will remember and repay their psychic debts to parents.

Drawing men into childbirth and child rearing is one way to merge the feminine and masculine and thus humanize men more fully. In China, it may be one way to counteract the apparently increasing problem of female infanticide in response to the One Child Policy. One way to protect infant girls is to encourage stronger initial attachment by their fathers, and direct participation by fathers in the process of childbirth can do this.

More fully humanized men are necessary in a sustainable society. The intimacy of the experience of childbirth and the process of early parent/ infant attachment are powerful socializing influences, even for most men who are less temperamentally suited than most women to empathic intimacy. Many a male "tough guy" has had the hard edges of his masculinity softened by becoming involved in the birth and care of his children. Social engineering is the key. Margaret Mead observed that motherhood is a biological necessity but fatherhood is a social invention, and this puts our social inventiveness to the test.

We shouldn't expect that the behavior of most males and females will ever become totally indistinguishable. Temperamental and historical differences will see to that it would seem. But it is possible to accomplish a great deal toward feminizing males (resulting in more empathic, caring men) and toward masculinizing females (resulting in women with greater respect for self). All in all, this would mean a more fully human population, one with a more qualitative and less quantitative orientation to family. Such people would be better suited to undertaking the transition to a sustainable society because they could better concentrate on enriching interpersonal, spiritual, and aesthetic encounters outside the narrow limits of the monetary economy.

Female Economic Traditions

Modernization has meant industrialization, urbanization, and an ever more monetarized society. The conventional view of society is increasingly at odds with basic realities because it does not recognize nonmonetary values. Elise Boulding considers the economic implications of this for women when she speaks of their "social invisibility."

In institutional modern accounting systems, women are economically marginal in modernizing societies and second-class citizens in the already modernized. They are a significant part of the cash labor force in societies like the United States, but they earn only about 60 percent of what men earn and contribute about 25 percent of (cash) family income. In modernizing societies these numbers look still worse.

The problem lies in the conventional economic perspective, however. The supposed economic marginality of women is one of several historical myths. Others include the myth that economic development always improves women's lives, and the myth that women are basically irrational in their childbearing decisions, and have always been "nonstop breeding machines."

If we consider, as Boulding suggests, not the official labor force of conventional monetarized economics, but actual day-to-day productive labor, the picture is dramatically different. Women dominate the basic economy of food (production and preparation), child care, and health care. From this perspective, basic units for economic accounting should be familial households, and the basic criteria for assessing value should be the meeting of human needs rather than the producing of services and commodities.

Fortunately for us as a species, meeting these needs and providing these basic human services are intrinsically rewarding in a human community that is a network of households that help each other in sickness and in health. That women are the cornerstone of a community so defined should be obvious, and empirically it is indisputable. It is true even in modern societies, where institutional productive and service facilities are important, yet women still care for the children and the elderly and manage households— even if they participate full or part time in the monetarized labor force. And it is undeniable in societies where the nonmonetarized economy holds sway. Valid "development" means improving these basic human systems first and foremost. Improve them, and then evaluate economic change—not vice versa. This puts society's goals before its instrumentalities, ends before means, method in its place, and social welfare systems paramount.

For example, as food production has slipped from the day-to-day control of women, its essential human function has eroded and been replaced by abstract formulations in which one-sided Economic Man is the paramount actor. Margaret Mead put it this way:

> Food today is treated as a commodity in large-scale production or as a weapon in economic negotiations. Its use at the local level as the main means of freeing human beings from hunger is being neglected. Half a harvest may be lost in a country where food is considered solely as a cash crop and where the traditional role of women in allocating part of the crop for local production is ignored. (1976, p. 10)

As Mead sees it, only if we restore the feminine voice to decision making about food will we remember that food is about feeding people—not about political and financial scheming. The large-scale industrial farm easily becomes a pawn in political and financial scheming. The small farm in which the growers are close to the land has a built-in bias toward food for feeding.

The point is twofold. First, by focusing on the traditional economic enterprises of women, we rediscover the real meaning of goods and services and thus unmask the pretentions of the monetarized economy. This perceptual shift is essential if we are to develop an economic perspective appropriate to a sustainable society. Second, traditional economic enterprises of women provide the infrastructure for the technological development we need in a sustainable society. We need better technology to feed ourselves and others—not more powerful industrial models of agriculture driven by financial and political interests rather than by nutritional needs. And we need it in both modernized and unmodernized societies.

In modern societies, the monetarized economy must harmonize with and support the nonmonetarized economy without harming the social and physical environment. In nonmodern societies we must resist efforts to dismiss or undermine nonmonetarized enterprises, instead enhancing their efficiency and effectiveness in a manner consistent with the dignity of the people (usually women) who operate them. Viewing these goals in light of the traditional female economy makes it clear that the conventional concept of economic development (increases in industrial and monetary enterprises as measured in dollars) is bogus. Real development is more accurately based on increasing human quality where it counts most—in actual lives of people in family households. This directs our attention to enhancing sustainable patterns of access to resources, and doing so in ways that encourage individual dignity and social connectedness.

The focus on women in development is all the more important because of worldwide demographic trends. Conventional economic development, in the rhetoric of Cornucopians, means ever wider prosperity as "undevelopment" withers away. In all likelihood, however, this is a false image. More to the point is the image of developed societies becoming relatively smaller. As Elise Boulding points out, in 1950—even if we include only women in the wage labor force—the percentage of all women "workers" who resided in "developed" regions was 42 percent, while in "developing" regions it was 58 percent. By 1975, these figures had become 36 percent and 64 percent respectively, and the International Labor Organization predicted a 29 percent-71 percent split by the year 2000. These disparities are even greater if we consider percentage of total world population: 34 percent vs. 66 percent in 1950; 28 percent vs. 72 percent in 1975; 21 percent vs. 79 percent in 2000. The quality of life for the 79 percent in the year 2000 will depend on how well we meet and respect economic needs of women in those societies. Neither traditional patterns that cast women in the role of beast of burden, nor conventional modern ones that treat them as financially second class citizens, will suffice.

Implications for the Transition to a Sustainable Society

Some years ago in *New Yorker* magazine, a cartoon appeared that said a great deal about the masculine and feminine perspectives. In it, two middle-aged couples were comfortably seated around a coffee table. One woman was saying to the other words to this effect: "George handles all the big issues, like war and peace, inflation, agricultural policy, and national politics. I handle the little things, like raising the children, cooking, paying the bills, and cleaning the house." The cartoon caricatures a characteristic dichotomy of interest, and it illustrates the improper denigration of the tasks of home and the false elevation of more abstract "macro" issues.

The historical separation of male and female domains has obscured some fundamental similarities by introducing artificial differences that have come to represent supposed deficiencies of women. Ten thousand years ago animals were introduced into agriculture, and their use was defined as a properly masculine activity. Likewise in the nineteenth and twentieth centuries, operation of agricultural machinery was defined as a male activity. The result has been to economically isolate and downgrade females from food producers to food processors and consumers. This trend, besides producing a decline in real prospects for sustainable agricultural productivity, has reinforced the false differentiation of men and women regarding technological competence. Of course women can operate agricultural and other machinery, and use it to good advantage, as demonstrated during wartime in many countries.

For the transition to a sustainable society to proceed, we must avoid sexist preconceptions and bring the characteristically feminine perspective to dominance in discussions of social policy and practice. This is not, of course, simply a matter of bringing women into public life. It is more a matter of changing the character of public life. But greater involvement by women who are confident in the validity of the feminine perspective is certainly essential. As things stand (and have long stood), females are usually forced to choose between public leadership and femininity. This is psychically unfair to women and a tragic loss to the community, which needs public femininity more than ever. Carol Gilligan recognizes that masculine leaders routinely sacrifice human relations for "systematic social action," be it in the service of abstract ideology or for the glory of God. For all the glorification of Ghandi, for example, we should recall that he largely abandoned his interpersonal commitments—e.g., to wife and children.

At a futurist meeting, the moderator led a group through an exercise on "utopia." Each participant was asked to list a characteristic of the ideal world. The usual big ideas came forth—truth, justice, freedom. From one woman came the suggestion: "no diarrhea!" Keeping the world's children safe from diarrhea would go a long way toward creating a utopia; it causes the deaths of tens of millions of young children per year in impoverished communities and societies. Such a practical grasp of human realities is most likely to be found among those who change society's diapers. Thus one way to improve the world's chances for sustainability is to involve men more fully in the day-to-day realities of child care, particularly infant care. So long as men are shielded from the day-to-day realities of the household, we face the prospect of a critical misreading of what the world needs to make a go of it in the twenty-first century.

Ernest Callenbach's novel *Ecotopia* describes a female-led ecology party based on caring and nurturance that becomes the dominant political force in the Pacific Northwest. The progressive area eventually secedes from the United States and a sustainable society is established there. One hopes that such a feminine-based ideological triumph is not just wishful thinking.

In any case, a focus on women and the feminine perspective is appropriate as we seek a sustainable society. Nonmodernized societies must repeal policies that undermine household economies with low environmental impact. Instead, policy should enhance and assist these household economies. A good start, as Elise Boulding suggests, is to reform accounting schemes so that women do not appear economically invisible—a fifth world beyond the fourth world of the very poor.

> The fifth world exists invisibly, uncounted, and unassisted, on every continent, in the family farms and kitchen gardens, in the nurseries and kitchens of the planet. The fifth world also sends its fingers out to the most poorly paid work spaces of business, industry, and the service sector. Within the rural and nonindividualized parts of that fifth world, women give birth to babies, produce milk to feed them, grow food and process it, provide water and fuel, make other goods, build houses, make and repair roads, serve as the beasts of burden that walk the roads and sit in the markets to sell what their hands have made. (1980, p. 5)

Boulding suggests creating new census categories (e.g., "home production worker") that include work outside the cash economy to account for the full work load of women and men. Such an approach also bases accounting systems and social indicators on the meeting of basic needs. This would do much to adapt census data to social realities.

She also recommends using the household, not the individual, as the accounting unit, and focusing on activities of the total family unit. One reason for doing this is that some (many?) women see individual recognition as a threat to their nurturant function (not to mention that it may also precipitate male sanctions). And using the household as the unit of economic analysis is better in accord with underlying empirical realities of day-to-day life—where it is the meeting of basic needs that counts, not some abstract or narrowly monetarized accounting of financial worth. She is confident that such an accounting systeem would more accurately reveal a society's basic economy and would better highlight the real costs and benefits of alternative paths of development than do conventional economic indicators. For example, based on United Nations data, Boulding estimates that women provide 99 percent of health maintenance services; yet they are economically invisible and may be disrupted by processes of conventional economic development. In the United States, the efforts of women as homemakers and mothers have permitted society to go about the business of industrial growth, confident that all was well on the home front.

A feminine perspective would also create and maintain a social and legal climate in which family quality is paramount. This would mean relying on the feminine ethic of caring in family planning (insofar as it is compatible with the carrying capacity of the environment). By and large, women will choose to limit family size within acceptable bounds when given the motive (economic power) and the opportunity (reproductive control) to do so. Their incentives derive from their natural "investment" in their children and the motive to do right by the living. Yet conventional economic development has generated pressure on many rural women to produce more rather than fewer children. Schemes that emphasize industrialization have undermined rural communities and their agricultural base. Industrialization and urbanization draw men away from farm work and leave women to tend the land alone, without technological aids that modern engineering might provide if it focused on their activities. As a result, women alone on the farm must struggle to make agricultural ends meet without sustained male help. The result is often decreased production and a strong incentive to "breed her own help" (to use Boulding's words). Population rises and agricultural productivity declines.

This trend in the "developing" societies has its parallel in societies like the United States, where increasing numbers of economically isolated and pressured women are responsible for children whose fathers are absent. Many refer to this as the feminization of poverty. According to government data, families with one parent (a woman) have less than half the median income of all families. Women alone with children account for 75 percent of all people living in poverty—a trend that is accelerating. Of 9.4 million American families headed by single parents, 35 percent live in poverty, versus 11 percent of all families. This works out to a poverty rate for children of 20+ percent overall—the "infantilization" of poverty.

Interestingly, this "recent" increase in the number of households headed by women may not be the modern creation many assume it to be. Legal criteria aside (e.g., the married woman whose husband is not present on a continuous basis), there have always been, worldwide, single-parent households. According to Boulding's calculations, between 20 and 50 percent of all day-to-day heads of households are women. The current worldwide figure is about 38 percent. Modernization does place special burdens on these women and their children, however.

History tells us that modernization has had ironically negative effects on many women in many parts of the world. True, it has often liberated women from traditional constraints. But it has been less than completely beneficial, because women's traditional economic rights and contributions— most typically in partnership with men or other women in agriculture and trade—have been devalued and made invisible. What is more, the shift from subsistence agriculture to cash crops disrupts traditional male/female partnership arrangements. Women and children may lose out in the process.

Historical evidence in many parts of the world reinforces this view. The International Labor Organization notes that many areas of Africa only began to experience food shortages in the 1960s and 1970s—apparently because urbanization and cash cropping schemes ripped away the economic base of rural women (e.g., taking their time and/or land away from kitchen gardens to service cash crops or industrial work, the cash from which does not purchase equivalent food). In the United States, as aggregate wealth has increased and women have entered the cash labor force, conditions for children are deteriorating seriously. More and more of them are placed in poor quality day care arrangements, are left without adult supervision in threatening urban environments, are experiencing the stress of single-parent households, are hurried into premature adolescence. More and more are slipping below the official poverty line. Modernization is replete with such apparent paradoxes—in which creation of wealth and increased social and economic impoverishment go hand in hand.

The biggest danger of masculine thinking is that it abstracts child-bearing, transforming it into a quantitative rather than a qualitative concern. This comes to a head in issues of contraception and abortion. The evidence suggests that we should trust the moral judgment of women in using these technologies wisely. The irony of those of the masculine persuasion worrying about whether those of the feminine will act responsibly is sometimes too much to bear. Of much greater concern on the whole is the ability and willingness of the male to perform responsibly—in contraception, in transcending a bias in favor of male children, in rejecting use of social or physical force to coerce women in childbearing decisions, and in meeting responsibilities for child support.

The One Child Policy in China has run up against serious problems on this score. The masculine bias is strong, and leads to tremendous pressure against women to produce male offspring (which is perversely ironic, because the male chromosome determines the child's sex). Women who give birth to daughters may be punished for their "error" by husbands, fathers-in-law, and even misguided female relatives (most notably mothers-in-law). The spectre of female infanticide has risen its ugly head (again) in China. Visitors to some remote villages have reported sex ratios of 5:1 favoring male infants. An American demographer analyzing the 1982 Chinese census estimated that 200,000 females were "missing"—presumably due to some combination of infanticide and hiding female births.

In China in early 1984 I saw and heard evidence to confirm all this. I learned also that the government is supporting an active campaign to bolster the value of female children—through propaganda, through institutional reforms to provide greater actual economic equality for females, and through prosecution of those who brutalize mothers or murder infant daughters. This awful situation reinforces the belief that the path to a sustainable society lies in empowering the feminine element and the females most likely to exemplify it—whether in China, where female infanticide is the issue, or in India, where sexist rejection of female children is compounded by fatal bride burnings related to the bride's inability to raise a sufficiently large cash dowry. One journalist reports two such burnings per day in the city of Delhi alone.

The feminine perspective puts family at the center of a web of relationships. The woman is most often the "kinkeeper." The needs of children are generally most efficiently met by the women in their lives. In Latin America, for example, researchers have found that a monetary supplement is translated into more nutritional calories for children if the payment is made to mothers. If it is made to fathers, they are likely to define it as discretionary income for their personal use. Recent United Nations reports reveal that efforts to reduce malnutrition can achieve major successes simply if mothers are provided with simple paper-and-pencil technology for maintaining growth charts for their children. Once they recognize malnutrition in the data on these charts, they can (in 60 percent of the cases in the Philippines, for example) redirect family food resources to counteract the problem.

In the United States, middle-aged women are the primary caregivers for the frail elderly as they are for children everywhere. Around the world, the health of women and children is a leading indicator of how well basic human needs are being met. It tells us how well society is doing in taking care of the most important business there is—family business. The masculine orientation threatens this. Men take women's work for granted, and women as well. The net result is a decline in social welfare and the wealth of families.

The devaluation of women has many sources, of course. Elizabeth Dodson-Gray has explored the theological devaluation of women in patriarchal religions that place females in third place after God and man. The psychological devaluation exposed by Gilligan is intertwined with economic relations. Women without a sound economic base are vulnerable to exploitation, coercion, and devaluation from men. Modernization erodes the traditional economic resources of women. A few women become marvelously independent because they are liberated for entrance into financially powerful careers. But many are left vulnerable—either totally dependent upon male breadwinners or left to the struggle alone with a marginal income of their own. If women and children are safe and secure, we will be better able to make the transition to a sustainable society.

Lest this argument be misunderstood, let me close this discussion by reiterating that the fundamental issue is the ascendancy of the feminine perspective. That perspective is not inaccessible to males. And the issue before us is inextricably linked to efforts to encourage the feminine orientation among men. It is the aggressive, exploitive, abstracted nature of masculinity that threatens us (as embodied in Economic Man). Masculinity, threatened by the "soft" path, fearing intimacy, seeks self-respect in the "hard" way. The soft definition of self (with important implications for the sustainable society) rests upon interdependence rather than competitive individualism. It is significant then that males speak of "the role of separation as it defines and empowers the self" while females speak of "the ongoing process of attachment that creates and sustains the human community" (Gilligan, p. 156).

Just as females have a natural affinity for the feminine orientation, males will tend toward the masculine perspective unless conditions change—unless the models and rewards that guide action change. Unless the feminine perspective is in the driver's seat, we are heading down the wrong road. But conventional models of economic development are a powerful engine, and masculinity is at the controls. The message is clear. If we are to move toward a sustainable society, we must alter our ideologies and our institutions so they will hear and resonate with the feminine voice. We must not permit these institutions to change that voice or drown it out. With this in mind we turn next to the world of modern private enterprise, where Economic Man feels most at home and the feminine voice is muted, if not completely silenced.

CHAPTER

8.

October 1982:

Hawaii

Business as Unusual: Private For-Profit Enterprise and the Sustainable Society

WHILE TRAVELING IN HAWAII I visited the Polynesian Cultural Center on the island of Oahu. It was created by the Mormon church's Brigham Young University campus in Hawaii to preserve and exhibit the cultures of Polynesia (Tahiti, Hawaii, Samoa) and to provide jobs for Polynesian students who attend the University. It is thus a blend of philanthropy, enterprise, and anthropology (something at which the Mormons seem to excel). The center itself teeters on the brink of becoming a Disneyland of the Pacific. The physical environment looks real from afar, but plastic, plastered, and fake up close. It does have real people, however. There are the student guides, who range from enthusiastic to blasé, and often seem unsure whether to be proud of their "primitive native heritage" or embarrassed by it. And there are some human artifacts—real traditional Polynesians who demonstrate their crafts.

In the Samoan compound one such human artifact was making a bowl from a slab of wood. The old man sat without speaking, hacking away at the wood with an adz, hollowing out the center. Later he would scrape it to create a smooth surface. Examples of the final product were on display: beautiful, smooth, richly colored brown wooden bowls used both ceremonially and day-to-day. "How long does it take to make one?" asked a visitor of the young student guide. "About two weeks from start to finish," she replied. A man near me shook his head and muttered, "Boy, you could turn them out in about half an hour with a good lathe. How the hell can he make a living like that?"

I was to think of this incident many times when I was in China two years later. The current regime's modernization campaign seeks to empower workers technologically and economically. After three decades of dramatic ideological mood swings, China seems to have committed itself to harnessing the power of individual initiative to spur economic development. Under the new Responsibility System, agricultural workers are allowed to market freely the fruits of their labor beyond the production quota established by the state (which retains ownership of the land). Furthermore, small-scale private enterprises such as shops and services, even small factories, are permitted. The result has been a boom, with incomes rising dramatically for those well positioned to profit from an eager market. This includes vegetable-growing communes near cities. If ever one needed evidence of the economic power of private initiative and enterprise, it is to be found in China.

But profit is not the whole story. In many areas, it seems, the communist principle "serve the people" is increasingly taking a back seat to "it is glorious to get rich." How will the social environment prosper when left to its own devices, in competition with the profit motive? And what about the physical environment? The goal of maximizing private profit seems to encourage increasing reliance on chemical fertilizers that contaminate ground water, mechanized vehicles that consume fuel, and conversion to cash crops of land once used for basic food crops. Rice is *the* Chinese staple, and the government sets a fixed price for it, a price that makes it a less attractive crop than some others. As more and more people make use of the freedom offered by the new responsibility system they seem to be concluding: "I can make more money doing other things. Let someone else grow rice. Why should I do it?" How does a society harness the power of private enterprise and at the same time preserve the common future?

It's become a tenet of our society that "The business of America is business," and the world has listened. We've heard it over and over: "What's the bottom line?" Discussions of the sustainable society seem to run aground on the shoals of profitability. Will this measure pay off? Will it maintain or increase dividends? Will such a program meet the payroll? No analysis of the sustainable society can proceed without accounting for the role of corporate economic enterprise—the private "for-profit" sector.

At the start, it's worth noting that private enterprise can be a powerful and marvelously humanizing force. But in a sustainable society, that power must meet basic material needs and provide satisfying work in environmentally sane ways. The task is to channel enterprise into sustainable lines of activity. Already modernized societies must become self-reliant and nonexploitive. We must decrease domestic consumption so that short-term "surplus" capital and other resources can be exported to impoverished societies to stimulate a sustainable social and economic order compatible with their resources. This is a moral and political challenge of the first order.

Private enterprise has much to recommend it. Garrett Hardin's concept of the tragedy of the commons and the lifeboat ethic argue persuasively for the moral value of private initiative *when set within a sustainable social milieu*. This contrasts sharply with Adam Smith's concept of the "invisible hand," in which it is *assumed* that the net result of unstructured individual initiative will be good. A sustainable society will most likely rest upon what some have called "guild socialism," in which small-scale groups compete as private enterprises. This would work, set within an economic climate in which sustainability is the net result, in which true cost rather than price is the dominant force, and in which the community is committed to maintaining access to social welfare systems for all.

When private enterprise provides scope for individual creativity, when it provides a sense of identity, when it offers a focal point for family activity, and when it is directed by realistic assumptions about energy use and resource transformation, it is a flexible, efficient, and sensible economic force. It can serve families well by providing economic continuity across generations, creating incentives to build lasting economic resources, and offering cooperative work for family members. Cottage industries and small-scale retail operations sometimes do this. Private enterprise can do all these things—and do them better than government-owned enterprises—*if* the ground rules protect the Earth and the future from unfair competition. In the proper context, private enterprise serves public goals. In the absence of an appropriate context, however, private enterprise is a sinister threat to social welfare and the sustainable society.

How do we assess the role of private enterprise as we currently experience it, when the distinction between "private" and "public" blurs? When some "private" enterprises are bigger and more powerful than some "public" ones? When private enterprises often seem to have all the prerogatives of persons without the moral obligations of citizenship? When private enterprise seems hell bent on consuming our environmental birthright for short-term profit? Where does private enterprise stand in the global moral order? How we are to trust the invisible hand, when a record 1,510 new grocery products were introduced to the marketplace in the United States in 1982 alone—including such basic human need-meeters as liqueur-flavored ice cream, kosher Kielbase, and "Beverly Hills Kitty Litter" made of $10,000 in shredded play money? Where is the redeeming social value in all this, when children in the United States and around the world are malnourished and don't have access to fully adequate sanitation? If the business of America is business, then whose business is this? It's an old question, but it wears well.

As many people see it, the "genius" of private enterprise is its ability to give people what they want. Black markets exist, of course, where official markets are not free to serve this function. Does this genius become an evil genius when it commands massive resources and private enterprise grows so large as to operate on a public scale? Can we accentuate the capacity of private enterprise to serve the sustainable society while finding ways to prevent it from devouring the social and physical environments? And can there be global justice if private enterprise is a dominating force in the world?

And while we're asking questions, is government-run business any better? Environmental degradation in the Soviet Union and China shows us that government ownership is no guarantee. Union Carbide produced the Bhopal disaster in India, but the Soviet collective economy produced Chernyobol. Government industries often have no external authority to monitor their performance. And they are often responsible for the most environmentally disruptive enterprises—e.g., electric power and mining. Both public and private enterprises may be geared to short-term payoffs at the expense of long-term sustainability. If we add to this the fact that imperious public works projects pursued in the name of modernization are themselves often very environmentally disruptive, we can see that the issue goes beyond simply public versus private ownership of the means of "production" (i.e., transformation).

The social justice of government-run business is not assured—at least not when it serves masters other than the common good and a sustainable future. Social injustice in state-run enterprises in profit-oriented societies like Brazil testifies to that. And, as we face the world problematique, we must recognize that nationalism may compromise the motivation and ability of government-run business to behave responsibly toward the world's social and physical environments.

In the interest of our moral health, we cannot accept the idea that rich nations, to sustain their affluence, must expect the rest of the world to live in abject poverty. Regional (and individual) differences in material affluence are probably inevitable, and they can be tolerated—provided each society has the material resources to meet basic human needs. Some can have fuel-efficient cars if all can have bicycles and buses. Some can have exercise clubs if all have adequate maternal/infant health care. Unless we see a radical transformation in the world of proportions never before accomplished, this sort of diversity within the context of universal adequacy is as much as we can hope for. Without significant changes, of course, even this modest hope will prove a pipe dream.

For our purposes then, the task is to work out an attitude toward private enterprise that is consistent with transition to a sustainable society. Accomplishing this will provide a sound foundation for social welfare systems and will promise to harness on behalf of families the awesome force of private initiative. It will, however, require that we banish Adam Smith's invisible guiding hand to the land of fairy tales, where it rightly belongs.

Advancing toward sustainability in modern societies depends on three issues: short-term return on capital investment, long-term return on capital investment, and impact on resources. Understanding these three concerns can go a long way toward clarifying the opportunities and limits of the private, for-profit sector of the economy.

Short-Term Return on Capital Investment

Certainly the most compelling issue is short-term return on capital investment. The drive to accumulate wealth is the critical dynamic. Growth is the norm. In conventional capitalist analysis, the alternatives are growth or decay. Like the shark that must always keep swimming to maintain a flow of oxygen-bearing water through its gills, the capitalist must always be using current capital to generate more. To stop is to drown. In conventional analyses, steady-state capitalism is a contradiction in terms— or at least a term that applies only to those relatively brief periods of stability between growth spurts and periods of decay.

This is why we must consider the compatibility of private for-profit enterprise with the needs of the sustainable society. Capitalism has an intrinsic, inherent drive that must be tamed and transformed, that must be channeled into sustainable paths lest it be world-destroying. By definition, an enterprise that does not succeed in growing and accumulating capital fails. It sounds simple, but it's actually quite complex, and hinges on the questions, "What is a good return on investment? And how do you calculate that return?" In the modern economy, the accounting for profit has become quite arcane, because monetarization has inextricably linked capital to money. In simple terms, to make a profit on one's capital, one must exceed the return one could obtain by lending its cash value to another enterprise. Thus private enterprise tends to generate an economic climate in which shrewd monetary investment displaces productive activity in a kind of economic musical chairs.

Robert Reich (1981) calls this "paper entrepreneurialism," and he says it is the natural outgrowth of monetarization. The system encourages clever manipulation of rules and numbers that only theoretically represent real assets and products. Paper entrepreneurialism is a creation of the highly automated accounting systems and esoteric tax structures that have evolved in modernized societies. It is socially destabilizing (encouraging such things as closing a financially marginal factory as a "tax write-off") and undermines families and communities. It is pseudo–private enterprise at its worst, but it is successful in the short run, from the perspective of the winner, because it meets the fundamental goal of accumulating money.

Actually producing something is a last resort when it is no longer possible to profit from moving capital around. In theory, this might seem helpful in the transition to a sustainable society, because money itself doesn't degrade resources. In practice, however, it doesn't help. The ever greedier money eventually comes to rest (if only briefly) in enterprises that physically *do* something, and then the pressure is on them to do something quickly that will feed the voracious interest habit of that investment. What is more, families and communities are disrupted and stressed at each step along the way.

The net effect is to encourage and reward enterprises that produce high short-term profits. The tax structure, fiscal regulation, and monetary policy all tend to reinforce this in one way or another. Only when managers have bound up their personal identity with their enterprise is there a dimension beyond short-run profit. If a business is someone's life and livelihood in the broadest sense—or it has some vivid psychic and historical link to a particular community—it has more than that single dimension. On the other hand, if one has no personal stake beyond a monetary investment, as is the case for many stockholders, maximizing short-term profit may be the be-all and end-all.

Fortunately, some of the measures needed to achieve a sustainable society are consistent with short-term profit. Either they permit an enterprise to move from unprofitability to profitability (e.g., by reducing costs or increasing sales), or they permit an already profitable enterprise to become more so. For example, no-till farming might permit a farmer to cut planting costs and thus increase profit, while at the same time reducing soil erosion to a sustainable level. Or a successful manufacturing firm might find a market for the waste resulting from its operations, and thereby add additional income without significantly increasing costs. Or a new enterprise might arise to profit from a new market created by a new technology.

Short-term profitability is a continuum. At one end stand the activities needed for a sustainable society that have a direct quick payoff in conventional terms. These activities require only technological development and transmission of information. At the other end are activities that don't add to short-term profitability for existing enterprises—activities that may even exact direct costs by reducing short-term return on invested capital. Requiring investment in waste treatment and pricing nonrenewable resources higher than renewable resources exemplify this.

One way to deal with this negative end of the continuum is what Garrett Hardin refers to as "mutual coercion mutually agreed upon"— regulation, voluntary or governmentally induced. Either approach can cancel out the competitive disadvantage of operating sustainably by imposing the same "penalty" on all competing parties. Emission controls on smokestacks are an example. If everyone must add to their costs equally, then the cause of the sustainable society advances without a *relative* decline in anyone's short-term return on investment. Of course, rarely if ever does such an effort really exact equal cost from all participants. Cheating from within the group and competition from unregulated outsiders can and often does upset the apple cart. Such regulation is only one compensation at this end of the continuum, however. Another is long-term profitability.

Long-Term Return on Investment

A private for-profit enterprise can have more than a short-term profit orientation. It can aspire to long-term success and see that goal as a mediator of short-term interests. At the simplest level, managers must plow back some returns to maintain the physical plant in the long run. They perceive a similar need with respect to the social plant—employee benefits, staff development, and community relations.

Looking more broadly still, they may see that they can enhance their future profitability by investing in resource-conserving strategies. For example, they may shift from petroleum-based to solar energy because they foresee a decline in profits in a petroleum-based system (although in the short term it costs less than the shift to solar). If they enter long-term operation into their day-to-day calculations, they may perceive elements of self-interest rather than altruism in efforts to advance the transition to a sustainable society. For some enterprises the issue is long-term profit because they can absorb short-run reverses. Fortunately, many such situations exist, and they complement the short-run profitability of other sustainable enterprises. Energy companies are one example. Some observers conclude that the statelike multinational corporations will lead the transition to a sustainable society for just such reasons. They are so enormous that they recognize the need for addressing the big picture in corporate planning. But even here long-range planning may not extend far enough into the future to take into account today's children. And that is where the crunch comes.

Impact on Resources

Conventional economics is tragically immaterial because it operates as if the monetarized economy exists apart from the resources of the material world. By and large, private for-profit enterprises do not consider their impact on resources, unless short- and long-term returns on investment dictate such a concern. Distinctions between organic and inorganic, between renewable and nonrenewable, have no economic significance. The transition to a sustainable society hinges on just these distinctions, however. We must identify existing enterprises that can use renewable and organic resources and still maintain short-term and long-term profitability. Next we must adopt voluntary or coerced efforts to control processes through which monetary prices are assigned to renewable and organic versus nonrenewable and inorganic resources, These measures include government regulation, modifying the economic behavior of consumers, and invoking the altruism and humanism of managers and investors—most of whom have children and perhaps grandchildren. Each path, all paths are important for the successful transition to a sustainable society.

The activities of private for-profit enterprises exist along three axes: short-term profitability, long-term profitability, and impact on resources. Of course, the location of activities along these axes is not fixed. Their positions may change through the action of technological innovation, depletion or discovery of nonrenewable resources, cultural shifts, and political directives that affect costs, prices, supply, and demand.

How far we can expect the private for-profit sector to go of its own accord down the road to a sustainable society? How much needs to be done in restructuring the economic and political environment to insist upon such progress?

Electric utilities. Only fifteen years ago, private for-profit electric utilities appeared to be enormous roadblocks on the path toward sustainability. According to analyses conducted by Amory and Hunter Lovins, however, they have begun to appear as potential leaders on this path, driven by demands of long-term profitability as well as pressures of short-term costs and prices. Writing before the temporary deflation of oil prices in the mid-1980s, they note:

> Price is driving the transition. Conventional oil products now retail at about forty to fifty dollars per barrel. Energy saved by more efficient use costs about zero to twenty dollars per barrel; well-designed renewable sources can now deliver a "barrel" for about five to thirty dollars. The alternatives—such as synthetic fuels at over seventy dollars per retail barrel, and electricity from new coal or nuclear power plants at about twice that price—are even less competitive than imported oil. Efficiency and renewables are simply winning the market's sweepstakes for the best buys—the cheapest ways to do each desired task. (Lovins and Lovins, 1982, p. 154)

This change is in the works, they argue, but is proceeding too slowly. The economic drain of current energy "production" and use on the United States is enormous—some 90 billion dollars per year exported to purchase imported oil in the early 1980s, before the temporary price decrease. Current patterns have paralyzed many economies, particularly those in the Third World not "producing" oil. Alternatives to the current threatening pattern are noteworthy for their ecological sensibility, their profitability, and their complementarity with family concerns. They involve conservation and alternative consumption measures implemented at the family, neighborhood, and community levels in concert with the profit-driven activities of the electric utilities themselves.

Although much is already being accomplished, several factors are impeding progress. People lack information about techniques and materials. Short-term incentives at the consumer level often are not organized to motivate behavior that would speed the transition. For example, if the landlord pays for heat, the tenant has no short-term incentive to conserve. Local policies often stand in the way of progress; zoning policies that inhibit residential use of "waste" heat from commercial enterprises impede energy efficiency. And government policies are biased against renewable resources: subsidies favor nonrenewable resources by a factor of ten to one. Capital investment as currently structured favors concentrated rather than decentralized use of resources; the latter is required for advanced conservation measures.

Amory and Hunter Lovins describe a series of practical steps to dislodge these roadblocks and speed the United States down the road to energy sustainability. The key is to reverse the investment strategy of utilities—to move them away from new power generation and toward efficiency and conservation, *and* away from financial ruin and toward profitability. The $25 billion per year spent on new facilities for power generation is an enormous step in the wrong direction. Such power stations are so capital intensive that each drains off enough needed resources to result in a net *decrease* of about four thousand jobs for the community, and impoverishes other enterprises that need capital and that promise more for the future.

The Lovins' plan is for electric utilities to lend money to increase conservation and efficiency *and thereby profit on existing generation capacity* rather than taking a loss in a climate of energy waste. The social and physical benefits of this alternative course dovetail so neatly with the financial benefits that it may be the single most dramatic example of private enterprise in a position to lead the transition to a sustainable society. But it is not guaranteed (what is?). It will depend on the proper regulatory climate to nurture, even demand, the needed shift in investment strategy, *and* on day-to-day support of consumers who must implement the conservation measures. If all the actors play their parts, the United States could move toward an electrical system that met all three criteria of sustainability. It could be based on renewable resources, could be centered in the family and community, and could be more just in relation to the rest of the world by becoming self-reliant rather than draining resources beyond its national boundaries. All this would be a major step in the right direction.

The Lovins' message may be getting through to public and private decision makers. A 1982 report indicated that the New Jersey Board of Public Utilities for the Public Service Electric and Gas Company had approved a plan to substitute conservation for new electric production and put it this way:

> Conservation is the safest, most reliable and least expensive source of energy New Jersey has. It is a "North Slope," an "uninterrupted pipeline" of energy supply in our own state, which this board intends to fully explore and develop.

It's a step in the right direction, albeit only one.

Industrial product life. "Product life" refers to the period during which products and goods are used. In Orio Giarini's analysis it is their utilization value, and it governs the speed with which they must be replaced. Thus, for example, a car built and serviced to last 20 years stands in a very different relationship to the sustainable society than does a car that lasts only 5 years. This concept has been elaborated and explored by Walter Stahel (1982).

In Stahel's view (and its validity seems clear), the currently dominant industrial model is the "fast-replacement system" in which the whole point is to produce goods that are cheap and nonreparable. Economic well-being thus depends on turnover. Profit becomes a kind of sales commission based on volume in which resource use is only evident in the cash price required to extract and transform raw materials into marketable objects. The results of this system have indeed threatened both the quality of human experience and society's prospects for sustainability. As Stahel sees it, instead of increasing real wealth we are devoting an ever larger proportion of our national and personal incomes to replacing products. Fashion and fast depreciation drive this system. It is the evil genius of private enterprise at its most diabolical.

Depreciation is an enemy of the sustainable society. That it is encouraged by current government tax incentives makes the government part of the problem rather than a leader in finding a solution. As for private for-profit enterprise, Stahel suggests that it is not ready to make the shift directly to a slow-replacement system of long-life products. Stahel sees a middle, transitional course: "product-life extension."

This approach encourages private for-profit enterprise to take up what have been called the "four Rs of appropriate technology": reuse, repair, reconditioning, and recycling. These are arranged hierarchically: in general, repair only when reuse is impossible; repair until reconditioning becomes necessary; and recycle after reconditioning. Such a strategy can be ecologically sound, in both the physical and social senses. Furthermore, it can be profitable in both the short and long runs. Specifically, it

- is available to small-scale enterprises and builds upon interpersonal initiative;
- results in a reconditioned product whose cost is considerably below the cash price of a new product (even under the ecologically unsound costing criteria of current industrial societies);
- leaves room to technologically upgrade existing products as part of the reconditioning process;
- shifts activity from capital-intensive, extractive, and industrially produc-tive enterprises to small-scale, labor-intensive, decentralized enterprises.

The data concerning product-life extension argue persuasively for its soundness. Stahel found that about 75 percent of all energy consumption in industrial enterprises is used to extract or produce materials like steel and cement. The transformation of materials into finished goods consumes only about 25 percent. The longer we keep the materials (and the finished goods) "in play," the more compatible are the enterprises that produce them with a sustainable society. Keeping the materials and goods in play is labor intensive, and that is good for families; because families need jobs to function and need to sustain informal social welfare systems while limiting demands upon formal social welfare systems.

Stahel offers several illustrative examples including the following:

- Rebuilding tractor engines and other parts permits conservation and profitable sales that last 80 percent as long as new tractors at half the price.
- Modernizing a residential building costs about 40 percent of building a new one (in the narrowest sense, not including the cost of a new location).
- Modernizing DC-8 jets with new engines produces an up-to-date aircraft at less than half the cost of a new plane.
- Societies at different stages of modernization can let products work their way "down" through the world's systems with a good performance-to-function ratio at each step (such as has been the case with DC-3 aircraft).

Perhaps the most telling example of the contrast between short-life and long-life products is captured in the contrast between what has come to be called the modern "world car" and Henry Ford's "everyman's car" (the Model T). The former is designed for quick and cheap manufacture, and relies upon nonreparable parts (including electronic "black boxes"). The Model T's relatively simple components were reparable by any local blacksmith. Fewer and fewer owners (and even mechanics) feel competent to repair the newest generation of cars. Many among us recall maintaining and repairing our own VW's in the 1960s, but we find the complexity of a 1981 VW daunting. A VW service manager once confided exactly the same sense of impotence. This makes neither economic nor psychological sense. People must feel empowered if the sustainable society is to work psychically. We need to be able to rely upon locals for service.

All in all, product-life extension is key in the transition to a sustainable society. It is the strategy of choice on grounds of short- and long-term profit and the best use of resources. It offers the prospect of meaningful, often family-based work because it is labor intensive and constructive in a way that many other forms of enterprise are not. And it promises to meet the basic need for work of the populations in most societies. Thus, it promises to help stabilize and justify both the physical and social ecologies. Many roadblocks now prevent implementation of this course—for example, tax disincentives and psychocultural biases that favor rapid depreciation and turnover. But once we recognize these issues, we can deal with them. Specifically, we need to change taxation policies that provide depreciation allowances and thus reward new production. We need to reverse the biases that currrently discourage reusability, manual labor, and self-reliance and encourage fashion, disposability, and conspicuous consumption.

Internalizing the externalities. Certainly one key in the transition to sustainability is the matter of "internalizing the externalities." Externalities are factors outside the priced costs of production and thus outside the enterprise's accounting. If private for-profit enterprises are to have a role in this transition, we must bring factors such as pollution, depletion, and impact on the social environment into the costs of doing business. Done fairly and homogeneously, this should *aid* in the profitability of competent enterprises. Otherwise, of course, it may threaten the profitability of enterprises receiving discriminatory treatment. If it is not done at all, the physical and social environments are at the mercy of altruism for prevention, of charity and government programs for rehabilitation. The tragedy of the commons is the probable result.

Constitutional lawyer Arthur Miller (1982) has argued for a change in the constitutional status of corporations as one way to compel responsible conduct by private for-profit enterprises. Their current ambiguous status, he argues, gives them too many privileges and not enough responsibilities. A change in constitutional status would provide a firm basis for requiring of corporations responsible conduct in relation to the environment. His analysis dovetails with others that stress the role of social responsibility in private for-profit enterprises as a force leading to innovating, developing, and implementing technological tactics for transition to sustainability. Social engineering, as the key to creating and implementing needed breakthroughs in physical engineering, makes sense.

At the core of social engineering is what we may call "corporate self-reliance," in which the private sector assumes full responsibility for social and environmental consequences of its actions in host communities. An economically sound production system should sustain and nurture host communities as much as it sustains physical raw materials. Corporate self-reliance proposes that we conceptualize, develop, maintain, and evaluate private enterprises in terms of their *total* costs and benefits to the planet's ecosystems—social as well as physical. This is a requirement to be met by enterprises as citizens, if we accept Arthur Miller's idea of explicitly recognizing the corporation as a special kind of citizen.

In the social sphere, corporate self-reliance by the private sector reconciles the roles of worker, family member, and citizen, developing the personnel needed for a sustainable society. These people will take an attitude of full responsibility toward the environment—an attitude that is the essence of adulthood. Socialization to adulthood means acquiring skills and attitudes necessary to assume such full responsibility in the workplace, in the home, and in the community. When the primary social roles of worker, family member, and citizen are out of kilter, the efficiency and productivity of all three settings (work, home, community) declines. When they are in harmony, all three function better in all dimensions in the long run.

A focus on the social context of private for-profit enterprise is necessary and appropriate. Those who work on global models (such as *The Limits to Growth*) have reached empirical and theoretical consensus on the proposition that the major variables in worldwide scenarios are sociopolitical rather than technological. Certainly technology has an important role in easing the necessary transition. For example, the work of the Intermediate Technology Group (stimulated by E. F. Schumacher) and the New Alchemy Institute can prove invaluable in implementing sustainability. But technology is not the critical issue. Political will and social organization are required if its wonderful tools are to be implemented. The Club of Rome has come to focus increasingly on sociocultural aspects of the world problematique for this very reason. The issue is, as always, human quality (Peccei, 1979).

The primacy of social rather than technological issues is consistent with corporate self-reliance and its implications for the community. Technological and social challenges differ in the degree to which they lend themselves to centralized, consolidated solutions. Technological innovations lend themselves to single-site development, testing, and dissemination (the success of various agricultural research laboratories is testimony to this). Technological innovations must be sufficiently consistent with local conditions to permit their use, of course. However, they can be centrally developed without necessarily violating basic human needs and values, without sacrificing essential human quality.

The same cannot be said of social innovations required for the transition to a society that combines sustainability and human quality. Here centralized development, testing, and implementation are not nearly enough. Social innovation is fundamentally much more closely tied to decentralized local research and development. Broad ideas and even society-wide "rules of the game" may come from central social laboratories. But full development of these ideas into patterns of behavior and belief must occur in response to needs, traditions, and ecological realities at the community level. The agricultural and retail "free market" as regulator of a society's economic life is a prime example. As a source of social creativity, the "free" and community-based society stands in refreshing contrast to the spiritually stultifying climate of highly centralized societies such as the Soviet Union. The complexity of the task—an ecologically sane approach to society— demands flexibility. This is fundamental for a socioeconomically sustainable society that is spiritually sustainable as well.

Cultural diversity is as important as biological diversity in enhancing evolutionary resilience and human progress. Freedom is the cornerstone of this crucial social edifice. Without it, negative influences inherent in the unsustainable society will prevail. A sustainable society is a free society; an unsustainable society must be an exploitive master enslaved to its exponential appetite ("Slaveship Earth"). And in such a society, private enterprise tends to be likewise exploitive.

Corporate self-reliance by the private sector stands in contrast to contemporary thinking that casts only government ("the welfare state") in this leadership role and asks of business only that it do no demonstrable social harm. The concept of corporate self-reliance is a major departure from the modern laissez-faire approach that has viewed both corporate responsibility and labor/management relations primarily in narrow monetary terms. In broadening corporate responsibility and labor/management relations to make them more consistent with the demands of a sustainable society, we must negotiate the fine line between corporate paternalism and corporate social neglect. Perhaps the image of corporate "maternalism" is apt, recalling our discussion of the feminine voice in Chapter 7. A nurturant and reconciling force is what we need, not a harsh divisive one.

Paternalism connotes authoritarian and judgmental regulation as the price one pays for concern and regard. Maternalism, on the other hand, connotes supportive discipline, meeting needs because they exist, and generally engendering allegiance and responsiveness through nurturing. Corporate self-reliance is the feminine voice in business, derived from the characteristically feminine approach to moral development and conflict resolution. The following analyses seek to show that it is ultimately in the best interest of the individual, the family, the community, *and* private enterprise.

Strategies for Corporate Self-Reliance[1]

Example 1: From Strike Town to International Model

One prerequisite of corporate self-reliance is the transformation of the traditionally adversarial relationship between labor and management into one of cooperation and mutual trust. This is part of what we need to establish guild socialism. An enterprise works best when participants share the same goals, seek solutions to the same problems, and agree to weather hard times together. But how do we attain such a state, given the traditional lack of trust between labor and management and their historically validated differences of class interest?

One idea is the labor/management committee, a new form of organization that has emerged in diverse communities in the United States over the last two decades. Their specific purposes differ, but in general their underlying goals are to improve the labor climate by enhancing productivity, reducing the likelihood of strikes, and maintaining the stability of the local work force. In this they resemble Japanese planning committees and the wage/price boards envisioned by Walt Rostow.

Jamestown, New York, is the site of one of the best known labor/management committees (JALMC). The JALMC was established in 1972 by corporate management, union leaders, and local government as an antidote to the gradual disintegration of the community's labor climate. At that time, the economic life of the area was in disarray. In the 1960s, 38 strikes occurred in Jamestown (population 40,000), costing 1,401 strike days; many businesses were relocating or ceasing operations.

The committee was made up of local government officials and representatives of labor and management from local factories. Working with consultants, the JALMC gradually transformed the community of Jamestown. They set up committees within companies to improve the quality of work life. They were problem oriented, composed of managers and workers who pooled their expertise to solve complex issues. The success of the JALMC is a matter of public record. Only 26 strikes occurred in the 1970s for a total of 490 strike days. New industry has come to the area, creating jobs and opportunities. Older companies once in danger of going under have streamlined operations and enhanced productivity, often with the contribution of workers' technical expertise.

Labor/management committees are just one strategy toward developing self-reliance at the corporate, community, and individual levels. They are not radical, in that the relative status of labor and management remains the same. The new elements, however, are cooperation, trust, and active participation of all involved. These themes weave their way through three other strategies for self-reliance.

Example 2: What's Small Potatoes to Sperry Rand
Is Bread and Butter to Herkimer, New York

When a plant is shut down permanently, it is too late for a labor/management committee. The issue is not the quality of work life, but loss of jobs and loss of revenue for the local community. Plant shutdowns have increased in the United States in the past decade. A plant is not always closed because it is not profitable, however. Frequently, it is owned by a large conglomerate with headquarters far away. As the conglomerate grows, it may liquidate small plants that make modest profits, writing them off as tax losses. Such an event is a business decision to the corporation, but it may signal economic disaster to employees and the local community, particularly in the case of towns and rural areas highly dependent upon the plant. And the community's economic well-being is the principal factor determining the character of its social environment.

One constructive response to the threat of plant shutdown is worker ownership. A case in point is the Library Bureau, a furniture factory in Herkimer, New York, that once was a subsidiary of Sperry Rand. In 1976 Sperry Rand decided to close the plant. Although it was making a considerable profit, it was less than the 22 percent standard of the conglomerate. In a dramatic example of community mobilization, the work force and the local community combined resources to buy the plant from Sperry Rand. Six months after announcement of the shutdown, ownership of the Library Bureau passed to employees and members of the community. As a result, the community has survived. More than that, it has triumphed and become more self-reliant, and has avoided a crisis in mental as well as economic health.

What is the role of the private for-profit sector in such community efforts? As the holder of title to such an enterprise, it is to facilitate, not oppose, community/employee purchase. As a member of the community, it is to join the effort to maintain community integrity. Of course, it would be naive to assume that employee ownership is always in the best interests of the workers, as Don Goldstein points out in a 1983 article in *The Nation*. In his analysis of employee ownership of the Weirton, West Virginia, steel plant, Goldstein shows that when remote and profit-hungry conglomerates are involved, the costs to workers may be so high they outweigh the benefits. As always, nothing is simple, and the possibility of being ripped off always exists.

Example 3: Getting Business in the Family Way

A third strategy for corporate self-reliance requires recognition by the private sector that corporate policies and practices have immediate and enduring consequences for the family and community lives of employees. This strategy involves institution by the company of specific "employer-based family supports"—a long-term investment in workers and the host community.

The interrelatedness of work, family, and community is the subject of a growing body of research. Work can provide support for families that goes beyond economic support. Innovative practices and policies by the private sector can enhance the social and psychological functioning of employees and their families.

Existing employer-based family supports fall into three categories. *Innovative scheduling* offers options such as flexible hours ("flex-time"), job sharing, and increased availability of part-time employment. *Corporate benefits* include maternity and paternity leave, flexible or "cafeteria" benefit packages, and programs aimed at reducing drug and alcohol abuse by employees. *Sensitivity to the needs of working parents* means special assistance for two-career families, work site child care, or other forms of family support.

Family and community can cause productivity problems for companies. In her study of a manufacturing plant, Ann Crouter (1980) found that mothers of children under six were the employees most likely to describe "negative spillover" from their family to their work lives. They poignantly described being absent from work to care for a sick child, being preoccupied at work worrying about unsatisfactory child care, turning down a transfer because hours were not flexible, and so forth. Home-based child care is probably most consistent with the needs of a sustainable society. It is more consistent, with greater emphasis on the family as an economically productive enterprise. However—at least during transition to sustainability—most parents will still require formal child care services.

High-quality company-sponsored child care would probably relieve many parents of considerable pressure and thus enable them to be more efficient and committed employees. In such a case no one loses. The company gains an effective, loyal employee. The parent receives social and economic support for child-rearing responsibilities. And the child receives quality care and supervision, a service many now go without. Companies that have implemented some form of child care (including Stride-Rite Shoes and Corning Glass) are enthusiastic about it. In some cases logistical problems have undermined success, however.

Example 4: Making the Whole Greater Than the Sum of Its Parts

For these three strategies to succeed, a fourth is probably necessary: worker participation in day-to-day decision making and problem solving. In the United States, such "participative" work usually involves semiautonomous teams that work together to perform a fairly large, complex task from beginning to end. Often individuals are rewarded for the number of skills they acquire, the goal being that all team members eventually will be able to perform all tasks involved in the job.

Where Ann Crouter conducted her research, teams managed their own inventory, monitored safety and quality control, handled performance problems, and hired new members. They were responsible for troubleshooting productivity problems, scheduling, meeting deadlines, and many other activities. This stands in dramatic contrast to traditional jobs with their stultifying routine, hierarchical supervision, and dearth of challenge.

A company that introduces participative work is usually motivated by the desire to enhance productivity or decrease alienation of workers. There are positive benefits for the individual as well. Studies have shown that self-direction at work actually can make an individual's intellectual functioning more flexible, a characteristic crucial in the transition to a sustainable society. Employees gain skills that are also useful off the job, including communication, problem solving, public speaking, listening, and decision making. It is not surprising that people in participative jobs are more satisfied than their peers in traditional jobs. They are more effective with others and better able to function autonomously in a complex environment. Such qualities make individuals more receptive to the life styles necessary for global sustainability and to what Duane Elgin (1977) calls "voluntary simplicity"—a conscious decision to live in a sustainable manner.

Implications of self-reliance by the work group or team are clear. By taking on tasks such as inventory or quality control once performed by specialists, the group gradually becomes a self-reliant collective, able to cope when a team member is absent, to plan ahead, and to perfect the work process.

The company benefits from such self-reliance. It gains a skilled, stable work force with high morale and improved productivity. As internal competence increases, the organization has less need for outside experts and becomes collectively more self-reliant. If the organization is better able to compete in the market, its chances for survival increase.

Finally, the community benefits from participative work and its effects. It is stabilized if local employers are able to reduce or eliminate layoffs and cutbacks. Job security strengthens families and breadwinners are able to generalize their new skills to their family lives. Many employees in the plant Crouter studied said participative work had helped them learn to listen to their children better, organize family life more democratically, and be more open with their spouses. This has important implications not only for child development but for marital quality and stability. Finally, the community benefits when employees extend their participation in volunteer community organizations. Community participation is all the more important today when high rates of employment of females have decreased commitment to the volunteer sector, an area traditionally dominated by women.

Without corporate self-reliance, labor/management committees, worker ownership, and employer-based family supports are unlikely to succeed. Such innovations cannot simply be imposed from above upon a work force or community. For example, employees often do not use work-site child care if they are not involved in planning it. The Head Start program is most successful when parents actively participate as partners with the teachers. Clearly, corporations have much to gain from restructuring the work process so that workers have a voice in decision making and problem solving.

Many of the strategies outlined here are relevant to all societies, but in some ways they seem most relevant to already modernized societies. When we turn to the rest of the world, there are additional special roles for private for-profit enterprise. These include agribusiness cooperatives, labor-intensive small businesses, and private investment for development.

Agribusiness cooperatives. In most of the Third World, the private for-profit enterprises most important for the transition to a sustainable society are agricultural. Agriculture is necessary to reduce food shortages and pressures for urbanization. Around the world, small farms in which the farmer has a personal profit motive are the most efficient food producers. The startling increase of production and real personal income among Chinese peasants in the wake of the new Responsibility System testifies eloquently to this. Small farms (1 to 5 acres) are the strategy of choice, particularly if they receive technical assistance, capital, and other support from corporate agribusiness. The "corporate core" provides access to technology while the small landholder provides the motivational anchor. This model can be adapted to many different settings, so long as the goals are related closely to meeting basic needs. David Hopcroft (1977), for example, has contrasted the commercial and economic wisdom of ranching animals indigenous to the African plains to the ecological and commercial folly of foreign cattle. Of the highest priority in Third World countries is the creation and maintenance of agricultural enterprises with high long-term profitability and low environmental costs. A partnership between small landholders and agribusiness can achieve those goals (and also provide an agrarian social order conducive to strong families).

*Small business.*The potential for job creation by small businesses even in a modern society has come under scrutiny in recent years. The Brookings Institution reported that businesses with fewer than 100 employees accounted for 51 percent of new jobs created in the United States between 1976 and 1980. A 1980 Massachusetts Institute of Technology study reported a 70-percent figure for the 1969–1976 period. Small businesses are farther removed from manufacturing and mining domains where economic slowdown translates most directly and quickly into unemployment.

Small businesses that make relatively small demands on capital are the natural choice for developing societies, where low-capital, labor-intensive enterprises are essential. Such enterprises can exist without the dangers of centralized direction, respond to local conditions, and provide a good labor-to-capital ratio to help stabilize the social scene. Like small farmers, small businesses can profit from the technical assistance and capital reserves of larger corporate entities. They are amenable to low-energy, low-capital appropriate technology, as has been determined by E. G. Schumacher and his colleagues. Efforts to stimulate such enterprises (e.g., by the Women's World Bank) are the core of the sustainable approach to economic development.

Private investment for development. As von Oppen (1982) has argued, developing societies face several investment problems. For one thing, they need capital for projects that are ineligible for government aid and unable to attract conventional private investment because they do not promise short-term payoffs. Von Oppen proposes private investment as a solution.

Such funds would permit individuals from industrialized societies to aid in promoting Third World development, without significant risk. With governmental underwriting of interest rates, the short-term profit to the private investor would be competitive with conventional investments. Simply marshaling capital is not sufficient for sustainable development. But it can play a pivotal role if the developing countries themselves have set a course toward sustainability through agricultural and business enterprises of the sort outlined earlier.

Prospects for the Future

"If the only tool you have is a hammer, you tend to treat every problem as if it were a nail."

This aphorism, attributed to Mark Twain and later expounded upon by psychologist Abraham Maslow, is apt. It highlights the fact that our tools shape the way we identify and define our issues and problems. For our purposes, we might reverse the aphorism to read: "If you define your problem as a nail, the only tool you will look for is a hammer." We need to expand our traditional concept of private enterprise and begin to see it as a tool to advance the transition to a sustainable society. For example, we must distinguish private enterprise based upon individuals from private enterprise based upon collectives (guild socialism). The trick is to broaden our conception of the issues and thereby see the relevance of *all* our tools. These issues appear to us now as unresolved problems and as questions for further study.

Much has been made in the popular and professional press of Japanese management. It is easy to exaggerate and overgeneralize the benefits of the Japanese approach, but it is a good model for developing management approaches geared to the needs of the sustainable society. Its keystone is a view of output that goes beyond short-term and narrowly defined worker productivity. Taking the long view, productivity is stimulated principally by reinforcement for competent performance, enduring worker-to-company and company-to-worker commitment, and linking together the fate and prospects of worker and company. If we add "sustainable environmental impact," we have an appropriate set of standards. Just as energy utilities are coming to see conservation as a major target for "productive investment," so in other industries reorientation toward long-term investment in human capital—*broadly conceived*—is an idea whose time must come lest our time on this planet run out. Business must assume responsibility for the social and community implications of its enterprise.

Sustainability puts short-term sacrifice in a different light than does cannibalization of the planet for the middle-run benefit of socioeconomic exploitation. Leaders must understand that while you can't take it with you, you *can* take future generations down with you. Unless we harness the profit motive on behalf of future generations, their only alternatives may be self-destructive capitalism or stultifying collectivism. Our great-grandchildren deserve better. Goals do matter in evaluating the costs of alternative means. If ends don't justify themselves, they can hardly justify the means used to achieve them.

One of the biggest unresolved issues facing the private for-profit sector is how to assume full economic and social responsibility for waste. As Giarini has shown, waste is the eventual result of all "productive" economic activity. The utilization value of products is the period of their accessibility and usefulness for meeting human needs. An implication for corporate self-reliance is that the private sector must develop "markets" for its waste. In fact, one criterion for judging a society's sustainability is its ability to prolong the utilization value of its raw materials. Thus, for example, when "waste" heat from one plant can be used by another, both enterprises have made a significant step toward sustainability. Similarly, when an expended product is recycled (either through its first producer or another alternative), the community experiences a net gain in sustainability. The same concepts apply to human beings, where durability and productivity stand against waste of human capital—i.e., the lives of individuals, families, and communities. Thus, in evaluating the worth of enterprises—in terms of tax and credit incentives—a careful analysis of waste, material *and* social, is imperative. If small is beautiful, so are durable, frugal, and efficient, in the broadest sense. And so may be private enterprise, when it operates in a suitable context.

All told, the private for-profit sector can do much to advance the transition to sustainability. As it is presently constituted, its activities can be consistent with short-term and long-term profitability. Even more is possible if fiscal and regulatory rewards and punishments are altered to create a climate of incentives. More still can be accomplished by the private sector through social engineering in internal operations and community relations. Done properly, such efforts will engender and sustain a sense of corporate self-reliance. And we all will profit from this business as unusual.

Footnotes

[1]This section is based in part upon a 1982 Mitchell Prize–winning essay written by my colleague Ann Crouter and me entitled "Corporate Self-Reliance."

CHAPTER

9.

March 1981:

Tokyo, Japan

The Politics
of Posterity

JAPAN IS THE SUCCESS STORY OF
the 1970s, financially, educationally, and socially. So say the weekly news
magazines, arbiters of popular myth and opinion. "These Amazing Japanese: How Do They Do It?" asks one story. How indeed? Japan shows me
two worlds: an ancient culture, alien to me, coming to terms with my country's modern culture. Many Japanese are enthralled with America—
McDonald's is here already, and a Japanese Disneyland is in the works.
How does one reconcile the old with the new? How does one accept the
modern and still embrace the traditional?

An alluring metaphor presents itself as I wander through the Meiji
Shrine in Tokyo, a parklike estate dedicated to the Meiji dynasty's restoration to the imperial throne in the nineteenth century. At its heart is a Shinto
temple, where I mix with the other tourists (mostly Japanese) and the real-
life devotees. A wedding party passes—priests in traditional garb, the others wearing the modern Japanese uniform, dark suits or tasteful print
dresses. Shinto tradition permits only the priests and the wedding party
into the temple for the ceremony. Continuing my self-directed tour, I am
charmed to watch a "christening" (to use the Christian term—my Unitarian-
Universalist friends would call it a "dedication"). Most families are represented by an ancient relative, usually a grandmother, who offers up the
child with obvious pride. It is a beautiful ceremony and I linger a few min-
utes after it ends. Later I observe the wedding party, now established in a
handsome reception room. In what seems a triumphant blend of old and
new, they are watching a videotaped "instant replay" of the wedding ceremony in living color on a Sony television. Who says you can't have your cake
and eat it too when it comes to culture and technology? Is this the path to a
sustainable society? Is this appropriate technology for a modern industrial
society that wants to respect its roots and honor its families? Is this how
the Japanese manage? I am tempted to answer "yes."

But then I am caught in a two-hour traffic jam between the hotel and the airport.

"Appropriate technology" refers to physical and social devices that seek to serve a sustainable society—one that is designed to endure permanently, that meets basic human needs, and that is just. Appropriate technology embodies ecological intelligence, socially, physically, and morally. It blends smart economics and humane social welfare systems. It nurtures and sustains the wealth of families.

Inappropriate technology violates one or more of the assumptions of a sustainable society. The most glaring violations voraciously exploit the planet's resources with an eye for short-term profit and a blind spot when it comes to justice. In general, the energy-intensive petro-chemical industries are inappropriate in this sense. They transform enormous quantities of precious material into ephemeral products that lapse into waste with alacrity. They are not built to last. And the community faces the task of coping with that waste, often in perpetuity. What a legacy for our grandchildren—all so *we* might have disposable bottles, razors, and phones.

But such physically inappropriate technologies are not the whole story. Also included are social institutions that methodically work against a life style that meets human needs. Modern society is increasingly suspect in this respect. Much of the work it offers is not satisfying or violates human circadian rhythms. Likewise inappropriate, in the unmodernized society, is the introduction of techniques that undermine the supportive social arrangements families rely on. Much of the modernization experienced by rural agrarian societies disrupts the economic and social resources of rural mothers and leaves them isolated and vulnerable.

Finally, where techniques inhibit the establishment of justice by reinforcing inequities, they are rightly called inappropriate. We see this when a government subsidizes energy- and capital-intensive agriculture that displaces family farms. This "modern" technique makes small farmers unable to compete with big farmers who have access to financial reserves for equipment and fertilizer. The result can be to drive out small farmers in the short run, when in the long run the small farm is more appropriate— because it provides more genuine work, coheres around families, and lends itself to recycling, reuse, and conservation. The same can be said (see Chapter 8) about other small businesses in contrast to large economic organizations.

What does appropriate technology look like? Of course, it varies depending on the situation, but in general a society fully committed to appropriate technology would have the following characteristics: decentralization, labor intensiveness, environmental soundness, and a self-reinforcing character. Each contributes to the effective stability of social welfare systems and the wealth of families.

Decentralization: Tasks would be accomplished first at the household, then at the neighborhood, then at the community, then at the regional, and only then at the national and international level. This would lodge the functions of both economic and social welfare systems as close as possible to day-to-day family life, where they belong.

Labor intensiveness: Work would provide dignified employment rather than simply short-term monetary return on capital investment. Sound and stable employment is the cornerstone of social welfare systems. Where unemployment is out of control, social welfare systems are swimming against the tide (or is it spitting in the wind?).

Environmental soundness: Economic endeavors would maximize conservation, recycling, and prolonged multiple use, and deemphasize extraction and the transformation of materials and "products" into waste (particularly nonbiodegradable waste). If our physical house were in order, it would be easier to put our social arrangements to right.

Self-reinforcing character: Tasks would be organized around incentives and penalties that together would reward ecologically intelligent behavior and cultivation of human quality. Human relationships form interlocking social systems, so we must structure our institutions to support sustainability.

Each of these elements demands further elaboration, for together they *are* the sustainable society. Without them prospects for families and their social welfare systems are grim.

Decentralization

"Small is beautiful." Schumacher's classic dictum rings true in general. Some tasks require large-scale operations, but most do not. Further, when full costs of operation are taken into account, smaller is usually more sustainable than bigger. Thus, small economic units are the policy of choice, unless proven otherwise. Whether it be food, health, housing, or manufacturing, large-scale bureaucratic and technocratic approaches have just about run their course in most areas. This is true of public-sector social welfare systems as well—most of which are lumbering giants, unwieldy and inefficient at best.

Household operations can very effectively meet multiple needs. Besides providing food, the fish pond or vegetable plot offers children an opportunity to learn responsibility, gives parents and their offspring a natural context for interaction, and provides children and the elderly with dignified roles that make economic and psychological sense. The same recycling scheme that reduces the volume of garbage also permits a parent to care for a child at home without facing a severe economic penalty for doing so. Restoring *real* productive functions to families will go a long way toward reducing demands upon formal social welfare systems.

The technology for achieving this is at hand. *The Integral Urban Household* (Farallones Institute, San Francisco) shows how food and energy can result from an ingenious network of integrated systems, all of which emphasize renewable energy sources and materials, smart technology, and recycling. Reading it, one is struck by how well the family's economic and social needs can mesh. An amazing degree of household self-sufficiency is possible with only a few hours of labor per week per family member for a family of two adults and two children (the appropriate family size in a sustainable society).

Such an approach is an appropriate alternative to pie-in-the-sky policies that seek "full employment" defined in conventional economic terms. The most practical solution to the employment crisis includes (but is not limited to) *withdrawing* people from the monetarized labor force. It favors genuinely productive work outside the monetarized economy (with, perhaps, part-time forays into the labor force for cash to supplement the family's nonmonetary "income"). This is not dreaming. It—not the conventional approach to employment—is the practical real-world alternative, as the coming decades will demonstrate with ever-increasing and irrefutable clarity. How do we translate this idea into practice? One way is to implement tax policies that encourage it. A second is to use existing public university extension systems to transmit the technology and reinforce the will to use it.

Of course, not all tasks are appropriate to the household, and we look next to the neighborhood. Many definitions of "neighborhood" exist, but one with special appeal bases itself on the walking range of a young child (perhaps holding a grandparent's hand). That makes sense. A neighborhood is the web of social and physical arrangements that surround one's household. And it manifests itself in what Kromkowski calls "pride in the neighborhood, care of homes, security for children, and respect for each other." Certainly a prime indicator of quality of life is how well social environments achieve these four goals (Bronfenbrenner, Moen, and Garbarino, 1986; Garbarino and Associates, 1982).

Stated this way, the significance of neighborhoods as support systems for families is clear. Ecologically sane enterprises appropriately located there reinforce each other and contribute to family well-being as well. They thus reduce demands upon formal social welfare systems at the community level. Being able to walk to work, shop, and play is an ecological virtue that harmonizes with family life. It also increases feedback and nurturance, essential elements of social support. Repeated face-to-face incidental contact with people leads to eventual associations, and ultimately to neighboring and even friendships. The more economically functional neighborhoods are (or become), the more socially cohesive they will be.

Unnecessarily driving a car is a misdemeanor against the Earth and posterity. Social policies that encourage driving and discourage walking are crimes against the planet. This may seem rhetorically excessive, but it isn't. It's only as dramatic as the issues themselves. This is, after all, a struggle for the future of the future.

A sustainable society includes economic and social cooperatives at the neighborhood level. Here families collaborate to meet productive and service needs that cannot be met at the household level. In doing so, they learn and demonstrate important social skills. What is more, they receive social support. Neighborhood-based enterprises need practical support from families. Tax policies, zoning ordinances, and public works allocations all can nurture neighborhood economic activities.

Some of these activities are child care, clothing exchanges, and shared use of tools such as chain saws, woodsplitters, ladders, and perhaps recreational equipment. The relevance of the neighborhood in meeting human needs is currently great in some communities, and it would become greater in a sustainable society. One way to increase sustainability is to decrease the use of automobiles. Fewer automobiles and less use of those that exist will increase the salience of the "walkable" and "bicyclable" environment—the neighborhood. Of course, in the short run, it will expose the social and economic deficiencies of many neighborhoods—highlighting the fact that they lack shops, work sites, recreation, and meeting places. Such exposure will demonstrate the need for social reorganization and political action—for example, instituting policies that strongly discourage (even penalize) owning two or more cars, that heavily tax gasoline, that restrict automobile access, and that reward communities that offer services within walkable distances.

For a start, all public services should seek to become accessible on foot or by mass transit, or by a combination of the two.

Community-level organization is necessary for transportation, formal education, industrial enterprise, and the like. And some social welfare systems (e.g., pension plans) also must operate beyond the neighborhood. But when households and neighborhoods become more sustainable, the need for many currently "essential" community-level activities decreases. For example, when recycling and conservation reduce waste to an absolute minimum, refuse collection becomes a much smaller matter. In modern societies, acitivity at the community level is likely to lessen. In nonmodern-ized societies, community activity will probably increase to provide services such as electrical power and sanitation, without overshooting the mark as modern societies have done.

A community's economy determines its social life. Before industrializa-tion and mass transportation, most communities had an agricultural base. Now, the variation is great. Some communities are based on an industrial plant. Others exist to provide a pleasant environment for workers who commute. Others are clustered around offices housing white-collar services. Most have lost any semblance of economic autonomy.

In a sustainable society, few communities will be wholly self sufficient. Most will trade for what they cannot achieve with local resources. This implies that appropriate technology will involve a regional component. For example, regional climatic variations mean differences in the need for a "heating industry." Passive solar heating could furnish virtually all the household heat needed in Los Angeles—but only 60 percent in New York, 57 percent in Boston, 52 percent in Seattle, and 42 percent in Madison, Wisconsin. Hydroelectric power can supply all electricity in the Pacific Northwest, but little or none in the Midwest. Appropriate technology is appropriate in its geographic scale. And it generates dignified employment.

Labor Intensiveness

Appropriate technology meets the requirements of the sustainable society by minimizing the use of physical resources and maximizing the use of human resources, while exploiting neither. A basic human need that it must meet is the need for dignified employment. Simply providing work is not enough. Premodern societies are labor intensive, but that labor is too often drudgery that breaks spirits and bodies.

Appropriate technology promises to pare away as much destructive labor as possible while leaving or creating as much dignified work as is needed. The plow developed by the Schumacher-inspired Intermediate Technology Group is a good example. It relieves the backbreaking burden of working an oxen-powered plow, but it is not a conventional tractor. In their clever arrangement, a small engine pulls the plow across the field using a wire, while two farmers use their skill and strength to guide it. The result is better plowing with a less expensive tool and provision of meaningful work. And of course, existence of permanent, ecologically sensible jobs at a relatively low capital cost per work site minimizes demands upon formal social welfare systems.

In the film *The Other Way* (1976), Schumacher recalled visiting an Indian industrial park and a nearby village. In the village he met a potter who worked a hand-powered wheel. At the industrial park he met a trainee learning to use an expensive modern machine. When he asked the trainee if he would be able to work locally using such a machine after graduation, the man replied, "No. I could never have the money to buy such a machine. No. I must go to the city to look for a job."

Schumacher's story remains relevant to conventional economic development projects, be they in Chicago or the Third World. A Brazilian economist/technocrat visited a government-financed industrial park in the desperately impoverished northeast, and the story he told perfectly mirrored Schumacher's. That industrial park, like the one in India, was inappropriate to the resources and needs of the peasant. Poor neighborhoods in the United States face many of the same issues. Their infant mortality rates are often comparable; their prospects for ascendancy to the middle class equally unlikely. And I have heard plans for their economic development that are as unrealistically large scale as what Schumacher observed in India.

The village potter's technology is insufficient to generate enough income for a modern standard of living. The trainee's technology requires an untenable capital investment. Both need a middle way—a technology more powerful than the potter's simple machine but not so grandiose and expensive as the trainee's. That middle way is appropriate technology, and modernizing societies often achieve it by blending traditional techniques with modern mechanisms.

The Chinese have an expression to convey this: "China walks on two legs: one traditional, one modern." (An observer witnessing the current modernization initiative might say China was limping a bit.) *Good Work*, the topic and title of Schumacher's final book, incorporates this two-leggedness.

It suggests using our highest technological insights to meet our profoundest human needs as lovers of labor. It appreciates and uses the magic of modern technologies, but husbands and cherishes their output rather than squandering it cavalierly. How do we encourage labor-intensive appropriate technology? Local, state, and national governments must formulate economic development policies that insist on it. These policies must require an accounting of "cost per work site" for all enterprises. The appropriate enterprises can receive public support and encouragement, while capital-intensive jobs can be discouraged through taxation, regulation, and public opprobrium.

Environmental Soundness

Appropriate technology must minimize impact on the physical environment, just as it must enhance the social environment by providing dignified work. This aspect is most clearly articulated and understood already. The engineering literature on renewability, conservation, recycling, and reuse is relatively well developed. Even here, however, application must proceed with intelligence, a conscious effort to seek the lowest level of environmental disruption possible, and a systematic plan to strengthen and support families.

A 1982 National Audubon Society report cautioned that devices needed to implement a renewable energy economy are not without dangers. These include hazards to birds and insects associated with large-scale use of passive solar collectors and pathogens associated with efforts to grow and harvest large quantities of vegetable matter. This suggests that our best hope is to reduce energy consumption, maintain a relatively small population, and simply shift to alternative sources.

There is no such thing as a free lunch, even if we *can* put the bill on our grandchildren's tab. We must remember Garrett Hardin's first law of ecology: "You can never do only one thing." The less we have to do to make global ends meet, the less we'll need to cope with unintended and unanticipated consequences.

Potential problems not withstanding, solar power, organic farming, wood, and natural fibers all are naturally the material centerpieces of appropriate technology and the sustainable society. They necessarily imply that a sustainable society will blend with the natural rhythms and appearance of the Earth. We must reverse the estrangement from nature so characteristic of most modern life styles, which implies some important changes in social and political orientation.

Many of our motives are sound, or at least benign. Particularly in their private lives, few people deliberately seek out socially and personally destructive paths. But modern technology's alluring promise that we can have our cake and eat it too (and not gain weight!) is dangerously seductive. Researchers in the late 1940s and early 1950s found that people most commonly purchased television sets "to bring the family together." The irony, of course, was that once brought together *physically* by the television set, they were then separated *psychically* by the experience of watching it.

Hardin's first law of ecology thus applies to the social as well as the physical environment. Perhaps the Amish recognize this in their efforts to remain aloof from the equipment of the modern life style. Perhaps we should respect their outlook, lest we be compromised by our gadgets. Like the Amish, we would do well to be cautious—even paranoid—about adopting modern technologies. We should consider their likely spiritual impact through their effects on social life in general and family life in particular. Choosing what we *should* do from amidst all that we *can* do is the modern challenge, particularly for the affluent. But even for the poor, the quality of day-to-day life can fluctuate depending upon the ecological intelligence they use in trying to make ends meet. One of the biggest challenges is to end the correlation between low income and developmental harm. We know from international research that this is possible in the domain of infant mortality and all that it means for the well-being of children and families. We can see it in other areas as well.

Perhaps appropriate technology is a fulcrum to move us onto the path toward sustainability—a kind of *homo sapiens ex machina*. Theology that defines the natural world as an obstacle to the assertion of human power is dangerous. One hopes that appropriate technology at the household and neighborhood levels will aid in the resocialization necessary to achieve an ethic, even a theology, based upon *harmonizing* human beings and other parts of the natural environment. We will not get very far until we as a society embrace an attitude of nurturant nonviolence toward the nonhuman environment—until we speak to the trees and listen to the birds. One is struck by the parallels in current economic and social welfare systems. Both suffer from a bigger-is-better attitude. Both are losing touch with basic human realities. Both stand in an unsustainable relationship with the human community. Reductions in one can help to facilitate reductions in the other.

A Self-Reinforcing System

Appropriate technology is as much social as it is mechanical and electronic. For a decentralized, sustainable society to function, a network of policies and practices must operate that reward ecologically sensible behavior and discourage irresponsible behavior. First, rewards for appropriate technology in the household must be consistent and powerful. Second, community-level enterprises (particularly businesses) must reward behavior that contributes to collective sustainability rather than to individual interests inconsistent with that goal. It is frightening and profoundly discouraging how far we have to go.

The benefits of appropriate household technology must be consistent and powerful enough to sustain motivation to engage in the required behavior. This means that decisions about taxation, subsidies, zoning, and the like must be made with an eye to supporting household sustainability. Immediate, clear feedback has a powerful effect upon behavior, as has been demonstrated by studies in which use of electricity is self monitored. In such cases electrical use declines. This principle has been applied to many human behaviors with comparable results. Whether it is lowering one's blood pressure, wiggling one's ear, reducing a child's temper tantrums, or cutting down on calories or salt, clear and immediate feedback goes a long way toward establishing self-control.

One obstacle to achieving sustainability is that so many consequences of our day-to-day way of living are invisible to us. Our garbage disappears each week. Our food appears. Turn on the tap or touch the switch, and water or electricity are at hand. This modern magic dulls our ecological sensibilities. The modern way makes us ethically flabby. To move along the path to a sustainable society we must sharpen our consciousness and rely on feedback systems that tell us, "Pay attention!" The benefits of household sustainability must be real and demonstrable, reinforcing people to do what needs to be done.

The need for community-level behavioral support is a tremendous challenge to social engineering. Hardin's classic tragedy of the commons tells us that the collective good suffers when people serve their self interest by exploiting a common resource at little or no short-term cost to themselves. The challenge is to harness self-interest in the service of the collective good. This means nurturing traditional value systems and social arrangements that already accomplish this and creating new ones if they do not exist or have been destroyed by modernization.

Where material frugality is valued we should nurture it. Where conspicuous consumption is valued we must discourage and penalize it. "Fashion" is an enemy of sustainability; "making do" is its friend. We need a web of values that emphasize nonmaterial avenues for expressing creativity, individuality, and mastery. Necessary material expression must be confined to areas consistent with steady-state environmental economics. For example, we should applaud and reward clever ways to recycle and brilliant ideas for substituting renewable for nonrenewable resources. But we must outlaw fashionable waste in whatever form it takes. We can't afford it.

Some Practical Utopian Thinking

Let us now examine the important features of day-to-day life in the sustainable society, with special reference to the role of social welfare systems in family development. To do this we must engage in utopian thinking—for the sustainable society is the modern utopia. Like utopias of old, it is a visionary solution to the essential problems of the age in which and for which it is created.

Day-to-day life will differ among cultures, of course, and especially between modern and modernizing societies. In already modernized societies, the shape of day-to-day life will be determined by current physical and social arrangements, albeit scaled down and redirected. For example, there is little likelihood that either the state or multinational corporations will wither away. To the contrary, strong social control is required to create and maintain policies that demand and reward ecologically responsible behavior by individuals, institutions, and businesses. Freedom will be absolute in the realm of ideas and expression, but minimal in the domains of environmentally threatening behavior. The community will be organized to speak and act in the interest of future generations (the only sensible meaning of "the future" to humans).

In unmodernized societies, day-to-day life will reflect a compromise between people's aspirations for material affluence and the realities of available resources. No one knows for sure, of course, what that will mean. But it seems unlikely that it will mean much more than possession of bicycles, access to schools and trains, use of telecommunications, and a guarantee of decent water, food and housing for all. In both societies, however, the family will be crucial. Four domains of day-to-day life bear on the prospects for success: population; transportation and housing; food and energy; and health and social welfare services.

Population

A stable population well within the society's carrying capacity is essential for long-term sustainability and to provide a cushion for cyclic ups and downs. This will mean comprehensive and pervasive family planning and careful monitoring of immigration to control population growth. At minimum, accomplishing this will require incentives for keeping family size at the replacement level, penalties for exceeding that level, and absolute right of access to contraception. It will mean two or less children per family—on average, at any rate.

The "natural" workings of the marketplace in the form of financial costs and benefits of child rearing can accomplish some of this task—and have, in most modernized societies. The high cost of rearing children tends to reduce family size. Surveys indicate that Americans will not forego parenthood because of cost, but they will reduce the number of their offspring. Is this enough? It may be, but then again it may not.

It may be necessary to back up individual choice with institutional management. Population specialist Kingsley Davis has suggested a childbearing license—a birthright that individuals could use, give, trade, or sell as they so desired. The net effect would be to set an upper limit on population. However, the implications of this approach for civil liberties and bureaucratic processes are disturbing. One suspects it will not happen except in times and places of clear, demonstrable population crisis. Even in China, the One Child Policy couples rewards and inducements with informal social pressure. The threat of penalties is real but mostly latent.

The key will be growing recognition that population control is fundamental to social welfare and the wealth of families. One can envision greater public willingness to reward small families and punish large ones through subsidies and taxation. The traditional and contemporary bias against the only child should be dispelled by more research and by better distribution of existing research that denies the negative stereotype of the only child.

In any case, day-to-day life in a sustainable society means a low ratio of children to adults. The number of children will be geared to replacement and adults will live longer, further decreasing the ratio in day-to-day social experiences out in the community. The community will view each child as a resource to cultivate, for it will need to enhance efficiency and allow a "no-growth" population to adequately support the elderly. Although this *should* lead to an institutional climate that nurtures and rewards responsible families, it will not do so automatically. The ratio of children to adults has declined in the 1970s and 1980s without any appreciably increasing societal inclination to cherish children. But as the dependency ratio grows more lopsided because there are more elderly in relation to adult workers, the importance of nurturing children to become effective adults will likewise grow. Efforts to educate political leadership to this fact will become increasingly important.

Transportation and Housing

For modernized societies, we can envision increased orientation to the neighborhood, more "complete" communities, and transportation services compatible with such residential patterns. When people can complete their missions (shopping, schooling, recreation, health and welfare services) on foot or bicycle within a mile or so of home, we can assign the automobile to its properly marginal role in day-to-day life. This will require education to redefine popular conceptions of what is a walkable distance. It has shrunk dramatically. One now sees the spectacle of people driving distances (as short as one-quarter of a mile) that only a few decades ago were walked. "Forget the fitness club! Walk more!" is the message. The effect will ripple positively through the family.

In *Helping Ourselves,* Bruce Stokes notes that "walking and cycling substitute food energy, a renewable resource, for petroleum, a non-renewable resource, as well as providing exercise and a sense of independence that no car driver experiences" (p. 45). Exactly. What is more, walking can be a potent force for mental as well as physical health (adopting for the moment what is really an artificial dichotomy between mind and body.). And walking and cycling can bring family members closer, since both encourage social interaction. Walking, particularly, could strengthen families who institute a tradition of an after-dinner walk in place of television viewing.

Another benefit would be to reduce the growing problem of obesity in children. The answer is not treatment programs for overweight youngsters, but rather a more healthy social environment. In 1987 Steven Gortmaker and William Dietz reported that between 1960 and 1980, the proportion of obese 6- to 11-year-olds nearly doubled (from 15 to 27 percent). Among teenagers the proportion increased from 15 to 22 percent. More recent research confirms this and points out that the general level of physical fitness has similarly declined. The transition to a sustainable society will promote a more healthy way of life for all of us (particularly children). And it will allow a pace better suited to the needs and capacities of children and the elderly.

The automobile-oriented real estate development of the post–World War II era has stood squarely against the transition to a sustainable society. It encouraged surburban "bedroom communities" that lack the infrastructure of a genuine community or neighborhood. What is more, they have been developed without regard for household energy conservation and food production. Houses aren't positioned to capture passive solar heat. Neighborhoods aren't "clustered" for energy-conserving architecture and landscaping; sometimes they don't even have sidewalks! Economic community life is based on the assumption of low-cost energy and the automobile as *deus ex machina*. More than being merely anachronistic, such areas may be harbingers of environmental and social ruin.

In a sustainable society, housing must keep neighborhood and community functions in mind, so that walking, cycling, and energy-efficient mass transit will be the logical forms of transportation. It's unreasonable to expect people to walk when there's nowhere to go, to cycle in dangerous traffic, or to take the bus when it won't meet useful schedules. Some residences need to be converted into commercial activities, including services and shops. Housing tracts will thus become actual small communities. And most if not all residences will become food and energy producers, individually or cooperatively. Zoning changes can also spur colonization of commercial urban centers so that they will include private residences. Geographic specialization will decline; heterogeneity will increase.

This will prove especially important in dealing with the emerging urban "underclass." As Nicholas Lehmann (1986) has demonstrated, heterogeneous urban neighborhoods make less likely the developmentally destructive habits that wreak human havoc in ghettos. Increasing homogeneity has been the trend in recent decades, in many cities. In the homogeneous model, demand far exceeds the capacity of social welfare systems. In a heterogeneous neighborhood, demand is reduced to manageable levels. This alone should tell us that the transition to sustainability is no romantic idealistic dream. Rather, it is a hard-nosed analysis upon which to build social policy.

Food and Energy Production and Use

In the sustainable society, food and energy production will be as decentralized as possible to increase self-reliance and decrease wasteful and unnecessary shipment. The role of middlemen will decrease. This means continuing the trend toward household gardening in modern societies and maintaining and enhancing household food production elsewhere. Here again we see profound need for a recognition of human interdependence and a resulting impulse for self-sufficiency (in part to avoid draining resources from other communities and societies). It is a special rendering of Buckminster Fuller's classic maxim to "think globally; act locally."

Household and community gardening can be very successful in producing fruits and vegetables, and in some cases even grain. Recall the World War II victory gardens. The same is true of energy production. Decentralized solar energy facilities can meet most energy needs in most places, most of the time. Particularly for nonindustrialized societies, biogas generators, wood lots, and agricultural waste are natural sources of energy. Food, productive labor, and energy are intertwined. Processed vegetables require a great deal of energy to grow, transport, and prepare for serving, unlike locally grown fresh vegetables. And, of course, growing food at home is family building, because it offers shared activities and productive labor for children and elderly.

Household food and energy production strengthen family functioning. They enhance the family's economic integrity by increasing the value of time spent as homemakers and by providing positive economic roles for children, who are mainly a cost when the family relies on purchased commodities. This is particularly important for poor families that cannot make it in the cash economy. We need innovative demonstration projects to lead the way.

The many family functions served by household food and energy production find parallels in neighborhood gardening. It brings households together in interaction that can support other collective enterprises regarding housing, energy conservation, crime control, and political action. What is more, in nonindustrialized societies and impoverished sectors of modern societies, it can enhance child health by improving nutrition. All these functions accrue further benefits by increasing the supply of—but decreasing the demand for—formal social welfare systems. In a sustainable society, all systems and policies are complementary.

In sum, in modernized societies, food and energy production by households and neighborhoods can reduce the need for capital- and energy-intensive agribusiness and its allied enterprises—processing, transporting, and distributing goods. In nonindustrialized societies, it can increase the likelihood of dignified subsistence. The net result is a better social environment for families and an increase in their real wealth.

Health and Social Welfare Services

A sustainable society will be a healthy one, in several senses. Its life style will promote physical and mental well-being. The family planning, residential, and food and energy production activities described create a day-to-day pattern that is demonstrably more healthy than either conventional affluence or impoverishment. In modernized societies, more walking, more vegetables, more physical labor, cooler houses, and smaller families *all* will reduce harmful physiological and psychological stress. In nonindustrialized societies, sanitation, better nutrition, access to technical information and energy, and family planning will have equally important benefits. In a sense, the transition to a sustainable society at this point in the history of humanity is an effort to ensure that each society has the best of whatever world it is part of.

The sustainable society will rely heavily upon informal social support systems to collaborate with professional health and welfare services. For reasons of both cost and effectiveness, there are real limits to the efficacy of health and welfare services as cash commodities. What most people need most often in times of stress or dysfunction is the highly motivated attention of a member of their enduring social network. Professional services are critical for some people some of the time, of course. A "home health visitor" can serve social and medical needs jointly. It is an appropriate professional role to bind together neighborhoods and demonstrate concretely the community's commitment to families.

But in a sustainable society professional services, rather than seeking to displace the informal social support systems of friends, kin, neighbors, fellow church members, and coworkers, would enhance and collaborate with them. In the sustainable society, such services blend together. Housing, transportation, food, and energy enterprises overlap. Relationships and institutions designed to meet one set of needs enhance enterprises designed to meet others. Formal and informal social welfare systems work hand in hand, resulting in a better psychological prognosis for the individual and a better sociological prognosis for the collective. Home health visitors can help to forge these links.

Utopian writers have already told us much about life in a sustainable society. Each real sustainable society will mix two visions: one traditional and agrarian, the other modern and urban. Few societies will approximate a pure form of either: in most, one or the other will predominate. The traditional agrarian society will set people in low-tech rural villages, and labor-intensive cultivation of subsistence (but nutritionally adequate) agriculture will be the predominant activity. It will combine the best of nineteenth-century state-of-the-art farm life with very selective inclusion of twentieth-century technology—e.g., electricity, telephones, and preventive medicine.

Most of the already modernized world will take a somewhat different path. There will be some return to the land, but the dominant social forms will be urban high-tech communities linked together by electronics. The power of modern technology will be turned to household energy and food production (the "integral urban household"). Microprocessors and sophisticated information processing systems will manage these complex operations efficiently and sustainably. In short, it will be an ecologically smart cousin of our current life style with a heavy dose of "voluntary simplicity." Austin Tappan Wright's *Islandia* (written in 1942) presents the low-tech traditional/agrarian path, while Ernest Callenbach's *Ecotopia* (published in 1975) presents the high-tech modern/urban format. These utopian works are simply and unabashedly that. But they are not fantasies or fairy tales in the same sense that Cornucopian writings are. Herman Kahn's vision is an impossible fantasy because it violates or denies the physics, chemistry, and biology of the planet. Wright and Callenbach propose social transformation set within ecological realities. This makes them utopias. As such, they serve the very practical function of showing us where to go.

How do we get from here to there? The *transition* to a sustainabale society, the attainment of a utopian vision, can happen on many levels at once and at a varying pace in many places. There are signs that components of the sustainable society are being envisioned, created, and field tested now and then, here and there, across the world and across the twentieth century.

Lester's Brown's *Building a Sustainable Society* identifies some of these components—e.g., population that is stabilizing in some countries. In *Helping Ourselves: Local Solutions to Global Problems,* Bruce Stokes cites hopeful progress in housing, energy, food production, family planning, and other areas. Duane Elgin offers a detailed picture of the significant number of North Americans who are creating and participating in a life style of *Voluntary Simplicity* that seeks to implement in families the day-to-day activities that would be universal in a sustainable society. By reducing personal consumption and waste, these pioneers both model the needed transition and make a real, though as yet numerically small, contribution to living lightly upon the Earth. Amidst all the bad news about global trends and against the evil backdrop established by the specter of nuclear holocaust, we see some bright signs.

The Institute for Appropriate Technology and the New Alchemy Institute offer many social and physical technologies that we will need. A comprehensive Southeast Asian plan to save endangered species focuses on saving ecosystems as habitats for endangered species and contexts for genetic diversity. Innovative planners are field testing clever ways to meet basic transportation needs without creating wasteful new systems—e.g., using existing postal delivery vehicles and routes to provide rural passenger service. The microelectronic revolution can offer new efficiencies and low-power smart services consistent with the needs of sustainability.

The core issue is hope versus despair. Faced with staggering political, military, demographic, and technological obstacles, despair seems the most plausible response. On the other hand, hope is the only reasonable strategy. Anyone who, like me, is a parent, whose children will be young adults in the year 2000, and who hopes to be a grandparent in the twenty-first century, has no other course but to work for the transition to a sustainable society. Do we want our grandchildren or their children to live in that "worthless state of existence" envisioned by Limits to Growth? What we need is not idle hope, of course, but active, intelligent hope. And that means politics—the politics of posterity.

August, 1981: Upper Canada Village, Ontario, Canada
I'VE COME TO THIS RESTORED NINETEENTH-CENTURY VILLAGE *to see a techno-logically simpler way of life in demonstration. Like Williamsburg in Virginia and Old Sturbridge Village in Massachusetts, Upper Canada Village uses architectural, agricultural, and manufacturing concepts and operations long since obliterated by energy- and capital-intensive technology. Of course, life was physically hard when Upper Canada Village (a composite of several villages, really) was contemporary. It's part nostalgia and part speculation. In any case, it's a pleasant experience, until a bit of personal past and present intrudes.*

In the brick mansion that serves as the Village's museum and centerpiece, I overhear a vaguely familiar, soft Southern voice engaging the official Village hostess. "Why don't you have places where people can stay here in return for working on restoration?" The hostess replies with something vague but pleasant. "Why don't you have a worker's collective to run this place? And, what about the real political history of Village life, of workers and ownership?"

The hostess smiles, says something, and extricates herself, looking for someone who will ask easier questions. I move closer, remembering the voice and now the face. She is a ghost from my undergraduate collegiate days. We were political science majors, were in the International Relations Club, and even traveled to Montreal together to attend a model United Nations (representing Taiwan when it still officially represented China). Then, she was a sweet and pretty and very idiosyncratic Southern belle, and I was the up-and-coming "campus radical." It was the 1960s, after all. She was a clear pool of her unusual self and I was busy starting the campus peace group, organizing the first political demonstrations on campus, and becoming the second independent since Kirk Douglas to be elected president of the student government.

She tells me she has spent the years since graduation in Europe working with leftist political committees and study groups. She's back in North America to pursue her political vision. "And you?" she asks.

I tell her about testifying before legislative bodies and consulting with government agencies on child welfare issues—child abuse and child care in particular. And I mention the Club of Rome, for some reason wanting to justify myself politically to this ghost who used to seem so soft and now has a hard-cutting edge.

"So," she says, "you've copped out politically. Isn't the Club of Rome a rightist kind of group for someone like you? But then, maybe you've changed."

That ends the conversation quite effectively. In a moment she's gone, not really interested in meeting my family. After she moves on I find myself remembering a joke I used to tell with political gusto and the confidence of youth in the 1960s:

Question: What's the definition of a liberal?

Answer: A radical with a wife and two kids.

Then my son and my pregnant wife return.

Is the transition to a sustainable society a political cop-out, a smoke screen for the "real" issues of economic and social justice? Or is it *the* political issue—and all the issues of conventional politics simply diversions? It seems to be the latter and it recalls another joke: "This is the pilot speaking. I have some good news and some bad news. The bad news is that we're lost. The good news is that we're making good time." Any political path that does not seek sustainability is a dead end—however speedily it is traveled.

Just what are the politics of Spaceship Earth? Defining the sustainable society partly in terms of justice begins to answer the question, of course. But the politics of justice are many splendored, and can support several ideologies. The politics of environmental permanence are even more variable. A right-wing scenario might have most of the world's people in subservient subsistence (low resource drain) while a small elite lived in energy- and capital-intensive material affluence. The result, Slaveship Earth, might be physically sustainable despite its moral untenability. A left-wing scenario might have everyone go down in environmental disaster together struggling for social justice, rather than permit enterprising elites to enjoy a privileged position at the expense of the masses.

And what about the politics of the actual transition? Are conventional right/left dichotomies relevant? One is tempted to say "no, but . . ." In today's world one sees examples of ecological soundness and madness from both ends of the political spectrum. Left-wing state-owned enterprises devastate the physical environment to modernize in the name of populist justice (China and Yugoslavia). Right-wing capitalist governments sponsor important reforestation projects (Korea). Effective and ineffective population control policies exist in both right and left politics. Multinational corporations run amok trying to generate profits while externalizing as many costs as possible; state-sponsored enterprises behave equally badly.

Concerning "pollution as the cost of doing business," it seems Eastern European societies are some of the grossest offenders. As a *New York Times* report (December 12, 1982) put it:

> In a system in which meeting or exceeding the official production plan takes priority over everything else, and which discourages an independent, vocal environmental lobby, there is little incentive for managers and Communist Party officials to install costly pollution control equipment that cuts down efficiency. (p. 9)

The specific examples are legion—Polish rivers so contaminated the water is unfit even for industrial use; East German industrial towns with levels of lead in the air several times higher than authorized maximums; an area in Bohemia in which whole forests are dying from power station emissions; Siberian cities with rising levels of pollution-induced infant mortality and congenital abnormality. These problems equal and often exceed the problems of capitalist societies. Perhaps the single most damning indictment concerns the Soviet Union's commitment to nuclear power. Reports indicate it plans to increase the proportion of its nuclear-powered electricity generation from 10 percent in 1982 to 25 percent by 1990. The chronically slipshod character of Soviet manufacturing, safety, and environmental efforts raises the specter of atomic accidents and pollution. The Chernyobol accident of 1986 is thus not at all surprising, and more such accidents are likely.

There are two clear political dangers. The first is right-wing totalitarian control that forces subsistence living on the masses so that elites may live in affluence. I want to call it the "Soylent Green solution," after the film version of Harry Harrison's novel *Make Room, Make Room*. Some envision such a scenario for Mexico in the wake of the bust that has followed the oil boom of the 1970s. In this case, societies could become steady state in the crudest sense of limiting environmental impact, but they would lack the moral stature of true sustainability. And they might be internally unstable, as citizens resist oppression, and externally disruptive, as people emigrate to seek greener pastures and thus complicate lifeboat ethics for richer societies.

The second clear political threat comes from left-wing efforts to establish Western levels of consumption on a massive scale under the banner of populist justice. The introduction of energy- and capital-intensive life styles to the mass of the world's population is a serious threat, because it represents a very narrow and shortsighted (however well intentioned) concept of justice. The intrinsic appeal of giving everyone access to the good things in life becomes a tragic flaw when it is linked to gross materialism of the modern sort. The seeming justice of the proposition that everyone should be able to live like the "best" do makes that proposition a very powerful political force. But the ecological madness of expressing the "best" in unsustainable material terms morally invalidates the proposition's claim.

These international contrasts have their domestic parallel in the United States. Although it's a caricature of sorts, it seems the Republicans play the role of the corporate elite, while the Democrats seek a more populist route. Neither party sets forth a program for the transition to a sustainable society. The former generally favors scaled-back formal social welfare systems; the latter typically seeks to expand those systems. Neither offers an approach that will reduce demand by creating a less stressed and less disrupted global ecology. Indeed, most conventional political debate is only a dispute over the means to achieve the same false ends.

Can we enhance both justice and ecological sanity? The answer is "yes," but only if we reject gross materialism and accept a *relatively* small population. If human societies and communities exist on a small scale, with a small population and minimal negative impact upon environmental systems, then (and only then) we can have *both* justice and ecological sanity. This is the life envisioned in *Islandia* and *Ecotopia* and in the early writings of Karl Marx. This is the human side of paradise, the steady-state society in which human dramas, triumphs, and tragedies may play themselves out without consuming the Earth.

Are we psychologically equipped for the needed politics of the sustainable society? Many say no. Psychologist B. F. Skinner (whose 1948 utopian novel *Walden Two* presented a blueprint for one sort of sustainable society) doubts we have the necessary political will. He argues that the "free" world has lost sight of the need for social control to encourage responsible behavior, while impoverished societies have lost sight of the mechanics for economic progress.

The political doubts are legion. The self-serving greed of profit-oriented corporations is well known and well documented in many cases. It exists in both capitalist and communist societies. How does this motive get channeled into sustainable paths? Political payoffs for short-term "solutions" to social problems are so great that they can preempt the meeting of long-term needs. From this perspective, it seems suicidal to entrust society's fate to conventional economic and political institutions. This is the premise of the worldwide Green Party movement, which seeks an authentic politics for posterity. While the frustrations of dealing with conventional political institutions have led to some excessive and wacky responses by "the Greens," the basic orientation is sound.

Futurists promise that space exploration and other high-tech invention will create new criteria and resources for sustainability. One example of this thinking is a special issue of *U.S. News and World Report* (May, 1981) that reeks of Cornucopian fallacies. Such comforting myth-making can only delay real, practical solutions to the future. Here, fantasy impedes reality.

Beyond this fantasy world is a narrow hedonism that discounts the importance of looking beyond tomorrow, arguing, "now is enough." For example, there is widespread subversion of policies designed to reduce use of leaded gasoline and thus airborne lead, a vicious pollutant. Many self-serve (and self-serving) gasoline customers are ignoring the prohibition against pumping lead-free gas into late-model cars. Instead they choose to use leaded gasoline, which costs less and offers slightly better performance. One customer, interviewed on television, said, "There's so much pollution out there already; what difference does it make if I add mine?" This is hardly the cultural base upon which to begin transition to a sustainable society. It reflects the same sort of baseness that litters public parks, despoils forests, and callously seeks short-run payoffs from environmental manipulation. It stinks.

April, 1987: Chicago
CHICAGO'S LAKE MICHIGAN SHORELINE *is the scene of a philosophical and ecological struggle. Narrow economic interests are always on the lookout for a way to dispose of parks and make a fast buck. This year the big defensive issue for environmentalists is resisting efforts to build a new football stadium on Lake Shore Drive. Environmentalists have also gone on the offensive to urge closing the lakeside airport (Meigs Field) and converting it to park land. On a more mundane day-to-day level, the battle pits the "do-gooders" against the "slobs." The latter wage a campaign of litter and graffiti; the former try to clean things up. As I walk along the shore it looks to me like the slobs are winning.*

Two mallard ducks are paddling close to shore. Three teenage boys approach, rocks in hand. One lets loose and misses the ducks, but not by much. I can't stand it, and make bold to intervene: "Hey, guys, don't throw rocks at the ducks. Don't hurt them. Isn't there enough pain in the world?" They hesitate; then one responds: "They belong to you?" What a fantastic question. How profoundly discouraging that someone should ask. Of course, these kids are merely expressing precisely the same attitude as their elders in high places and low. They would exploit and degrade the whole planet with the same cavalier selfishness these boys show as they stone the ducks.

Yeah, they belong to me, and I to them.

What stands against this armada of forces allied in ecological darkness? Are there constructive spiritual forces strong enough to overcome the dark side of materialism? Perhaps our Hare Krishna friends are right to assert that we must countermand the bad karma our way of living generates by transcending materialism and seeking a path of pure spirituality. Perhaps there can be a politics that respects the spirit and the land. On the grossest level, political action is afoot to unite disparate groups in a campaign to thwart self-interested efforts of individuals and groups who seek transitory financial gain through environmental madness.

In the United States, environmentalists are building bridges to other political organizations. For example, Environmentalists for Full Employment is seeking to overcome the purported conflict of interest between organized labor and environmental protection. Its 1982 report, *Fear at Work: Job Blackmail, Labor, and the Environment* reveals that capital-intensive modern industrialization *reduces* employment, in contrast to labor-intensive appropriate technology. This is the basis for a natural alliance. Of course, the link is only half formed at present and impeded by the "job blackmail" mentality exploited by management in time of economic crisis. And the problem is intrinsically unsolved as long as "environmentalism" is defined as a special interest (as if it were merely another lobby).

More broadly, in congressional elections the "green vote" has helped to elect some environmentally sane candidates. The League of Conservation Voters claims that in 1982, 46 of 63 candidates it backed were elected, while the Sierra Club claimed a success rate higher than 80 percent for the 158 candidates it endorsed. The 1982 "green vote" was a promising sign at a time when national leadership presented an image of willful and callous hostility toward the concept of a sustainable society.

Another potentially promising sign comes from opinion polls. A 1982 survey conducted by Research and Forecasts, Inc. of New York reported that 49 percent of the general public in the United States believed we must accept a slower rate of economic growth to protect the environment—and only 24 percent believed we must relax environmental standards to achieve economic growth. About 55 percent supported pollution standards even if it slows down energy production. However, 60 percent want their local communities to continue to grow economically, and 80 percent say "a strong national economy" is among their top priorities.

Is the glass half full or half empty? Should we be encouraged that about half the people have a vague (perhaps unreliable) commitment to environmental protection and a glimmer of understanding about some of the costs of conventional economic growth? Or should we be discouraged that after all that has been said and done, the general public is still of a mind to have its economic cake and eat it too? In 1965, only 17 percent identified pollution as one of the three highest priority national problems. In 1970 (right after Earth Day), 53 percent did so. In 1980, the figure was 24 percent. So it goes.

As public opinion ebbs and flows we need to return environmental concern to the front burner. To some extent this means seizing the "opportunities" presented by environmental crises for progress toward widespread public understanding and commitment to the transition to sustainability. And it means that we need a massive, ongoing program of public education to improve popular understanding of what it will take to live in a sustainable society.

While some people delight in voraciously gobbling up the Earth for short-term private gain, others hug trees and find political channels to express their respect for the world. The forces for life achieve small triumphs amidst the forces of death and chaos.

Because children are special targets for the forces of environmental madness, family is the most promising focal point for the forces of light. Protecting children can become an important focal point for a political coalition aimed at the sustainable society. Freedman and Wier have reported on this struggle in a 1983 article entitled "Polluting the Most Vulnerable." They begin with a damning assessment of how efforts to dismantle environmental laws "have drawn little notice" and proceed to note that

> In particular, signs of the growing health crisis for children, who are substantially more sensitive than adults to the toxic effects of many pollutants, have been all but ignored by reporters and regulators alike. (p. 600)

They proceed to chronicle the grisly story of what *The Nation* calls "Reagan's War on Children"—increased efforts to reverse protection of children and expedite industry's search for profits to their detriment (child health is expendable because it is a financial externality). The overall dismal record is brightened only by the occasional successes of political coalitions fighting rearguard actions to slow the forces of greed and madness. One example is found in the defeat of efforts to relax the standard for lead emissions in the atmosphere. The overall picture is dominated by commercial profit-making first; the interest of children is a very distant last. A political climate of "anything goes" in the search for profits means virtually unrestricted introduction of toxins into the environments of children, with no required testing even on young *animals*. How much insight does it take to say, "This is wrong!"

Only by shifting our attention to children and their families will we have a consistent focal point for the politics of a sustainable society. As anthropologist Margaret Mead saw it, family provided the individual with a concrete historical perspective. Her words are worth recalling here.

> As in our bodies we share our humanity, so also through the family we have a common heritage . . . the task of each family is also the task of humanity. This is to cherish the living, remember those who have gone before, and prepare for those who are not yet born. (1965, p. 11)

We must help people and societies project that vision of connection forward and outward from ourselves and our children to form a politics of posterity. If we can truly establish the foundational concept of the "family" in the "community of nature," we will have the spiritual resources we need for a politics of transition.

This is most evident in what Duane Elgin calls voluntary simplicity. His survey of those who are moving toward "a way of life that is outwardly simple, inwardly rich" gives concrete examples of the politics of posterity and a covenant with nature—e.g., the Greenpeace Movement and the New World Alliance. Elgin observes that

> A majority of those pioneering a life of conscious simplicity are not strongly identified with any traditional political dogma. What seems to bind this group together is not political ideology but an appreciation for the dignity and preciousness of all life. (p. 69)

But would it be fun? Many people wonder whether all this political action, sensibleness, conservation, and eschewing conspicuous consumption would be boring. Certainly this concern could be a disingenous ploy. But it might be genuine. A student once expressed this in a particularly forceful manner. "I don't want to hear any more of this!" she said, after a reading assignment and class discussion of revisionist economist Georgescu-Roegen. "It's paralyzing to think that we can't enjoy *anything* without feeling guilty that we're wasting *something*. I hate it!" The reaction is not unlike the backlash against cancer warnings: "To hell with it. Living gives you cancer. I'll damn well enjoy myself rather than being careful all the time."

Would life in a sustainable society be fun? It might not, if it is imposed in a totalitarian political context and a Puritanical cultural climate. (Of course, if we wait too long, that might be the only technically feasible approach—or at least it might seem so in the face of widespread environmental crisis.) But we can be confident that a sustainable society would permit a flourishing of fun. By holding the physical environment in a steady state, we could free human experience for what poet Lawrence Ferlinghetti called "a rebirth of wonder." We could afford to concentrate on enhancing relationships, on spiritual development, on playing, on *being* with a wondrous intensity.

With demands on formal social welfare systems at managable levels, we could afford to concentrate upon human "actualization." That *would* be fun. Many of those who Duane Elgin describes as having chosen the path of voluntary simplicity report just such a rebirth of wonder. One says:

> My life is suffused with joy, and that transforms even the ordinary day-to-day unpleasantries that come along. (p. 60)

Another reports:

> The most satisfing thing is that you can see life right in front of your nose—feel it all around you—running through you and continuing on. (p. 81)

Elgin himself puts it this way:

> The overriding objective of the industrial era has been to maximize one's personal pleasures while minimizing one's personal discomforts. Life has been lived as a constant process of "pushing" (trying to push away from discomforts) and "grabbing" (trying to acquire or to hold on to that which gives pleasure). With the loss of inner balance that accompanies a largely habitual "pushing" and "grabbing" approach to life, a deeper pain ensues. . . . By choosing balance we can more easily negotiate a skillful path through the world. (p. 84)

This message runs through both *Islandia* and *Ecotopia*. In *Ecotopia*, characters often speak about their freedom to indulge themselves emotionally because of the social stability of their steady-state society. They dig deeply into the essentials of life—love, work, and play—because the material ephemera of life are arranged and do not distract them.

Islandia conveys this message best of all, however. The essential passages of human experience are direct, simple, universal, and unchanging: mating, childbearing, child rearing; puberty, adulthood, old age, dying. *Islandia* envisions a society in which technology is *selected* to permit a life style in which these fundamental human concerns are the principal agenda, an agenda unencumbered by false issues of materialism and conspicuous consumption. Family is central, backward and forward in time, with the generations ahead and behind in the hearts and minds of those currently occupying the planet. And it is an emotionally and spiritually rich life. An Islandian speaks for this life when he says to his American friend:

> We are put in a world of nature, of wind and sun, rain, clouds, growing trees and plants, of other animals and of other human beings. We are out of tune if we alter our natural environment too much. At least so we think here, though you foreigners often don't think that it matters or don't think at all. In this natural world we have natural desires—hunger, love, exertion of our powers in our minds and in our muscles. If the natural satisfaction of those desires is in any way checked we are out of tune. But we have simplified our problems greatly. We have a mode of life that gives us satisfaction of hunger and as full an opportunity as we wish to exert our minds and our muscles. You foreigners have built up for yourselves an environment that makes the satisfaction of those desires less easy, for its complexity makes the desires complex, and its

diversity makes the desires of the mind confused and obscure. . . . [I]t
is so hard for you—harder for you than for us. (p. 395)

What Next?

So what are we to do? An agenda for the transition to a sustainable
society might include the following items:

1. *Support "green" politics.* The "green movement," based as it is upon
a realization of the world problematique, can become a worldwide force for
ecological sanity and lifegiving reform. The transition to a sustainable
society is fundamentally a political enterprise. Existing groups such as Sierra
Club, National Wildlife Federation, Audubon Society, and Global 2000
Coalition are crucial, particularly in coalition with progressive and *genuinely*
conservative political actors. Those who want to find a way to participate
should consider subscribing to the *New Options Newsletter* (P.O. Box 19324,
Washington, D.C. 20036; phone 202-822-0929) and reading *Green Politics*
(Capra and Spretnak, 1984).

2. *Support policies and institutions that maintain family functions.*
Family is at the heart of the matter. Faced as we are with unsettling trends
in family formation and dissolution, it becomes all the more important that
the community invest in family life. One way is to insist that communities
set a high standard for child care and help parents meet those standards.
Communities share custody of children with parents. We must resist the
current trend toward the "feminization of poverty." First, we can encourage
household energy and food initiatives as a matter of basic social policy.
Second, we can support efforts to improve family life education, including
mediation services for estranged spouses. Third, we can require "registration
and inspection" of young children so the community can monitor child
development and not lose track of the children for which it is responsible.
Fourth, we can involve men more fully in child rearing, particularly in the
intimate details of infancy. This will help "tame" men and prepare them for
the nurturant roles needed in a sustainable society. With these experiences
they will be better prepared to speak in and listen to the feminine voice. In
the family, as in social life in general, each of us should know the nitty gritty
details of life—from changing diapers to taking out the garbage. Thus will
we be empowered to see things clearly and be protected from the imaginary
world that the mass media so often presents to us. Our families offer the best
grounding in what really matters.

3. *Insist upon responsible procreation.* Knowing as we do that population growth is one of the engines that drives the world problematique, can anyone who gives birth irresponsibly make a moral claim on the world? The exact meaning of responsible procreation is open to some debate, of course. But the presumption must always be that having more than two children requires some special justification, for it makes special demands upon the world. At this point in history, how can any couple justify anything more than replacing itself in the world? For some that seems like strong, perhaps distasteful medicine. But we need to take it. Concentrate on quality rather than quantity. That's the message.

4. *Support programs that encourage household and neighborhood projects to grow food and conserve energy.* Almost every family can grow some of its own food and conserve energy; every neighborhood can also accomplish significant things in this regard. Its symbolic and practical significance is not to be taken lightly. The technology for doing it becomes more clever and ecologically sensible all the time. Among several useful guides are *Gardening for All Seasons,* produced by the New Alchemy Institute, and *The Integral Urban Household* by the Farallones Institute. Locally grown food rather than food transported over long distances is cousin to home-grown food, of course. Here too we must look to social policy for support, in the form of zoning, tax, and subsidy policies.

5. *Support programs that plant trees and cherish the natural environment.* Each of us can strengthen the natural ecosystem and our spiritual union with the chain of being that links our fate to the fate of the Earth. Planting trees is one very practical way to demonstrate this union in a caring way, and it helps children learn their place in the world. One big sugar maple tree can in one year remove the lead emissions from 1,000 gallons of gasoline burned in automobiles. Planting trees to commemorate family occasions further strengthens the connection between family and Earth. And even if you feel foolish at first, hugging a tree is one way to express the fellowship of being. Another is to join the Native American Indians in offering "special greetings and thanks" for the natural wonders of day-to-day life. This spiritual dimension is important. Putting it into political practice through support of environmental action groups is the next step.

6. *Vote for local governments that seek to restructure community life to promote mass transit, walking, and cycling, and to discourage driving.* Individuals can look for ways to drive less. Most of us could walk and cycle more than we do. Keep track of miles driven and periodically examine the record to find ways to put the automobile in its proper place—in the garage.

Take a family walk around the neighborhood rather than a ride around town. Walk or cycle to work. Walking and cycling are good for the spirit and the body; driving is wrong for both. Every gallon of gas used is lost forever. Avoid trivial uses of the Earth's nonrenewable resources. Don't rob our children's children so you can escape the pleasure of strolling on foot rather than rolling under gas power. Use these personal experiences and insight as the basis for local politics. Every community makes decisions in these domains every week. Are they part of the problem or the solution?

7. *Endorse the campaign to reject fashion.* Fashion is an enemy. Consumerism is a disease. We are bombarded daily by the message that buying new things is a matter of cultural and economic patriotism. But we have a higher loyalty. Virtually everyone in a modernized society has more material possessions than he or she needs, and buys replacements and additions on the basis of fashion. Individuals can resist fashion. Governments can penalize it (e.g., by levying special taxes on new products when old ones exist). As a start, each of us can forego at least one significant purchase per week as an act of defiance against fashion and consumerism. We can put half the money "saved" into meeting the *real* basic needs of a truly impoverished family in a Third World country through Oxfam, UNICEF, Save the Children, or Foster Parents Plan International, and half into political campaigns to advance the domestic transition to sustainability.

8. *Base decisions on true cost.* Remember that the true cost of any purchase is *not* the money that changes hands, but the transaction's effect on our global ecosystems. Anything made of nonbiodegradable plastic costs more than something made of wood, no matter how many dollars change hands. Anything crafted by human hands costs less to the world than something made on energy- and capital-intensive machinery. The same object made locally usually costs the world less than it would if transported over long distances. Each of us can do something to contain the cost of our presence on the Earth. We all make choices every day as we select or reject plastics, processed/packaged "convenience" foods, and petro-energy. We can translate this insight into community life by insisting that local governments use true cost, not price, in decision making. Think of it the next time you see a worker using a gasoline-powered leafblower instead of a rake, a snowblower instead of a shovel.

9. *Insist upon economic indicators that reflect true wealth.* Measures such as GNP simply reflect cash transactions. We must reject any such system of accounting in favor of efforts to measure wealth in terms of the utilization value of goods. What is more, simple averages (such as per-capita

income) are beside the point if they obscure polarized discrepancies between haves and have-nots. Social accounting comes before economic accounting: infant mortality, literacy, life expectancy, child maltreatment—these are the crucial measures for families. Gear accounting to the issue of supply and demand for formal social welfare systems.

10. *Build professional roles in ways that harness and enhance the human ecology of families and neighborhoods.* Social support systems work through social networks of kith and kin. They are the primary structures to sustain families. As such, they are informal social welfare systems. Professionals should seek to build up and collaborate with these networks. Techniques for doing so are understood (Garbarino, Stocking, and Associates, 1980; Whittaker, Garbarino, and Associates, 1983). We must go beyond the mechanics of collaboration between formal and informal social welfare systems, however. We must strive to harness the synergy that comes from a way of life that is ecologically responsible. In such a way of life, the economic/physical/biological dimensions of life are in harmony with the social and psychic.

This is the overriding message: the future of social welfare systems and the wealth of families depends upon the progress toward a sustainable society. The alternative is physical, social, and moral disaster. Which will it be?

References

Chapter 1

Adams, B. H., *The Education of Henry Adams*, (1914)

Aldiss, B., *Galaxies Like Grains of Sand*, (1974)

Bronowski, J., *The Ascent of Man*, (1974)

Brown, L., *Building A Sustainable Society*, (1980)

Carson, R., *Silent Spring*, (1962)

Elkind, D., "Strategic Interactions" in J. Adelson (Ed.), *Handbook of Adolescent Psychology*, (1980)

Forrester, J., *Urban Systems*, (1980)

Geogescu-Roegen, N., "The Entropy Law and the Economic Problem", in H. Daly (Ed.), *Economics, Ecology, Ethics*, (1970)

Giarini, O., *A Dialogue on the Wealth of Nations*, (1981)

Gilligan, C., *In A Different Voice*, (1982)

Hawrylshyn, B., *Road Maps to the Future*, (1980)

Jacobs, J., *Cities and the Wealth of Nations*, (1984)

Kahn, H., *The Coming Boom*, (1982)

Lawrence, D.H., *Lady Chatterly's Lover*, (1928)

Lesh, D., "Summary of the Limits to Growth" (1978)

Meadows, D., and Meadows, D., *The Limits to Growth*, (1972)

Meadows, D., Richardson, J., and Bruckman, G., *Groping In The Dark*, (1982)

Mesarovic, M., and Pestel, E., *Mankind At The Turning Point*, (1974)

Peccei, A., *The Issue Is Human Quality*, (1976)

Simon, J., *The Ultimate Resource*, (1983)

Smith, G., "The Telelogical View of Wealth: A Historical Perspective" in H. Daly (Ed.), *Economics, Ecology, Ethics*, (1980)

Stokes, B., *Helping Ourselves*, (1981)

Veblen, T., *Theory of the Leisure Class*, (1912)

Chapter 2

Brown, L., *Building A Sustainable Society*, (1980)
Christopher, R., "Changing Face of Japan", *New York Times Magazine*, March 27, 1983
Elgin, D., *Voluntary Simplicity*, (1979)
Giarini, O., *A Dialogue on the Wealth of Nations*, (1981)
Grant, J., *State of the World's Children*, (1986)
Harrison, H., *Make Room, Make Room*, (1962)
Huxley, A., *Brave New World*, (1948)
Kahn, H., *The Coming Boom*, (1982)
Kahn, H., *Global 2000 Revisited*, (1983)
Orwell, G., *1984*, (1948)
Potter, A., *People of Plenty*, (1954)
Rostow, W., *Stages of Economic Growth*, (1964)
Sager, M., *Autobiography of Margaret Sager*, (1938)
Savard, R., *World Military and Social Expenditures*, (1982)
Schell, J., *The Fate of the Earth*, (1982)
Simon, J., *The Ultimate Resource*, (1983)
Wattenberg, B., *A Dearth of Children*, (1987)

Chapter 3

Auel, J., *The Clan of the Cave Bear*, (1979)
Becker, G., *A Treatise on the Family*, (1981)
Bernard, J., "The Good Provider Role", *American Psychologist*, (1981)
Brown, L., *Building a Sustainable Society*, (1980)
Campbell, D., "On the Conflicts Between Biological and Social Evolution and Between Psychology and Moral Tradition", *American Psychology*, (1975)
Caplan, G., *Support Systems and Community Mental Health*, (1974)
Cherlin, A., *Marriage, Divorce, Remarriage: Changing Patterns in the Post War United States*, (1981)
Davis, N., "Children and Single Women in Early Twentieth Century America", *Family Issues*, (1982)
Dodson-Gray, E., *Patriarchy as a Conceptual Trap*, (1982)
Ehrlich, P., *The Population Bomb*, (1967)
Elshtain, J., "Feminism and Family", *American Educator*, (1983)

Eron, L., "Prescription for Reduction of Aggression", *American Psychologist,* (1981)

Etzoini, A., *An Immodest Agenda,* (1983)

Friedan, B., *The Feminine Mystique,* (1968)

Garbarino, J., and Assoc., *Children and Families in the Social Environment,* (1982)

Grant, L., and Tanton, J., "Immigration and the American Conscience", *The Environment Fund,* (1981)

Greer, C., "Six Views of the American Family", (1976)

Hardin, G., "The Tragedy of the Commons" in H. Daly (Ed.), *Economics, Ecology, Ethics,* (1980)

Houseknecht, S., "Voluntary Childlessness", *Family Issues,* 1982.

Mead, M., and Heyman, K., *Family,* (1965)

Meadows, D., Richardson, J., and Bruckman, G., *Groping in the Dark,* (1982)

Mills, C.W., *The Sociological Imagination,* (1963)

Reiss, I., *Family Systems in America,* (1980)

Stinnett, N., Chersen, B., and DeFrain, J., *Building Family Strength,* (1979)

Trivers, R., "Parent-Offspring Conflict", *American Zoologist,* (1974)

Van Den Berghe, P., *Human Family Systems: An Evolutionary View,* (1979)

Winn, M., *Children Without Childhood,* (1983)

Chapter 4

Bronowski, J., *The Ascent of Man,* (1974)

Campbell, A., *The Sense of Well-Being in America,* (1981)

Dodson-Gray, E., *Green Paradise Lost,* (1980)

Elder, G., *Children of the Great Depression,* (1974)

Elgin, D., *Voluntary Simplicity,* (1978)

Elkind, D., "Strategic Interactions" in J. Adelson, *Handbook of Adolescent Psychology,* (1981)

Erdman, P., *The Crash of '79,* (1976)

Etzoini, A., *An Immodest Proposal,* (1983)

Ewen, S., *Captains of Consciousness,* (1983)

Finkellor, D., *Child Sexual Abuse,* (1984)

Fromm, E., *To Have or To Be,* (1955)

Hazard, S., *The Transit of Venus,* (1980)

Heilbroner, R., *Business Civilization in Decline,* (1978)

Hirsh, F., *Social Limitations to Growth,* (1981)

Hollander, C., "Thanks for the Recession", *Newsweek*, (7/25/83)

Huxley, A., *Ape and Essence*, (1948)

Krutch, J., *The Modern Temper*, (1956)

Leiss, W., *The Limits to Satisfaction*, (1980)

Maslow, A., *On Becoming Human*, (1951)

Peccei, A., *The Human Quality*, (1977)

Sahline, M., *Culture and Practical Reason*, (1982)

Schumacher, E.F., *Small is Beautiful*, (1974)

Scitovsky, T., *The Joyless Economy*, (1981)

Steinbeck, J., *The Grapes of Wrath*, (1939)

Stinnett, N., Chesser, B., and DeFrain, J., *Building Family Strength*, (1979)

White, L., "Historical Roots of Our Ecological Crisis", (1967)

Wright, A.J., *Islandia*, (1942)

Chapter 5

Bell, D., and Kristol, I., *The Crisis in Economic Theory*, (1981)

Boulding, K., *Evolutionary Economics*, (1981)

Daly, H., *Steady State Economics*, (1980)

Georgescu-Roegen, N., "The Entropy Law and the Economic Problem" in H. Daly, *Economics, Ecology, and Ethics*, (1980)

Giarini, O., *Dialogue on Wealth and Welfare*, (1981)

Hewlett, S., *The Cruel Dilemma of Development*, (1980)

Lamb, R., "The Economic Pie Isn't Growing, But More Americans Need Shoes", (1982)

Reich, R., *The Next American Frontier*, (1983)

Rostow, W., *Stages of Economic Growth*, (1962, 1972)

Schumacher, E.F., *Small is Beautiful*, (1973)

Seuss, Dr., *The Lorax*, (1971)

Skinner, B.F., *Beyond Freedom and Dignity*, (1970)

Skinner, B.F., *Verbal Behavior*, (1952)

Thulow, L., *Dangerous Currents*, (1983)

Turner, F.J., *The Frontier in American History*, (1817)

Chapter 6

Boulding, K., *Evolutionary Economics*, (1981)

Daly, H., *Economics, Ecology, Ethics,* (1980)
Friedan, B., *The Feminine Mystique,* (1963)
Giarini, O., *Dialogue on Wealth and Welfare,* (1981)
Reich, R., *The Next American Frontier,* (1983)
Shannon, G., and Cromely, E., "Settlement and Density Patterns", in J. Wohlwill and W. Van Vilet (Eds.), *Habitats for Children,* (1983)
Smil, V., "China and the Environment", (1983)
Toffler, A., *The Third Wave,* (1982)
Winn, M., *The Plug in Drug,* (1985)
Wynne, E., *Growing Up Suburban,* (1977)

Chapter 7

Blumbery, R., "A Paradigm for Predicting the Position of Women", in *Sex Roles & Policy,* (1976)
Boulding, E., *Women: The Fifth World,* (1980)
Callenbach, E., *Ecotopia,* (1979)
Dodson-Gray, E., *Patriarchy as a Conceptual Trap,* (1982)
Ferguson, C., *The Male Machine,* (1976)
Gilligan, C., *In A Different Voice,* (1982)
Gordon, S., "The New Corporate Feminism", *Nation,* (1983)
Mead, M., and Heyman, K., *Family,* (1965)
Rosenblatt, R., "The Male Response to Rape", *Time,* (4/18/83)
Rossi, A., "Transition to Parenthood", *Journal of Marriage and the Family,* (1968)
Tinker, I., *Women and World Development,* (1979)
Trivers, R., "Parent-Offspring Conflict", *American Zoologist,* (1974)

Chapter 8

Crouter, A., and Garbarino, J., "Corporate Self Reliance and the Sustainable Society", *Technological Forecasting and Social Change,* (1982)
Crouter, A., "Participative Work and Personal Life", (1982)
Elgin, D., *Voluntary Simplicity,* (1979)
Goldstein, D., "Saving Jobs But At What Price?" *The Nation,* (12/10/83)
Hopcroft, D., "Commercial Applications of Indigenous African Animals", (1979)

Lovins, A., and Lovins, H., "Electrical Utilities: Key to Capitalizing the Energy Trovertion", *Technological Forecasting and Social Change*, (1982)

Miller, A., "Constitutionalizing the Constitution" *Technological Forecasting and Social Change*, (1982)

Reich, R., *The Next American Frontier*, (1983)

Stahl, W., "The Product Life Factor", *Technological Forecasting and Social Change*, (1982)

Von Oppen, M., "Toward Private Investment Funds For Development Aid", *Technological Forecasting and Social Change*, (1982)

Chapter 9

Bronfenbrenner, V., Moen, P., and Garbarino, J., "Families and Communities" in R. Parke (Ed.) *Review of Child Development Research*, (1984)

Brown, L., *Building The Sustainable Society*, (1980)

Callenbach, E., *Ecotopia*, (1979)

Capra, F., and Spretnak, C., *Green Politics*, (1984)

Elgin, D., *Voluntary Simplicity*, (1979)

Farallones Institute, *The Integral Urban Household*, (1979)

Freedman, T., and Weir, P. "Polluting the Most Vulnerable", *The Nation*, (1983)

Garbarino, J., and Assoc., *Children and Families in the Social Environment*, (1982)

Garbarino, J. Stocking and Assoc., *Protecting Children From Abuse and Neglect*, (1980)

Harrison, H., *Make Room, Make Room*, (1966)

Kromkowski, J., *Neighborhood Deterioration and Juvenile Crime*, (1976)

Lehmann, N. "The Underclass", *Atlantic*, (1986)

Mead, M., and Heyman, K., *Family*, (1965)

New Alchemy Institute, *Gardening For All Seasons*, (1983)

Shumacher, E.F., *Good Work*, (1985)

Skinner, B.F., *Walden Two*, (1948)

Stokes, B., *Helping Ourselves*, (1981)

Whittaker, J., Garbarino, J., and Assoc., *Social Support Systems in the Human Services*, (1984)

Wright, A.T., *Islandia*, (1942)

Index

Population growth, 7, 17, 18, 19, 40-41, 45-47, 79, 159, 224, 228-229, 237
  modernization and, 77, 83
  rates, 76, 79, 80, 82, 83
  standard of living and, 19, 79, 84
Poston, Dudley, 77
Potter, Alan, 43
Potter, David, 95
Poverty, 50, 104, 105, 111, 159
  feminization of, 185, 244
"Prayerfull economics," 49
Presser, Harriet, 143
Private enterprise, 192-195, 198, 201, 205, 212
  social responsibility of, 203, 204, 207, 208, 213
Productivity, 128, 212
Product life, 200-203
Profit, 196-199, 200, 201, 213
Progressive conformity, principle of, 177
Project on the Predicament of Mankind, 17
"Psychological Man," 132
Psychological support, 63, 65, 66, 102
Public sector, 10, 194, 236

Rape, 173
Recycling, 201, 219, 222
Regulation, 198
Reich, Robert, 121, 138, 196
Reiss, Ira, 59
Religion, 96-99. See also Christianity
Research, 48
Resources, 10, 17, 33, 40, 83, 198, 200
Responsibility, 10
  corporate, 10, 203, 204, 208, 213
  System (China), 137, 142, 158, 192, 211
Revolution, 20, 22
"Revolution of rising expectations," 38
Richardson, John, 87
Rosenblatt, Roger, 173
Rossant, M. J., 130
Rossi, Alice, 170

Rostow, Walter, 42, 116, 117-120, 122, 126, 128, 132, 133, 135, 206
"R's," (of appropriate technology), 201
"R" strategy, 74
Ruskin, John, 15, 16

Sahlins, Marshall, 109
Sanger, Margaret, 29
Save the Children, 246
Schell, Jonathan, 31
Schell, Orville, 142
Schumacher, E. F., 96, 98, 99, 111, 116, 120, 123, 204, 211, 219, 223
  Intermediate Technology Group, 204, 223
Scitovsky, Tibor, 109
Scotland, 107
Self-reinforcing system, 226
Sense of Well-Being in America, The (Campbell), 107
Seuss, Dr., 124
Sexual abuse, 60, 103
Shannon, Gary, 159, 160
Sierra Club, 240, 244
Silent Spring (Carson), 17
Simon, Julius, 15, 22, 42, 72, 85, 89, 128
Simplicity, 36-37, 98
  voluntary, 37, 100, 233, 242
Sinclair, John, 107, 109
Single-parent households, 62, 185
Sivard, Ruth, 53
Skinner, B. F., 107, 132-133, 238
"Slaveship Earth," 39, 40, 236
Smil, Victor, 142
Smith, Adam, 193, 195
Smith, Gerald, 15
Snowbelt, 161
Social conditions, 7, 40, 70
Social innovations, 204-205
Social security, 105
Social welfare, 1, 13, 20, 45, 61, 219
Social welfare systems, 2, 5, 7, 64, 99, 232
  affordability, 3, 52